The
GAMING
INDUSTRY

The GAMING INDUSTRY

Introduction and Perspectives

International Gaming Institute

University of Nevada, Las Vegas

William F. Harrah College of Hotel Administration

John Wiley & Sons, Inc.

New York • Chichester • Brisbane • Toronto • Singapore

This text is printed on acid-free paper.

Library of Congress Cataloging in Publication Data:
The gaming industry : introduction and perspectives / International
   Gaming Institute, University of Nevada, Las Vegas.
          p.   cm.
     Includes bibliographical references.
     ISBN 0-471-12927-5 (cloth : alk. paper)
     1. Casinos—United States—Management.   2. Gambling—United
States.   I. University of Nevada, Las Vegas. International Gaming
Institute.
HV6711.G35   1996
795'.068—dc20   95-50583

Printed in the United States of America

10 9

Contents

Preface

Gaming has been of interest to a variety of academic disciplines, and gaming concepts have been used as tools for effective teaching for many years. Recently, increased public interest in gaming, as an acceptable form of recreation, as a means to raise revenues, and as a way to revitalize ailing economies, has focused attention on casino gambling as a field of study that is itself worthy of extensive treatment.

Historically, the perceptions of gaming make it more than just another form of recreation. Various academic disciplines have studied gaming from their unique perspectives—history, psychology, economics, marketing, law, sociology, mathematics, criminology, anthropology, urban planning, and hotel administration. It is obvious that a single approach to gaming education is not possible or desirable. Most disciplines, however, do not treat the subject beyond a research interest or as a specialized course in the implications and ramifications of gaming or gaming behavior for the individual.

The primary purpose of this book is to analyze gaming as a course of study intended to develop future professionals for careers in the gaming industry. An additional purpose is to introduce hospitality professionals to gaming as an integral part of the hospitality industry. The emphasis is on gaming as a major entertainment industry.

The book is divided into four parts. Part One, "Introduction," orients the reader to the historical development of games of chance and the gaming industry. Part Two, "Casino Operations," presents the complexities of gaming operations in relation to various casino functional areas. Part Three, "Gaming," deals with gaming mathematics and utility analysis. And Part Four, "Casino Management and Gaming Education," focuses on gaming careers and the preparation for them.

This book is a beginning. Its 12 chapters were written by faculty members of the UNLV International Gaming Institute (IGI), which is committed to being the leader in gaming information and gaming resources. The acquisition and integration of the exhaustive Royer Collection of books and other resources into the institute's International Game Technology Library, coupled with the existing gaming collection at the UNLV library, create a gaming information resource unmatched in the world. This book of readings is the first textbook offered by the Information Center of the institute. *The Gaming Research and Review Journal,* now in its second year, is an ongoing source of new material.

Gaming education is in its infancy, but the rapid development of the gaming industry indicates that it may well be the growth segment of the hospitality industry in the twenty-first century.

We would like to acknowledge the authors featured in this book for their hard work, expertise, and contribution, to the William F. Harrah College of Hotel Administration and the UNLV International Gaming Institute.

David J. Christianson, Dean
William F. Harrah College of
    Hotel Administration
University of Nevada, Las Vegas

Vincent H. Eade, Director
UNLV International Gaming
    Institute

The GAMING INDUSTRY

 *Part One*

Introduction

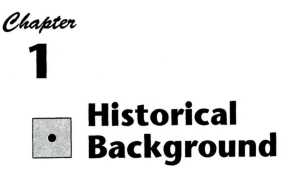

Chapter 1

Historical Background

INTRODUCTION: BEFORE THERE WAS A UNITED STATES

There was gambling at the foot of the Cross for the robe of Christ. But the history of wagering does not start there. Adam and Eve, as they considered taking a bite of the apple, were actually contemplating the first wager of life. Additionally, according to Messick and Goldblatt,[1] there is a school of thought that suggests that Eve ate the apple to settle a bet she made with the serpent as to the number of seeds the apple contained. Unfortunately, she swallowed one of the seeds and therefore lost the wager. Also unfortunately, she became pregnant. The belief, therefore, that "the urge to gamble is as old as woman and as powerful as the sex drive," has been around a long time and perhaps has more converts today than ever, since it offers a quick-healing salve for the fever blisters of the soul.

Another commonly held tenet is that one of the reasons gaming consistently wins out over love and sex is that it is itself an expression of virility. This, however, does not explain the millions of women who play, and it is counter to the view of many psychologists who believe that gambling is really a sex substitute for men and women who are trying to find a way of losing with grace.

The Egyptians attest to the association of gambling and sex in their mythology. When the Goddess Rhea (Earth) became pregnant while having an illicit affair with Saturn, the Sun in his rage ruled that she could not be delivered of her child during any month or year. Mercury, who also loved Rhea, came to her rescue by making a wager with the Moon "at tables" and won from that goddess one-seventieth of her light. Out of this light, he fashioned five new days, which Rhea used to give birth to Isis and Osiris. These five new days, when added to the then 360 day calendar, were thereafter observed by the Egyptians as the birthdays of their gods. The ancient temples of Egypt have yielded "ivory dice" known as "astragals," which may symbolize the dice that Mercury used in his duel with the Moon.

The Bible also tells of gambling. Moses made decisions about the division of the land of Canaan by the casting of lots. This gambling technique provided him with the necessary alibi in that the result of casting lots could be considered the will of God, not Moses' doing. The Jewish people were so convinced that gambling was a form of divine revelation that they tried to punish all mortals who used it for mercenary purposes. The Jew who won something of value from another Jew was guilty of theft, but anything won from a gentile was not considered a crime. This might also indicate that "the swindler" has been on the wagering scene for some time as well.

The Moslems classify gambling and wine together. The Koran clearly states that "in both there is great sin, *and also some things of use unto men,* but their sinfulness is greater than their use." Given this loophole, many Moslems are great gamblers.

Because of their urge to gamble, humans have always provided themselves with loopholes in divine laws and, for sure, in their own laws in order to continue with the practice. The Greeks considered gambling a great sin, but there was so much gambling in Greece that Aristotle noted, "thieves and robbers at least take great risks for their spoils while gamblers gain from their friends to whom they ought rather to give."

The passing of centuries seems to have done little to stop or curb the human desire to gamble, even though from time to time much effort has been spent in the attempt to control gambling through decree, contract, or treaty.

From the beginning of the first crusade through the Middle Ages and up to the discovery of the New World, those in power have tried to regulate gambling.*

The first laws in England relating to gaming date back to the Middle Ages, when Ordericus Vitalis (1075–1143), a clergyman, wrote of the fondness of the clergy for "dice-playing." At the same time, John of Salisbury (1110–1183), a monarch, decried the "damnable art of dice-playing." Commencing in 1388 with the Statute of Richard II, six monarchs and Cromwell of the Interregnum each expressed their will in statutes, none of which were enforced to the degree necessary to prevent great wealth from being transferred based on the roll of the dice. Prior to 1700, it was generally accepted that the legislatures could not modify the basic principles of Common Law. Like the Common Law itself, the early statutes merely penalized any game that was in itself, or owing to the manner of its playing, injurious to society or to the state. It was, therefore, not the game that was attacked, but its consequences.

---

*For a complete discussion of the history of gambling regulation, see Massick and Goldblatt, cited above.

THE STATUTE OF ANNE (1710)

The ambiguities of the 1664 statute were rectified in 1710 by "An Act for the better preventing of excessive and deceitful Gaming," popularly known as the "Statute of Anne." This statute was the most important development in English gambling law prior to the American Revolution (one that would be introduced in its entirety in some southern colonies in America).

The Statute of Anne sought to constrain the impact of gambling on the English social system. Because it resulted in large transfers of wealth, gambling disrupted England's land-based society. The purpose of the statute was, therefore, to protect the landed aristocracy from the consequences of their own folly; they were viewed as especially prone to gambling's vices and particularly susceptible to its ruin. The first and most significant section of the statute made "all Notes, Bill, Bonds, Judgments, Mortgages, or other Securities or conveyances whatsoever" given in payment of gambling debts "void, frustrate, of none Effect to all Intents and Purposes." The law did not affect wagers of less than £10.

According to Messick and Goldblatt, a good record of the depths to which gambling had brought the depraved appeared in the July 29, 1713, issue of *The Guardian*. The writer complained that "A night of gambling ruins a woman's looks. I never knew a thorough paced Female Gamester hold her Beauty two winters together." There was also another problem spelled out quite candidly: "All Play debts must be paid in specie, or by an Equivalent. The Man who plays beyond his Income, pawns his Estate; the Woman must find something else to Mortgage when her Pin Money is gone. The Husband has his Lands, to dispose of, the Wife her Person." One problem was the chauvinism of that era. The article continues, noting, if the woman lost her looks from too much gaming, her "Person" might not have been worth very much.

In England and France, men and women continued to gamble despite the usual stories of sore losers and swindlers. William Crockford, the son of a London fishmonger, might even seem to herald the history of Bugsy Siegel of *Fabulous Flamingo* fame in Las Vegas, which also offers a touch of *deja vu*. Crockford, a skilled mechanic of wist, piquet, and cribbage, as well as a bookmaker, founded one of the first lavish gambling houses of the period in London, which bore his name. *The London Times* described the scene as follows:

> On entering from the street, a magnificent vestibule and staircase breaks upon the view, to the right and left of the hall are reading and dining rooms. The staircase is of a sinuous form, sustained in its landing by four columns of the Doric order, above which are a series of examples of the Ionic order, forming a quadrangle with

apertures to the chief apartments. Above the pillars is a covered ceiling, perforated with luminous panels of stained glass, from which springs a dome of surpassing beauty; from the dome depends a lantern containing a magnificent chandelier.

And this seemed to be only a first glance. The article continued to describe the state drawing room as "baffling perfect description of its beauty, but decorated in the most florid style of Louis Quartorze." It was indicated that the upholstery and other decorations were said to be "imitative of George IV."

George IV was not impressed, however. A *Times* article entitled "CROCKFORD's HELL" (January 1, 1828) reports that "the monarch . . . in his usual nervous style, denounced such infamous receptacles for plunder as not only a disgrace to the country at large but the age in which we live."

George IV may have been critical, but England was not. Statesmen, authors, soldiers, and poets were proud to be members, and visitors, such as Prince Talleyrand, belonged. Upon his death in 1844, the son of a fishmonger had become one of the richest men in England.

England and other European founders of the new world exported not only gamblers but also the antigambling sentiment. Upon their arrival they found that the Native Americans had been gambling for over two thousand years, as indicated by petroglyph writings in caves not far from what is known today as the "Entertainment Capital of the World"—Las Vegas.

Messick and Goldblatt conclude their work on the ancient history of gambling with a reference to the present as follows:

[I]t isn't necessary to study the relics of the past to understand that as civilization evolved, as wealth piled up unevenly, as men become frustrated and bored, gambling promised excitement and offered the illusion of hope. [And] [s]teadfastly, we refuse to learn by experience. No need to wonder . . . why man continues to throw good money after bad. We need only to turn to a friend of George Devol, one "Canada Bill" Jones. Marooned one night in a river town, Jones went looking for some "action." He found it in the back room of the barber shop. Warned that the play was crooked, "Bill replied: "I know, but it's the only game in town."[2]

One might wonder whether or not there may have been a Bingo game on the *Mayflower's* voyage to the new world—strictly for entertainment, of course. The answer would naturally have been a resounding "NO," the obvious reason being that the game had not yet been invented.

THE NATIVE AMERICANS

Although gaming was a significant part of the history of the development of the United States, centuries prior to the White man's appearance on the scene the Native American seemed mesmerized by gambling, taking a chance at anything that could have an unknown outcome. Archaeological discoveries dating back 2,000 years have been uncovered in Clark County, Nevada, indicating that "the contest" was even part of sacred Native American rituals. Such discoveries also indicate that since the beginning of their culture in North America, Native Americans spent a considerable time wagering on games of skill and chance. As a result of their own culture, the white man's law had little or no effect on Native American gambling, since in most cases, Native Americans gambled among themselves in a manner adopted by their people hundreds of years before.

Zuni myths tell of holy men being patrons of divine chance, gambling the entire future of a tribe or nation as a form of recreation. It was a mythical belief that all men inherited their desire to gamble from these patrons of religion, considered by Native Americans to be the first gamblers. Many sacred artifacts discovered at Zuni burial grounds are similar to, and may be the forerunners of, latter-day gaming equipment.

In more recent times, contests such as foot races, lacrosse, and contests of warrior skill earned their winners prizes of baskets, eagle tail feathers, jewelry, buckskins, rabbit skin blankets, and, of course, horses.

The Chippewa were known to have gambled intensely by playing checkers. Their stake were weapons and smoking pipes, which tended to give an air of seriousness to their game. The Crow tribe was reported to wager cartridges on sleight-of-hand games. To win, the contestant tried to guess which of his opponent's hands held an object, a game sounding like the forerunner of Three-Card Monte.

The first sailors to the west coast were reported to have observed Coastal Native Americans wagering for animals with tokens resembling dice.

Some of the first fur traders to the Pacific Northwest returned with stories of Native Americans who played a game similar to dice. One game featured a form of doubling the wager. It started with a minor token matched by the opponent's token. The winner then wagered his original bet with his winnings against a second item of considerably more value than the original items of the first wager. The game continued until one or the other contestant lost everything. At certain points of the game, a return of some of the spoils occurred allowing the loser to continue with the game. Usually, however, games ended when one winner took all. Games could last days without pause except to eat and possibly to sleep. Some victims lost everything they had of value—horse, dogs, cooking utensils, lodge, wife, even wearing apparel. The loser was then obliged to get an old skin from someone to cover himself and to seek shelter in the lodge of one of his relations.

If a wife was gambled and lost by her husband, she could say nothing about the outcome. She merely took up residence with the winner.

Possibly one of the most unique forms of wagering was reported to have occurred in Austin, Nevada, by the Reese River Reville. According to the report, one of the most modest wagers ever seen was by three Piutes playing a Native American form of poker—the stakes were chewing gum. To make a bet, a player nipped off a piece of the gum he was chewing and placed it in the pot before him. The winner of the pot took all the pieces of gum and put them in his own mouths for storage until he bet on the next outcome.

Today Native Americans and their reservation treaties regarding the conduct of gaming on reservation lands are in a position to exert great influence as gaming proliferates. Vast territories of the United States may feel the tremendous influence that Native American gaming can exert on the economies of surrounding communities. Some of the largest casinos are operating under the auspices of several Indian nation counsels and are providing healthy support to Indian reservations. The question naturally arises, when it is recognized that it is not Native Americans playing in their casinos but white men and women: Who regulates these casinos, and are the proceeds taxed by the several states?

American Gaming Law 1776–1976

The information that follows was derived in part from a project on the development of the law of gambling. The purpose of the project was to provide policymakers with the historical and legal context within which to evaluate proposals for the suppression or decriminalization of gambling.

English materials were reviewed as part of the project and an effort was made to place legal developments in their economic, social, and political contexts. General findings of the study concluded that there was a need to examine each form of gambling on its own terms: public and private lotteries, wagering on sporting and other events, machine gambling, and casino-type operations. Consideration was also given to the operators, participants, levels of participation, methods of promotion, places of participation, and degree of regulation.

The preface of the study, concluded in 1977, made the following observations:

> Winds of change are sweeping across the legal horizons of the world of gambling, which was once virtually universally condemned by law. The federal government and the states are now in the process of reconsidering their traditional prohibitions of its various forms. The final outcome is yet in doubt, but the emerging design seems clear; it embraces the *de facto* decriminalization of various forms of illicit gambling, along with the socialization of selected games. The nation seems to be heading for the worst of both worlds. Illegal gambling will flourish in a twilight zone between formal prohibition and halfhearted enforcement. By its side, legal games will develop—first lotteries, then off-track betting, finally perhaps state-run, or at least state-regulated, casinos. Gambling policy will have changed in a hope to increase tax revenue and reform law enforcement, comparatively little income will be realized, organized crime and professional gambling will endure, and the corruption and inefficiency of law enforcement and the obstruction of courts will continue.

THE NORTHEAST

Although attention is paid to the South, the Midwest, and the West, there is strong correlation of all areas with the development of gambling in the Northeast, particularly New York City. Considerable time, therefore, will be devoted to investigation of gambling in New York City and in the state of New York.

The English legal system played a leading role in shaping the development of American legal thought and its institutions, and so it was with gambling laws both prior to and after the American Revolution.

John Winthrop's Puritans were among the earliest settlers of the North American continent. Those who settled in what is now Massachusetts condemned gaming from the start, but their disapproval did not originally rest upon the belief that such activity was evil per se or directly contrary to the teaching of God. The Puritans were basically opposed to idleness. According to Puritan doctrine, all law derived its force and validity from the word of God. That "word" had only one rightful source, the Bible. While theft and adultery were specifically prohibited, the Bible did not expressly condemn gaming.

Nevertheless, in its first year of existence, the Massachusetts Bay colony outlawed the possession of cards, dice, and gaming tables, even in private homes. In addition, although games in general were not expressly banned, they clearly fell under the idleness statute of 1633. The early colonists opposed any unproductive use of time, and game playing was condemned as one form of idleness. Other prohibited diversions included dancing, singing, and all unnecessary walking on Sunday.

Connecticut's laws followed a similar course and denounced game playing whether or not gambling was present, because it prompted". . . much precious time to be spent unfruitfully."

Several factors combined to produce the Puritan opposition to entertainment reflected in and exemplified by this early Northeastern legislature: The harsh and unfamiliar American wilderness, the danger of hostile Indian attack, and the possibility of starvation or disease. Later statutes considered other problems: the welfare of innocent families, public safety, and juvenile delinquency.

In 1721, a New Hampshire act against gambling, for example, spoke of a need to prevent the unnecessary impoverishment of the gambler's family. Moreover, a New York statute expressed concern for the financial ruin of the gambler and the violence connected with gambling ventures, while a 1748 New Jersey act equated idleness and immorality with fraud and the corruption of youth.

Lotteries also migrated from the earliest of times onto the American scene. However, they occasioned an argument derived from the Bible that specifically condemned such activity. Although the growth of a working, nonreligious class in the Puritan midst led to a weakening of the religious influence, the Puritans did not take their loss of political power lightly. Prominent Puritan theologians began to interpret recurrent misfortunes as signs of God's anger with the degradation of Puritanism. Cotton Mather developed a biblical position against gambling that centered on the concept of a lottery. Appeals to chance, he argued, usurped God's power and were, therefore, profane. Since the lot was used several times in the Bible to determine God's will, the use of chance events for other purposes was a profane assumption of God's authority. Despite these arguments, moves to finance public projects through authorized lotteries were generally successful in the 1700s. One reason was that taxation in the colonies was poorly organized and produced little revenue. The several colonies of the Northeast that condemned lotteries on moral grounds such as those outlined above continued to operate them despite their supposed immoral nature.

Horse racing also continued to be treated like the lotteries. Finally, in 1771 the General Assembly of Rhode Island passed "An Act to Prevent Horseracing," ostensibly as a wartime measure. Although probably designed to ensure that all available horsepower would be devoted to the American Revolution, the act prohibited wagering on horse races, fixed a fine of £100 for violations, and further provided for the forfeiture of horses run for a bet or wager.

Opponents of gambling also attempted to control those who directly fueled the common passion for it—professional gamblers. Most Americans at this time felt that the only acceptable occupation was one in which the individual contributed a useful service to society through disciplined and honest work. The professional gambler represented the antithesis of this ideal, for he was lazy, undisciplined, and dishonest, and gained his wealth through the victimization of others. The full time gambler was regarded as a parasite and a thief; as the Pennsylvania gambling law of 1847 indicates, he was found to be a nuisance to the body politic.

Private game playing by the average citizen did not necessarily arouse strong disapproval, and neither did the results of its efforts. There was no fault in an innocent and moderate recreation provided by the playing of games, but they were not to be played for something of value.

Maine's major gambling statute, patterned after Massachusetts', also emphasized the illegality of keeping a gambling house. The courts in Maine determined that there were two separate offenses: keeping a place for gambling and permitting persons to play any games for money in a house under one's care.

At the turn of the twentieth century, the demographics of the Northeast began to change. The migration of Irish and Italian Catholics to the new world had become significant. Although they brought with them a habit of hard work, they held to their age old traditions of gaming as a form of relaxation. With the new industrialization migration to the cities and the development of factories, tension grew between the traditional legal minds and newer popular attitudes toward gambling, and enforcement of antigambling statutes became progressively more difficult.

New York

The story of New York is in itself the story of the Northeast from 1830 to the 1970s. The pressure of the times was the evangelical Christian reform movement experienced in different forms in many parts of the country, whose impact was felt most strongly in the northern and western portions of the state, probably because of the large number of New England Protestants who had settled in those areas. Liquor, slavery, the lack of institutions for the poor, and women's status as second-class citizens all came under attack.

Liquor evoked more concern than any of the other evils because of its reputed popularity among the people, particularly among the rapidly expanding class of urban poor. Reformers such as Horace Greely led what began as a temperance movement in the 1830s and reached a peak of total abstinence by the 1850s.

Gambling underwent similar treatment during the reform era. In 1851, the New York Association for the Suppression of Gambling was established. Founded by Greely and led by Johnathan Green, this organization sought to "expose" gambling establishments. The "Green Law" of 1851 represented New York's toughest gambling law up to that time, mandating minimum fines for anyone found guilty of keeping a gambling establishment, exhibiting gambling devices, or assisting in any banking game. The law also called for the destruction of gambling devices.

Despite its tough language, the Green Law failed to achieve its goal of eradicating gambling. The continued popularity of the activity under attack led both public officials and citizens to defy the law. Moreover, gambling was not just a favorite passtime in urban areas. An estimate 6% of all New York City dwellers looked to the gambling industry for their employment.

Between 1825 and 1855, New York State experienced a doubling of its population, primarily as a result of immigration. Many immigrants came from Eastern Europe with a Catholic background, and they brought with them none of the Protestant tenets against gambling. Further, the bulk of this increase occurred in urban areas. By 1855, one-fourth of the state's population and nearly one-half of Manhattan's inhabitants, were foreign born. The majority of them came from Ireland and Germany. Densely populated enclaves of immigrants developed in the cities. The crowded conditions in which they lived, their poverty, the difficulty of coping with a new language, and cultural barriers contributed to making these people prime supporters of the corrupt machine politics that were to characterize many of the government agencies of New York City and state throughout the last half of the nineteenth century.

Lotteries and numbers were not a major source of concern during most of the twentieth century. Rather it was a game known as "Policy," an offspring of the lottery, that attracted attention. The courts were liberal in determining which of a wide variety of schemes constituted Policy; however, it was not statutorily defined until the 1965 Penal Law declared "Policy" or "the numbers game" a lottery in which the outcome is not determined by any act of the players or promoters.

Despite the laws on the books, Policy continued to flourish in New York City, primarily because it was ingrained in the ghetto neighborhoods of the cities. In Brooklyn's Bedford-Stuyvesant section, for example, the amount the Policy operations handled in 1970 exceeded $36 million. Of that sum organized crime withdrew an estimate $11 million from the community. If the $51 million that was spent on heroin in 1970 is added to that figure, the total organized crime take from Bedford-Stuyvesant in 1970 exceeded $62 million, $6 million more than the federal government received from it in taxes. On the other hand, organized crime was also a major ghetto employer. In 1970 policy alone provided some 15,000 jobs in Bedford-Stuyvesant.

Lotteries have been an on-again-off-again form of legalized gambling since the first gambling laws were enacted, and they remain a dilemma for New York City. In December 1974, Congress dropped its ban on broadcasting lottery information. Since that time several states have instituted major television and radio coverage of their lotteries. In July of 1975, New York joined this trend, in a return to early nineteenth-century practices. Based upon a popular television game show, New York's first lottery broadcast was a half-hour prime-time affair featuring finalists in the state's super $1 million lottery. Billed as the "largest giveaway in history" and hosted by a popular television celebrity, the broadcast attempted to create a sense of drama to entice the playing instincts of the viewers. The lottery is still in effect.

Bookmaking, like gambling and lotteries, continued to grow throughout the twentieth century as a business of organized crime. The drive to stop betting on races was not appreciated by track owners, who had come to rely on the large amounts of money that bookmakers paid to owners. To preserve this revenue, track managers developed a system of "oral betting," which was held to be exempt from the bookmaking law. Again, the court acted to protect betting as entertainment. The bookmaking statute was defined in the 1965 Penal Law as "accepting bets from members of the public as a business, rather than in a casual or personal fashion." Also included as an offense was the possession of flash or water-soluble paper. The only defense available to a possession charge was that the item was neither used nor intended to be used for bookmaking or Policy.

Decriminalization regarding on-track betting came about to stem the persistent illegal gambling and the increased profits that organized crime received from it. New York began to investigate the possibility of returning to the earlier pattern of legalizing certain forms of gambling that could be carefully monitored by public officials. The need for increased revenues that arose between the two World Wars, combined with the invention of the pari-mutuel totalizer, prompted New York to pass a constitutional amendment in 1939 by which the legislature was empowered to authorize pari-mutuel betting on horse races. Such betting was to yield impressive revenues to the state.

In 1940, the legislature enacted the Pari-mutuel Revenue Law, which continued the state racing commission. The commission was empowered to license pari-mutuel betting on horseraces and steeplechases conducted by incorporated racing associations, to set the rules governing such betting, and to investigate all cases related to race betting by subpoenaing books and records. To ensure the honesty of the betting system, the associations were required to be bonded, and precise standards for bookkeeping, bet paying, and information posting were imposed. Betting was limited to on-track transactions, which proved to be a financial boon to track owners.

During the Wagner administration in New York City, a series of fiscal crises inspired the city to lobby for legalized off-track betting (OTB) as a means of solving its financial problems. Advocates claimed that it would raise at least $2 billion annually. While the city pushed for OTB, the state legislature, reflecting race track interests, opposed it. Public opinion in New York City ran three to one in favor of OTB, and one 1963 public opinion poll revealed that few New Yorkers worried about the morality of race betting. The city quickly exercised the local option provided in the law and established the New York City Off-Track Betting Corporation, a public benefit corporation "operated along the lines of a private enterprise business whose profits accrue to the taxpayers in the form of public revenue."

The OTB system is able to accept and transmit bets placed throughout the state into the pari-mutuel systems at the tracks. Thus, only a single pari-mutuel pool is required, and the result is a single parimutuel payout price. The extent to which OTB has accomplished its dual goals of raising revenue and combating organized crime cannot yet be fully evaluated, but a preliminary verdict is that OTB has succeeded in increasing government revenues as well as redistributing them. The irony of the OTB phenomenon is that many horsemen and track owners say that it is slowly destroying racing. They claim that it has caused on-track attendance to sag and that it is responsible for the growing number of racing injuries. Trying to keep up with the minimum figure of $5,600 for the yearly upkeep of each of their race horses, owners no longer give their good stock a rest. Tired horses and tired jockeys make mistakes.

One conclusion about New York gambling would be that despite ventures into legalization and state control, New York has not succeeded in putting organized crime or illegal gambling out of business. In 1973, one study recommended that New York also legalize casino gambling, slot machines, and pari-mutuel betting on jai alai, claiming $1.15 billion per year could be raised as a result of legalization. A study conducted by the Fund for the City of New York, however, found that the goals of trying to raise substantial revenue and compete with organized crime were contradictory. While some forms of gambling were considered manageable by government, others, such as sports betting, were not because the state could neither extend credit nor enforce loans the way organized crime could. The study concluded that "legalizing some forms of gambling as a contribution to the battle against official corruption and organized crime is worth a try. To achieve a measure of success, there will have to be sustained pressure on criminal gambling operations from two sides: the economic competition of a higher-payout legal game and the unacceptable costs of stiff fines and jail terms for those convicted of illegal gambling operations."

The study went on to caution that "it would be a mistake to expect too much to result. Real solutions to such basic problems will require much more basic and far-reaching efforts." The legislature apparently feels that such efforts have been made. In early 1976, it held hearings for a bill to amend the state constitution to allow gambling in state-operated casinos. Most speakers favored legalization; the Speaker of the Assembly, echoing the usual reasons justifying almost all forms of legalized gambling, asserted that casino gambling would strengthen sagging city and state economies and would weaken the grip of organized crime. New York, therefore, seems to be on the verge of returning to its earlier days when most forms of gambling were generally legal, subject only to public order limitations.

It is ironic that today the largest casino in North America is operated not in New York but in Connecticut by Native Americans.

THE SOUTH

Early efforts to control gaming in the southern colonies aimed at the "nuisances" arising from gambling rather than at gaming itself. The earliest enactments of southern colonial legislatures, preoccupied as they were with the more pressing problems of frontier defense and settlement, dealt with gambling only when activities associated with it threatened to disrupt the social order. Thus, the first statutes passed concerned cheating, fighting, or the disruption of the economy caused by large gaming losses. These laws had the effect of promoting hard work and thrift among colonists, who, in the early years, were more interested in gold (metallic or in the form of tobacco) than in producing sufficient food to support the colony. But unlike the laws in Massachusetts, these laws did not embody a work ethic as such. Disorder, not idleness, was the foe.

The earliest enactments of these legislatures generally involved (1) the explicit reception of the Statute of Anne, which declared gambling transactions to be unenforceable and gave a loser of over £10 a right to recover his losses, and (2) passage of local legislation criminalizing various disruptive activities associated with gambling.

The landed gentry controlled politics during the colonial period, and they saw no reason to criminalize the very pleasures that represented an honored part of their life style. More important, no countervailing public movement opposed gambling, and so no token gestures toward antigambling feeling were made. Even Virginia, which prohibited public gambling, did not really strike a blow at the way of life of the tidewater aristocrats; if anything, prohibitions of public gambling struck at the pleasures of the poor, who, unlike the rich, did not have space in their own houses for large-scale gambling. Thus, as the South entered the Revolution, gambling was not condemned by the masses, but was celebrated by the few as part of the "good life." To the degree that the law concerned itself with gambling, as in England, issues of public order and the maintenance of economic stability were of paramount concern.

The lottery, as it was first in England, became a revenue-raising device. Legislators were aware that lotteries did not offer a perfect solution to the problems of raising funds for infrastructure. One early Delaware law, attempting to regularize the chaotic lottery system that had sprung up in the state, talked around the point but did not ban all lotteries.

South Carolina effectively banned all lotteries in 1762; and Virginia and Georgia followed.

The American Revolution joined three different classes from three different areas of the new land: lawyers and merchants from New England; great landowners from the South, particularly Virginia; and frontiersmen, present in most of the colonies, who saw the Revolution not only as an effort to break away from Britain but as a democratic uprising against the social order of many of the colonies themselves. These three classes started the Revolution and then proceeded to create a new nation in a struggle among themselves. Not surprisingly, it seems that all three groups had quite different opinions regarding gambling.

The frontiersmen in what are now the states of Kentucky, Tennessee, Alabama, Arkansas, and Mississippi, borrowed from the laws of gambling that came from the settled area from where they originated. Thus, lawmaking on the southern frontier did not involve a unique process of creating new laws to fit new conditions.

At least one prominent Tennessean welcomed the decriminalization of horse racing. Andrew Jackson, ironically the man whose name would one day be attached to a strong antigambling position, was a lover of horse racing and a frontier politician. In 1788, he participated in a horse race that almost led to his premature demise. Jackson matched a prize horse against a horse owned by Colonel Robert Love in a race that drew spectators from miles around. When Jackson's horse lost, the impetuous young lawyer challenged Love to a duel. Jackson's friends intervened and removed the hot-tempered loser from what might have been a fatal encounter.

In 1811 there was an attempt to legislate against wholesale gambling, to punish those who encouraged gaming and to provide for the forfeiture of liquor licenses of tavern owners who encouraged gaming. Most states in the western South followed the Tennessee-Virginia pattern, and by 1829 Florida and Kentucky had passed the Statute of Anne and prohibited the operations of gaming tables. In Arkansas, similar ends were served by the 1829 statute, although by 1855, Arkansas moved to criminalize all forms of betting. In Mississippi, gaming was a much more visible evil than it was in other states. Natchez was a veritable Las Vegas on the Mississippi in the 1830s and 1840s.

Jackson and Vicksburg were also infested with gamblers during this period. In 1835, Vicksburg citizens rose up in revolt and told the gamblers they had six hours to leave town. When the gamblers refused the "friendly invitation," 400 men gathered to drive them from their lairs. Two gamblers objected to the seizure of their property and killed one of the leaders of the mob, a prominent physician. The mob was satisfied only when the two gamblers were lynched without benefit of clergy or counsel.

By 1860, Tennessee, Kentucky, and Alabama were being settled, and they repeated the pattern of the older states: Gaming was allowed, but any gambling that could cause a public nuisance was prohibited; nonetheless, all of the states gave their blessing to betting on horse racing.

There was always a distinction between private and public gambling. Private gambling was legal and always allowed, but public gambling among Whites and Blacks received harsh punishment. In 1837, Georgia penalized Whites who gambled with free or slave negroes with a one- to five-year jail term. Alabama enacted a similar law in 1852, although the penalties were higher. These punishments were designed to discourage contacts with Whites that might give Blacks troublesome ideas about equality. Ironically, slaves could not be prosecuted for their violations of gambling laws. The Florida Supreme court held, for example, that as a matter of law, a slave was not a "person" (but property) and therefore, since he owned no property, could not be convicted under the state's gambling laws.

Louisiana is an exception to all generalizations concerning the development of gambling law in the South. The South in this era was generally Protestant dominated and rural; Louisiana, at least around New Orleans, was Catholic and urban. English common law formed the basis of most gaming laws in the Northeast and South, but the Napoleonic Code and French law were the root of the legal system in Louisiana, especially New Orleans. These differences can be exaggerated, though, considering that Louisiana was a typical slave state, agriculturally dependent on cash crops.

Political development in Louisiana paralleled that in the rest of the South. In 1806, the territorial legislature passed an act directed at professional gamblers. This act, however, like those that followed, exempted New Orleans from its reach, and thus gambling was indirectly legalized in that city, with predictable results. New Orleans became an open city and a gambler's paradise. It soon taxed gaming houses to produce revenue for the New Orleans Charity Hospital, and gambling promoters consistently pointed to the aid given to the hospital as justification for the continuation of the New Orleans exemption. Public gaming was simply not seen as an evil by its citizens. In the 1840s, however, the city licensed casinos and taxed them in direct violation of state law. Nothing was done about the violations; thus, an attitude of toleration came to be reinforced by lax enforcement. The *laissez-faire* attitude toward gaming that developed in early Louisiana would have important consequences later.

Although most states, after a bad experience with state lotteries, moved toward strict prohibition of gambling in the post-war period, Louisiana moved in the opposite direction. In the 1860s, it actually relaxed its already liberal attitude toward gambling offenses and allowed the birth of the infamous Louisiana State Lottery, otherwise known as the "Serpent." In 1866, the state licensed the Louisiana State Lottery Company (LSLC), the charter of which seemed at first glance to offer the state particularly good terms. The company was given a monopoly for 25 years. In return it was to pay the state $40,000 a year in lieu of taxes. Since there was no guarantee that the lottery would be profitable, the state seemed to have struck a good bargain for itself. With its power confirmed by law, however, the lottery proceeded to corrupt the state in order to maintain its privileged status.

Instead of losing money or breaking even, the lottery became the most profitable enterprise in the state. By 1877, the LSLC began selling tickets in every state in the nation, and the house took a 20% to 40% cut on all revenues produced. Profits were spent to promote the lottery. When reconstructionist Republicans began to lose power, lottery managers shifted with the political winds and poured a quarter of a million dollars into the campaign of a Bourbon Democrat. In 1879, in response to cries for reform, the charter of the LSLC was withdrawn and the sale of all lottery tickets criminalized.

By skillful maneuvering, the Lottery Company induced the Constitutional Convention of 1879 to produce a document that included a provision expressly authorizing the legislature to charter lotteries and mentioning the LSLC by name. The courts construed this as a reinstatement of the lottery's charter. The Serpent was back in business, but several states began to fight it. The Philadelphia *Times* led an aggressive anti-Serpent campaign in Pennsylvania, so the LSLC tricked the *Times* publisher into a trip to Louisiana. Upon arrival, he was served with process in a libel suit instituted by the LSLC. Faced with the inevitability of a losing judgment in the Serpent's home jurisdiction, the publisher forced a settlement of the case by threatening to take it to the then hostile United States Supreme Court. The uproar resulting from this episode helped to bring about the banning of lottery materials through the mails. The lottery was never thereafter as profitable as it had been, and the Serpent was killed by statute on January 1, 1894.

For a while, corruption surrounding the lottery's activities strengthened Louisiana's antigambling forces. Legislation ensued, but the courts refused to read the laws broadly. They held that if skill was involved, a game was not prohibited. Despite legislation to the contrary, gaming continued unabated in Louisiana and gambling flourished in New Orleans until World War I. Indeed, the Kefauver Congressional Committee on organized crime reported that New Orleans remained an "open city" until the 1950s.

A horse race law was enacted to raise revenue for the state through a licensing procedure. By 1940, with the state's cut of the pari-mutuel take, the Louisiana Racing Commission was formed.

Louisiana's relaxed policy is in great measure due to the continuing existence of a large constituency that looks with favor upon gambling. Most all legislation against gambling has been against the professional gambler, not at the bettors or social gamblers. Habitual gamblers have been declared to be vagrants; nevertheless, given the state's long history of tolerating gambling, current legislation decriminalizing gaming is not unexpected.

The National fight against lotteries in the 1830s and 1840s was, in large measure, part of the general movement against both "sin" and monopoly. In 1842, Democrats came into power because of their opposition to lotteries. The lotteries in turn were portrayed merely as an adjunct to a corrupt monopolistic banking system dominated by the wealthy Whig power elite. The great moral fervor of the 1830s produced many reform movements among people both in the North and South. Many states attempted to ban all "unauthorized" (non-state-operated) lotteries.

The movement against lotteries had two significant effects. For the first time, legislatures found that they could not effectively separate the nuisances produced by gambling from the activity of gambling itself. Efforts to criminalize only the nuisances had failed. This, in turn, led to a re-examination of the whole approach of segregating the "excesses" produced by gaming from criminal treatment. Second, since the reform movement produced in most states a constitutional amendment banning lotteries, an important new weapon was placed in the hands of prosecutors and courts in their efforts to prosecute gamblers.

After the Civil War and beyond Reconstruction, the South periodically attempted to become more "Northern" by industrializing and diversifying its agricultural systems. These efforts were only moderately successful, and today, despite constant talk of a "New South," the region remains what it has always been: unique.

Prohibition and Criminalization

The states that have developed a rigid antigambling policy—Mississippi, Alabama, Georgia, Tennessee, North and South Carolina, and, until very recently, Virginia—have, on the whole, done so gradually. For most of them, the inclusion of an antilottery clause in the state constitution marked the beginning of the development of public policy opposed to gambling. Today, Mississippi has completely reversed itself with the implementation of Riverboats, of which there are nine.

Florida. Florida's experiments with legislation have been a direct response to the decline of the tourist industry in the 1920s. Little, if anything, in Florida's previous history would lead one to expect that the state would turn to gambling as a source of revenue in hard times. Once pari-mutuel gambling at race tracks was allowed, however, further state promotion of gambling followed.

Florida had experimented with licensed casino gambling in the years after 1879, although a local option provision gave cities the authority to prohibit such activities if they wished. Courts upheld the licensing system, but it never took hold in any significant way. By 1895, a reform legislature acted to prohibit the operation of gaming houses and also criminalized participation in all games of chance. By 1895, Florida seemed to have moved into the camp of the strict prohibitionists.

The policy of Florida continued on this strict course for the next thirty years. In 1905, for instance, those who frequented gambling houses were declared vagrants, and private citizens could obtain injunctions to close down a gambling house. The courts enforced these laws vigorously. Betting on horse racing was declared to be illegal gambling.

The state might have maintained this rigid antigambling posture but for two of the worst hurricanes of the century that occurred in 1928, devastating Miami and Fort Lauderdale.

The publicity from these storms paralyzed the Florida tourist industry. Moreover, the state was faced with the task of raising large amounts of revenue to rebuild the ruined cities. Since the state constitution forbade an income tax, alternative sources of revenue were necessary.

Faced with these crises, Florida turned once more to licensed gambling, hoping to raise revenue and attract Northern tourists to the state. A regulated system of licensing for pari-mutuel horseracing, dog racing, and jai alai was established. Betting outside the pari-mutuel system was forbidden, and racing days were controlled. This revenue-raising device largely fulfilled its purpose.

Florida's experiments with legalized gambling came to a halt after 1937. This was partly because of the public's awareness of the problems of organized crime. The pari-mutuel system was a major exception to the rule, but the official policy of the state seemed to swing back in the direction of antigambling.

Today, Florida's form of legalized gambling is the state's sixth largest revenue source. Although casino gambling has appeared on referendums many times in the recent past, the public, and therefore the legislature, holds firmly against it. Because of the recent downturn in the national economy and the added proliferation of gaming in other states, Florida has once again inaugurated a state lottery, and there have been very recent indications that it may consider casino gaming in a more favorable light.

Other States. Of all the Southern states, only Louisiana, Florida, and Maryland have experimented with legalized gambling on a large scale in the modern era. In other southern states the exceptions to general prohibition have been narrowly drawn. West Virginia prohibits all betting, either public or private, and the prohibition extends to all games, whether or not skill is involved. In 1933, the state permitted pari-mutuel betting at race tracks and in 1935 established a racing commission to oversee the operation of the system. Racing was a temporary response to a crisis, and the state has shown no signs of expanding the exception.

Kentucky, too, has legalized pari-mutuel betting, but here again the exception is due to the size and power of the state's horse-racing industry, and it is a clear exception to the antigambling policy. While the state's Legislative Research Commission has recommended the adoption of off-track betting, no action has been taken on the proposal. There is no evidence that Kentucky's laws are expanding beyond horse racing, as its position against gambling otherwise has remained firm.

Delaware has generally stringent laws against gambling. In 1951, betting itself was criminalized. Thus, the legalization of pari-mutuel betting in 1935 seemed, for a while, to represent a distinct exception to the general rule and can be explained only by the Great Depression.

Arkansas legalized pari-mutuel betting in 1935 in response to the Depression and a state commission was established in 1957. In the same year, pari-mutuel betting on greyhound racing was expressly permitted by the state. Although it was never legalized , Arkansas did tolerate the existence of large-scale casino gambling in Hot Springs for a significant period of time, until *The New York Times* picked up on the close working relationship between Arkansas politicians and the casino operators. State officials were finally forced to reconcile their expressed public policy with their private action and suppress the casinos. The casino operators attempted to reopen by gaining passage of a statewide referendum legalizing their operation, but the antigambling feelings of the people and the state's apparently strict antigambling policy won. The unique allowance of casino gaming in Hot Springs was probably due to the tourist business generated by visitors from St. Louis and Chicago. Since the closing of the casinos in Hot Springs, no further moves have been made to decriminalize gambling. The prospect for further legalization seems remote, especially since the population remains rural and Protestant.

THE MIDWEST

Early gambling statutes in the Northwest Territory closely paralleled those in the East. The preamble of the 1790 Northwest Territory Act, the first antigambling statute affecting the Territory which reflected a philosophy characteristic of much of Puritan-derived legislation, articulated the danger seen in continued gambling activity. The 1790 act declared gaming contracts to be void, and any person who established or permitted the establishment of "any species of gaming" where money might be wagered could draw a $200 fine. In the absence of organized law enforcement on the frontier, the statute encouraged the prosecution of violations by private individuals through a provision that reserved one-half of all the resultant fines for the private prosecutor. The act also prohibited tavern keepers from keeping billiard or other tables. Those who violated the ordinance risked losing their licenses.

Lotteries never enjoyed the popularity in the early Midwest that they enjoyed in the East and South, perhaps because they were not a financial necessity as they were in the early days of development in these latter areas; where they were used to raise revenue. By the time Midwestern towns needed capital for major improvements, the newly chartered banks of New York and other Eastern cities could provide it. Lotteries had, therefore, lost their most viable rationale by the end of the eighteenth century; only their gambling aspects remained.

Before 1800, the only route west from Ohio was the Ohio River. After 1800, overland roads were built, but they were at best "rock-strewn, precipitous roadways over the mountains" or "rutted or muddy courses through the lowlands." Thus, most settlers continued to rely on the river for at least the first 20 years of the nineteenth century.

River travel increased remarkably with the development of the steamboat. The first steamboat on the great central rivers, *The New Orleans,* was launched by Nicholas J. Roosevelt in 1911 at Pittsburg. By 1815, another steamboat, the *Enterprise,* made the long upriver journey on the Mississippi between New Orleans and Louisville in only 25 days.

Only ten years later, there were 75 steamboats making regular journeys on the Mississippi and Ohio rivers.

Improved river transportation gave rise to the massive westward migration of the 1820s and 1830s. The steamboat not only brought population and prosperity to Midwestern river cities, it brought gambling as well. Professional gamblers regularly worked the steamboats of the Mississippi and Ohio; the boats were an ideal setting for the victimization of unsuspecting travelers. On land, the town tavern of more rural days was replaced by the "wolf trap," a primitive form of casino. Cincinnati, an early population center and the chief port on the Ohio River, was particularly infested with these river-borne hustlers.

The citizens of Ohio, however, were not pleased with the influx of gamblers. Antigambling fervor increased throughout the 1820s and 1830s. In the wake of antigambling riots and lynchings, Ohio river towns expelled gambling hustlers. In Cincinnati, an angry mob threatened to burn down all the gambling houses and hang their occupants. Only the intervention of Mayor Sam Davis saved the lives of the gamblers and, perhaps by design, the gambling industry itself.

Settlements on the Mississippi River generally lagged behind settlement of the Ohio Valley by about 30 years. In the mid-nineteenth century, many of Iowa's settlers came west from Ohio, apparently wishing to escape the rapid population growth. Indeed, many of the Iowa pioneer families of the 1840s had been Ohio pioneer families between 1790 and 1820.

Missouri was settled much earlier than the rest of the land west of the Mississippi because of its location on the lower Mississippi and its proximity to the Gulf of Mexico. In fact, Missouri's settlement coincided closely with that of the Northwest Territory. During the eighteenth century, French Canadian trappers and traders roamed the region, but after 1815 pioneers poured in, especially along the Missouri and Mississippi. Thus, gambling and antigambling activity west of the Mississippi originated in the territorial days of Missouri.

In 1814, the Missouri Territorial Legislature passed its first law prohibiting gambling. Section 3 of the act prohibited the keeping of any gaming tables and subjected violators to a fine not exceeding $500. This 1814 provision is identical to the current provision except that two additional forms of gambling were brought within its prohibition: keno in 1881 and slot machines in 1901. Sections 5 and 7 of the 1814 law have also been retained with little modification. Reflecting the Statute of Anne, Section 5 declared that debts and other commercial transactions that were based on gambling were null and void. Section 7 fined the owner of any building who was convicted of permitting gambling on his premises.

Iowa's first gambling statute was not enacted until 1838—24 years after Missouri's—and reflected the later period of settlement of the Iowa

Territory. In general, migration upriver from St. Louis was slow because the United States continued to recognize Indian title to the region, even after the Louisiana Purchase.

Iowa was pronounced a U.S. Territory the same year gambling was declared illegal. At the same time, and in sharp contrast to the laws of other areas, Iowa made gambling debts collectible. These were defined as "any valuable thing won by gambling or playing at cards, dice, or other games of hazard whatsoever." Despite the collection provision, the law was designed to discourage gambling. The statute also provided a procedure by which gambling losses could be recovered for use by the county by any person. The 1838 law made it a misdemeanor to keep gaming tables and to "induce, entice, or permit any person to bet or play" dice.

With the passage of time, new laws enacted by the newer territories were more sophisticated than the ones enacted by their predecessors. Instead of simply prohibiting the possession or use of gambling devices, for instance, Iowa introduced a nuisance law and provided for the seizure and destruction of gambling devices. Similarly, witness immunity was made available to law enforcement officials in Iowa but not to those who were trying to suppress gambling in the Ohio River Valley. Iowa was also the first Midwestern jurisdiction to declare that any person who "does or is suspected to get his livelihood by gaming" was a vagrant and subject to imprisonment.

In 1843, the Iowa legislature expanded the Territory's gambling laws to include more of the traditional provisions. Lotteries, never popular in Iowa, were outlawed. Also, all gambling debts were declared void, thus repealing the contradictory provision in the 1838 law. Losers could sue for recovery of losses within six months, and if a loser failed to sue, any other person could do so. An element of private enforcement was thus introduced.

Minnesota was the next territory to be formed from the land bought in the Louisiana Purchase. It was established in 1849, and the Organic Act of Minnesota immediately became law. This act provided that the laws in force in the Territory of Wisconsin at the date of Wisconsin's admission as a state were to "become valid and operative in Minnesota until altered, modified, or repealed by the legislature."

Minnesota did not pass its own gambling provision until 1851. Its antigambling statute forbade keeping, using, or betting on gaming tables and rendered all gambling contracts void. Minnesota also introduced nuisance concepts into its gambling law, but, unlike Iowa, required search warrants to be issued before an alleged gambling device could be seized. In the same year, the state granted municipalities the independent power to suppress gambling.

After the territories enacted these first provisions, the legislatures remained silent on the subject of gambling for 20 years. The courts also refrained from active involvement in the development of the law of gambling at this time. The only noteworthy decision was an Iowa case that held that horse racing was not a game of chance as defined by the statutory prohibitions on gambling and, thus, not forbidden by law.

Lotteries, the only significant gambling activity west of the Mississippi, were played in Missouri. In fact, Missouri was an important exception to the Midwest's relative lack of lottery activity, perhaps having been influenced somewhat by the constant lottery activity of its downriver neighbor, Louisiana. In the first decades of the nineteenth century, the Missouri legislature periodically authorized lotteries. In 1835, however, it began to show its disapproval of them by prohibiting all those not authorized by the state. In 1842, the legislature attempted to eliminate all lottery activity in Missouri by repealing lottery authorization enactments. A Missouri court, however, found the new statute unconstitutional. The court affirmed the lower court's ruling that the statute violated a federal constitutional ban on laws impairing the obligation of prior contracts.

As a result of this court decision, lotteries that were previously authorized continued to flourish in Missouri. The most notable of these was the New Franklin Road Lottery, which had been franchised in 1833 to raise $15,000 to build a road from New Franklin to the Missouri River. The lottery continued to flourish into the 1870s long after New Franklin had been abandoned and the road had collapsed into the river. Finally, in 1880 the Missouri court declared that the franchise of the New Franklin Lottery had finally expired. The state could then constitutionally enforce its lottery ban.

The mid-nineteenth century was a period of increased judicial definition of gambling law, which broadened the reach of existing laws. Although the enforcement of gambling law in the Midwest was never efficient, prosecutions were numerous enough to allow courts to clarify the artfully worded statutes. Laws were strengthened with added clauses about cheating and use of gambling devices.

In 1819, Michigan banned horse racing and declared it a public nuisance. It was not until 1882, however, that Michigan courts were forced to define gaming. The definition imposed by Judge Cooley was simple: "Let a stake be laid upon the chances of a game, and we have gaming." After 1860, Michigan entered a stage of development experienced by Ohio 30 to 40 years earlier. Betting on elections and betting by minors were both outlawed. In 1877, Michigan specifically banned gaming on railroad cars and increased various gaming penalties.

Antigambling sentiment in two of the last Midwestern states to be populated—Wisconsin and Minnesota—reached a peak in the 1870s and 1880s. Wisconsin banned gambling on railroads in 1875 and forbade Policy in 1883. In 1888, a Wisconsin court decision upheld the legality of horse racing for prizes, but declared that the prize offering could not be mere subterfuge for betting or gaming. In 1870, Minnesota augmented earlier territorial gambling prohibitions by introducing nuisance laws and municipal enforcement. The state banned railroad and steamboat gambling in 1874 and sought to curtail swindling in an 1877 enactment. In 1878, Minnesota added special provisions to protect minors from gambling and banned gambling in taverns.

By the mid-nineteenth century, lotteries had been prohibited in the Midwest for years. Gambling opponents were not content, however, until antilottery amendments were added to all the state constitutions.

The opposition to lotteries in the Midwest can be understood by examining the then prevailing Jacksonian ideology. Authorized lotteries were a form of legislatively bestowed privilege and monopoly that the Jacksonians fiercely attacked. Because the people saw the state charter lottery system as a conspiracy between legislative representatives and private interest groups, statutory prohibition against lotteries would not suffice. Constitutional provision, however, could forever prevent a legislature from suddenly repealing an antilottery statute and enacting a lottery authorization. Thus, the passage of the antilottery provision was a matter of the people checking the legislatures rather than the legislature curtailing the activities of the people.

Jacksonian opposition to state-authorized lotteries was part of its opposition to the Second bank of the United States. To the Jacksonians, the bank was a monstrous symbol of privilege and speculation that threatened political equality by promoting the creation of a special class—a money aristocracy. Although there was never any real threat that the United States would develop a society as class-locked as that of Europe, the Jacksonians were vigilant about preventing privileged groups from getting rich by any means other than their own labor.

Jackson's sentiments on banking could sum up equally well his followers' opposition to lotteries. Antilottery sentiment was motivated by a strong "money-for-labor" philosophy. No one should expect to get rich by a lucky draw, and the lottery operators should not reap a fortune by collecting the nickels and dimes of farmers and washerwomen. Just as the Jacksonians were against the federal government granting privileges to one bank, they were also against the states granting privileges to lottery companies. The Jacksonian belief firmly held on the frontier and in the West, that all property should be earned through work, echoes earlier Puritan edicts against idleness.

To some extent, this was a morality of necessity. The harsh conditions in both seventeenth-century Massachusetts and early-nineteenth-century Illinois would not support shirkers. The only way for a frontiersman to pull himself out of poverty was through hard work, discipline, and temperate habits.

In the late nineteenth century, a new gambling evil was feared in the Midwest: commodities speculation. Trading in futures was seen as extremely dangerous to the economic health of the region and the entire nation. While the panics of 1837 and 1857 were commonly blamed on wild land speculation, the panic of 1873 was seen as the consequence of commodities speculation. In response, dissatisfied Midwestern farmers forced the passage of antispeculation legislation and abandoned their traditional Republican Party to form small third parties. These parties eventually coalesced into the Populist movement, led by Wisconsin Governor Robert La Follette.

One of the problems confronting the agricultural states during this unstable periods was the apparent contradiction between the need for a market in futures commodities to provide capital and the tendency of speculators to use that market for gambling.

Indiana was the first Midwestern state to tackle the futures problem. In 1865, its Supreme Court held that dealing in futures was not illegal gambling, but it later held that commodities speculation *was* illegal if, at the time of making the contract, neither party intended the actual delivery of the goods. The court was attempting to ban "bucket shops" and speculation, but to permit legitimate futures contracts.

As a national center of agricultural trading, Illinois's experience with the futures problem is particularly important. By 1860, Illinois had a population of 1 million. Chicago had surpassed St. Louis as the Midwest's largest city and Cincinnati as the nation's leading center of meat packing. Northern Illinois industries, many of them serving agriculture's need for manufactured products, made Illinois third in the nation in manufacturing.

Against this background, the Illinois legislature banned all futures contracts in 1874. One year later, however, the courts modified this prohibition to allow futures contracts where at least one party intended delivery. Nevertheless, this view was later discarded in favor of a more stringent interpretation of the statute. An 1889 case, *Schneider v. Turner*, held that *all* option contracts were unlawful. The court noted the purpose of the statute: "It manifestly is to break down the pernicious practice of gambling on the market prices of grain and other commodities." Whatever the purpose of the statute, it was apparently not effective. In an 1890 case, *Soby v. People*, the court observed: "The evil it was aimed at, continued to increase with wonderful rapidity through the state . . ." To remedy the statute's ineffectiveness, another act was passed in 1887 to suppress bucket shops.

In 1990, judicial course was again reversed, when the court in *Booth v. People* held that suppression of market gambling was within the police power of the state, and that suppression need not embrace each and every contract for options, "but only those which are at the root of the evil which threatens the public safety and welfare." This decision opened the way for a legitimate commodities market with state regulation.

Politically, the Midwest was a Republican stronghold from the Civil War to the 1930s. It was not until Franklin Roosevelt and the New Deal that the GOP lost its political monopoly and the Democrats made major inroads. The changing political allegiance in the Midwest was due in part to a changing population. Between the two world wars, immigrants came from Europe, Canada, and the southern United States. Moreover, southern Blacks arrived in the northern industrial cities in great numbers. Today these cities have significant Black populations; however, the Midwestern states without major metropolitan areas remain essentially White.

Religion, too, changed the Midwest. While Protestants continued to be the majority, the number of Catholics and Jews has increased significantly since 1900, particularly in the cities.

Finally, the Midwest economy changed from largely agricultural in the nineteenth century to primarily industrial in the twentieth. The midwest still produces much of the nation's food, but more Midwestern workers are engaged in manufacturing than in farming. These social and economic changes may account for a softening of the Midwest's traditional attitude against gambling. In contrast to the blanket prohibition of the nineteenth century, various states now allow pari-mutuel betting, state-authorized lotteries, and Bingo for charity. The urban states (Illinois, Ohio, Michigan), with their more diverse economies and populations, generally have the more liberal gambling laws. In contrast, Indiana, which is still largely rural, retains its earlier, more conservative prohibitions.

Nevertheless, the Midwest remains more opposed to gambling and the liberalization of gambling laws than the Northeast. Although the twentieth century has brought cultural and economic diversification to the region, the old religious and rural influences are still strong enough to form significant resistance to gambling liberalization.

Because of the recent economic downturn of the late 1980s, liberalization and decriminalization of gaming have been considered. The proliferation of riverboat gambling from Iowa to New Orleans, and lakeside casinos in Chicago, is an indication of this trend.

Chicago was incorporated in 1833, and by that time "the mud hole of the prairie" already had its share of gamblers. By the 1840s, there were far more gambling houses in Chicago than in St. Louis or Cincinnati, even though the city on the lake was only half the size of either river city.

Committees of town fathers were formed to rid Chicago of this growing vice, but they were unsuccessful until "Long John" Wentworth became mayor in 1857. At that time, there was a notorious vice section north of the Chicago River known as the Sands. Newspaper articles reported that untold numbers of strangers were lured to the gambling dens there and robbed and murdered. Despite repeated efforts to clean up the area, it continued as a haven for hustlers, thieves, and other undesirables. Then, one afternoon in 1857, an advertisement of a dogfight in another part of the city lured all the male inhabitants away from the Sands. While they were gone, Wentworth sent in a sheriff and 30 policemen to demolish and burn down 15 tumbledown buildings. By destroying their nest, the mayor's men effectively scattered the gamblers all over town. Not content to stop there, Wentworth raided a gambling house on more respectable Randolph Street. Policemen entered the building through the roof and chased the gamblers and employees out to the street, where they were captured and arrested. The contents of the building—gambling equipment and furnishings—were then confiscated.

Wentworth and other Chicagoans continued to fight gambling, but during the Civil War their energies were necessarily directed elsewhere. Once again, gamblers flocked in and set up shop. After the war, Chicago's sporting circle was dominated by Mike McDonald, the purported originator of the phrase "There's a sucker born every minute." As a young man in New Orleans in the 1850s, McDonald had become enamored with the glamour of gambling and resolved to take part.

By the 1880s, McDonald had also achieved considerable political influence: He engineered the campaign of Mayor Carter Harrison (a mayor who did not have Wentworth's reformist tastes) and became the leader of the Cook County Democratic machine. Despite his part in the graft of city building contracts and scandals involving his two wives, McDonald successfully combined the two roles of gambling czar and political broker until his death in 1907.

In McDonald's time, vice and urban politics were dominated by the Irish, but by the early twentieth century, crime had become more ethnically diverse. Figures on Chicago's underworld in the 1930s show that 30% of the bosses were Italian, 29% were Irish, 20% were Jewish, and 12% were Black. Not one leader was listed as a White American of native-born stock. This is undoubtedly because organized crime—defined here merely as the distribution and sale of illegal goods and services—has traditionally served as an avenue of upward social mobility for new groups in America. After an ethnic group has spent several generations dealing in gambling, prostitution, drugs, and (during Prohibition) liquor, it moves on to legitimate businesses and professions.

Organized crime did not originate with bootlegging during Prohibition. Rather, it began with gambling syndicates in American cities after the Civil War. As illustrated by the career of Mike McDonald, gambling had close links with urban politics. One reason for this connection was the common Irish background of the gamblers, police, and politicians of the late nineteenth century. A more important reason, however, was that the gambling syndicate and the political machine were often part of the same neighborhood organizations. Gambling operations such as numbers, depended upon a large number of runners who cultivated friendships with the local citizens in much the same way that a precinct captain did. Thus, organized crime was entrenched in Chicago and other American cities long before the passage of the Volstead Act in 1920.

Prohibition ushered the Italians into organized crime and probably accounted for the myth that *all* organized crime began with bootlegging. By the time Italians began immigrating to the United States in large numbers, most areas of illicit activity had already been monopolized by other groups. The Irish, for example, dominated gambling and racketeering, and the Blacks controlled policy.

Bootlegging gave Italians their opportunity, but not all bootleggers were Italian. In fact, there were twice as many Jews as Italians involved in the distribution of illegal spirits. Whatever their ethnic background, however, bootleggers were almost all newcomers to the underworld: young men in their twenties who had grown up in urban slums.

Once Italians and other bootleggers made their entry into organized crime, they branched into other areas, particularly gambling. Almost from the beginning, bootleggers invested in gambling operations and continued to expand long after repeal. Since Prohibition lasted only 13 years, most bootleggers were still only in their thirties and had amassed extensive capital when alcohol became legal again. In most cases, the bootlegging entrepreneurs invested in the existing gambling structure, but seldom replaced the gamblers already there. The system could absorb these newcomers, although not always without muscle and violence, because gambling opportunities expanded during the 1920s and 1930s.

Increased use of the telephone altered bookmakers' methods of operations, and the legalization of pari-mutuel horse racing gradually eliminated the bookmaker's role at the track. Many bootleggers also found it convenient to go into slot machines as a sideline. Since the machines were often placed in speakeasies, it was easy to service them as trucks went from place to place delivering liquor. In the years after the repeal of Prohibition, ex-bootleggers also played a significant part in the creation of regional gambling centers: Miami, Florida; Hot Springs, Arkansas; and, most notably, Las Vegas, Nevada.

Blacks and Organized Crime

In the past 40 years, Italian dominance of organized crime has declined. As Italians enter legitimate businesses and professions and become assimilated into the mainstream of American culture, Blacks, and in some cases Puerto Ricans, are assuming control of the nation's gambling, prostitution, and narcotics. Although Black participation in the entire spectrum of organized crime is a recent phenomenon, Black control of policy is not. Originating in Black neighborhoods in the nineteenth century, Policy was contemptuously labeled by White racketeers as the "nickels and dimes game of the poor." Even so, in New York it was eventually taken over by Whites in the 1930s. In Chicago, however, it remained in Black hands until 1952, when it was wrested from them by Sam Giancana, a late Mafia chieftain.

One reason given for Chicago's long period of Black control was the close political connection with Mayor "Big Jim" Thompson from 1915 to 1931. In the same kind of symbiotic relationship that existed between gamblers and politicians in the nineteenth century, Thompson and the Black organization were mutually helpful. The Blacks paid $500,000 a year to his machine, and Thompson gave protection to the Blacks' operations. In addition, Black underworld employees registered Black voters, got them to the polls, and served as election judges. It has been asserted that Blacks must again establish the same type of political connections before their organization can succeed like that of the Italians.

Other Forms of Gambling

A twentieth-century gambling phenomenon was the movie house "bank night." Motion pictures became commercially significant around the turn of the century, but the Depression was hard on the movie industry. Along with other struggling businesses, it was forced to create new marketing devices to survive, and one of these was bank night, where a ticket bought admission and a chance to win a prize.

Clearly, the bank night looked like a lottery, and most Midwestern states had constitutional prohibitions against lotteries. Even so, the legal status of bank nights was not always clear. Prizes might include cars, refrigerators, stoves, and other items of varying values. Clever promoters found ways to get around the fact that bank nights were defined as lotteries, however, and 33 years later the court found ways to get around this definition. A theater gave a cash prize to a person whose name was drawn from a list of everyone who had previously registered. Thus, to win a person did not have to pay admission to the theater on the night of the drawing. Nevertheless, the court held that the scheme was a lottery, saying that to abide by previous decisions to the contrary would be to join hands with those who would attempt to defeat the lottery laws and evade the state constitutions. As a result, such pronouncements stunted further growth of bank nights. Since the 1930s, lotteries such as this have been all but eliminated.

What was meant by a gambling device was not always clear. Slot machines were generally found to be gambling devices; a 1937 Missouri court easily reached this conclusion by applying the traditional test of whether skill or chance was the dominant element. The status of pinball machines that offered free replays, however, was more problematic.

Courts had noted that gambling had three necessary elements: (1) consideration or risk; (2) chance; and (3) reward or prize. However, in conservative Indiana the law took a different course. In 1955, the legislature excluded pinball machines that gave only the right to an immediate replay from the list of prohibited gambling devices. Two years later, the Indiana court held that this distinction between free-replay machines and other types of machines had a rational basis. While some machines provided unearned monetary gain, free-replay pinball machines provided only free entertainment, so the distinction was not unconstitutional. By 1960, however, the Indiana court held that pinball machines that *recorded* the number of replays won were gambling devices. The court even went further to say that pinball machines were gambling devices because free replays were a thing of value.

Legalization of Gambling

The twentieth century has produced two major periods of financial need for some Midwestern states: the Great Depression and the fiscal crises of the 1970s and 1980s. In response to the Depression, Illinois legalized pari-mutuel on-track betting in 1927; Ohio and Michigan followed suit in 1933. The legislatures of these states created regulatory agencies and specified operational guidelines. This followed a period when horse breeding and racing were becoming popular, especially in nearby Kentucky. All of these changes followed the development of the technical necessities for the pari-mutuel system. In the late 1970s, instances of reported race fixing had been reported as far west as Illinois. Nevertheless, Illinois was fourth in state revenues from horseracing, behind New York, California, and Florida.

Despite the recent institution of income taxes in some states, Ohio, Illinois, and Michigan again found themselves in stiffening financial straits. Wisconsin and Missouri also expressed doubt about the ability of current revenues to meet increasing needs for social services in their larger cities. One typical response to these revenue demands was to follow the lead of New Hampshire, New Jersey, and New York by establishing a state lottery, and this course was followed in Michigan, Ohio, and Illinois. Attempts to establish state lotteries in Wisconsin and Iowa, however, failed in the 1970s.

Gambling prohibitions have been relaxed in other areas. Among these are the recent exemptions of charitable, religious, and fraternal organizations from the ban on Bingo and similar games. States have drafted guidelines for the games that specify maximum prizes and the frequency of game nights. Church Bingo and similar games have generally been well received in the Midwest.

Most changes in gambling laws during the twentieth century have been attempts to suppress the involvement of organized crime. States have also singled out organized, illegal gambling by distinguishing between social and private gambling, and commercial and professional gambling.

In Iowa, the problems with the 1973 gambling law prompted the legislature to pass a comprehensive revision in 1975. The new statute is not intended to resurrect Iowa's former prohibition against all gambling. Rather, it permits the social and charitable gambling that is popular in the state yet curtails commercial gambling that attracts organized crime. Gambling is now regulated through extensive licensing. Iowa aptly illustrates the course of reform being pursued in a number of states as it begins to reconsider old legislative traditions.

THE WEST

Before 1850, the West was generally inhabited by strays—cowboys, prospectors, miners, and fur traders. It was a crude region, populated almost exclusively by men. There were no laws and no formal government to restrain antisocial behavior. In fact, the early West was more a collection of individuals than any sort of coherent society. When these loners did gather, it was often to conduct such riotous rituals as the "rendezvous" of the fur trappers.

> For several days, while a whole year's business was transacted, celebrations and merriment were also in order. Horse races, gambling, drinking, dancing, story telling, and swapping Indian wives were as much a part of the *rendezvous* as was the barter of beaver. Often the mountain men, who were an improvident carefree lot, would lose the result of a whole year's grueling work in a few days of a riotous *rendezvous*.[3]

Such periodic debauchery also appealed to the miners and the cowboys who followed the trappers as the West's chief inhabitants. A combined casino, bordello, and saloon, the "CBS" was a fixture wherever there was extra money to be spent. Gambling, whoring, and drinking took place openly and was welcomed in the early boom towns for the fat profit it yielded.

As one author crudely put it, "Four things indicate prosperity in a mining town—Hebrews, gamblers, common women, and fleas. Hebrews, gamblers, and common women are accurate thermometers of ready money and prosperity. When Jews and gamblers pull stakes for another town, it is a safe guess that prosperity is also going."

Gambling was not considered socially degrading in these impromptu communities. Moreover, until these areas garnered enough residents to win formal territorial recognition, problems of law and order were settled by local people, who set up rudimentary policing functions.

But cheating, and the violence it spawned, had to be controlled in the early West. Too often, this meant a vigilante hanging or two. Vigilante justice quickly become as loathsome and as unruly as the evils it sought to correct. Slowly, even the cowboy and the miner came to see the need for law. Yet it was not the cowboy or the miner who brought the restraints of civilization to the old West.

After the Civil War, settlement of the West by farmers and their families was actively promoted. The war had resolved the conflict over whether future Western states would be slave or free. Sizable areas of the Kansas, Nebraska, and Dakota territories were already well populated by the 1850s, but other more distant regions awaited the coming of the railroads for large-scale immigration. Until the end of the nineteenth century, however, the journey west was extremely dangerous. Most settlers had to cross the continent in wagons or on foot.

The constant threat of violence from Indians and other settlers was another hazard of the Western wilderness. In 1873, an Arizona vigilante group called the Law and Order Society lynched four alleged murderers on one of Tucson's busiest streets. Even later, in 1881, the Earp brothers and Doc Holiday settled their dispute with the Clantons in a gunfight at the O.K. Corral. Ultimately, private law enforcement was replaced by a formal government only when there were enough immigrants to warrant territorial recognition by the federal government. The territory's residents would elect a legislature, and the federal government would appoint a governor and judges.

Characteristically, one of the first acts of the newly elected territorial legislatures was to pass antigambling statutes. This was particularly true on the Great Plains, where the legislatures were dominated from the beginning by farmers. Kansas and Nebraska, for example, both gained territorial status in 1854, and by 1855 the sodbusters had triumphed over the veteran frontiersmen by passing a comprehensive gambling law.

Unlike other Western states, Utah never experienced conflict between new settlers and old. The Mormons were the first pioneers to reach Utah, and the first territorial antigambling law was enacted without significant opposition. This legislation was reminiscent of the laws passed in the Puritan colonies in the seventeenth century. For example, the mere playing of games was forbidden, regardless of whether the players placed wagers. The laws were theologically derived.

Alaska is another Western state that experienced little conflict over gambling in its early years. The Yukon gold rush of 1896 led to an increase in gambling and lawlessness, but the gold rush eventually ended, and the hordes stopped coming. Throughout most of its history, Alaska was largely regarded as a government outpost, and federally appointed officials simply decided which laws should be adopted.

Typically, early territorial statutes were modeled on the existing laws of most eastern states. For example, the Kansas Act of 1855, which was identical to a Missouri statute passed in the same year, outlawed all games of chance. Specifically prohibited were setting up or keeping games of ABC, Faro Bank, E.O., Roulette, or Equality. Conviction under the statute was limited to cases where the accused kept a prohibited device and permitted someone to play it. The maximum penalty was one year's imprisonment and a $1,000 fine.

Gambling laws in the West were not passed in the spirit of Puritan attacks on idleness, as they often were in the East. Thus, even in legislatures dominated by Methodist farmers, zealous antigambling campaigns were not crusades against greed and sloth. Rather, as in the South, they were intended as methods for controlling the abuses of public gambling only. The majority of Western states, like Virginia, tolerated private, social gambling; they attempted to outlaw only the public, commercialized variety. Even when individuals were caught in public gaming houses, they were only lightly fined or not held liable at all.

Texas law illustrates the general Western distinction between private and public gambling. The Penal Code of 1856 acknowledged that a private room in an inn or tavern did not come within the intended ban on gambling in public places. Further, the code did not prevent individuals from indulging in games of chance for their own amusement.

The Texas courts restated this distinction between private and public gaming. An earlier court explained that the blanket prohibition on gaming tables and banks was due to their purely commercial nature. Western gambling laws were meant neither to save gamblers from their own folly nor to condemn wicked and wasteful behavior. Like their counterparts in the South rather than in the Northeast, the laws were enacted in an effort to curtail the worst abuses of public and commercial gambling.

As legends of the Wild West recount, gambling often resulted in disorderly conduct and violence. Those abuses had to be controlled before farmers would move their families into the towns. Since lawless behavior was directly associated with gambling, gambling was declared illegal as part of a concerted effort to eliminate the prevailing unruliness.

Recently, however, some historians have questioned whether gambling's excesses really posed a serious enough threat to warrant a blanket prohibition. One writer asserts that only 15 homicides occurred in notorious Dodge City between 1870 and 1885, and few of these were related to gambling. Bat Masterson, the redoubtable lawman hired to tame the unruly in Dodge City, in fact killed no one in his several years as sheriff. Although gambling was almost exclusively town centered, contemporary newspaper reports indicate that violent crimes in Western towns such as Dodge City were relatively infrequent. Thus, while myth implies that the frontier townsfolk were besieged by armed desperadoes who flocked to the casinos, brothels, and saloons, the record suggests that this was not the case.

Indeed, the frontier towns, even with their gambling, were comparatively safe. Town entrepreneurs, interested in the steady growth of these communities, had to be assured of an orderly, stable place to conduct business. Even the proprietors of gambling establishments—often the owners of more legitimate businesses as well—were in favor of curbing gambling abuses, although clearly they did not want to prohibit gambling altogether. When the town did become unruly from time to time, it was still easier to control the crime and violence there than out on the open plains.

Nevertheless, many Western states and territories passed stern measures against gambling. It is difficult to explain why Nebraska, which had a fairly negligible problem with gambling abuses, would adopt such radical prohibitions. It would seem that the state never considered a more discriminating approach, such as a licensing system to regulate and restrain gaming.

Apparently, Nebraska's agrarian interests, reflecting its Eastern origins, dictated an absolute ban on gambling as soon as they gained control of the legislature. The opposition to gambling, however, was more than a pragmatic objection to the growth of crime. Rather, it was a demonstration of political anger: Gambling was a speculative enterprise designed to take advantage of the hardworking but unwary farmer. Once again, the Jacksonian influence was seen in operation.

The response to gambling in the Far West—the Rocky Mountain states and the Southwest—was quite different from that on the Great Plains. In Wyoming, Montana, and Arizona, there was no incipient clash between old-timers and newcomers. Farmers never came to these states in great numbers, so there was never great opposition to the gambling establishment. Unlike the farm states, the Far West did not prohibit gambling altogether, but many legislatures did pass licensing and regulation measures.

The licensing scheme passed by the Montana territorial legislature, for instance, was typical of those enacted by most Far West states. The owner of each house where gambling tables were kept or games of chance were played was to pay a fee of $50 per month. The fee schedule was adjusted in both 1873 and 1877, and from its increasing size one may infer that profits to gambling house operators were substantial. The 1887 law required each operator to pay a $100 general fee every three months plus $40 per month for every Faro table and $250 per month for every Poker or Roulette table.

Despite regulation, many Far West gambling operations bordered on fraud. The governor of New Mexico described the house advantages as being "enormous," the player having a 250% less chance of winning than in some of the more respectable casinos. In Montana, where certain types of casino games were welcomed, Three-Card Monte, strap games, Thimble-Rig Black and Red, the Ten Dice game, Faro, and "any other game where fraud or cheating was practiced" were nonetheless banished. The penalty for violators was severe: up to five years in the county jail, a maximum of $1,000 fine, or both. Gambling fraud was considered a serious offense not only because innocent players were fleeced, but also because suspected cheaters—along with a few bystanders—were often shot.

The Statehood Era

The Far West. The desire to achieve statehood eventually moved even reluctant states to adopt a ban on commercial gambling. In a 1907 conversation with New Mexico's newly appointed territorial governor, President Theodore Roosevelt personally outlined the terms of statehood: "Captain, I know your ambition is to have New Mexico made a state, but before you can get statehood, you must clean house in New Mexico and show to Congress that the people of New Mexico are capable of governing themselves."

The implication was that the territory would have to dispel, among other things, its general reputation for lawlessness by prohibiting gambling. In most Far Western states, the years just before statehood were marked by conflict between the federally appointed governor and the popularly elected legislatures. The governors, who were often outsiders, tried endlessly to direct the legislatures toward banning gambling. The legislatures' reaction was usually to balk at being told what to do.

The Farm States. By the time Kansas and Nebraska were granted statehood, the small farming community had become the dominant political unit on the prairies. The cowboys farther west continued to tread lightly on gamblers, but the farmers redoubled their efforts to banish gambling completely. One form singled out for special attack was the lottery. The original constitutions of many of the farm states included express provisions against legislatively authorized lotteries. Since lotteries were never prevalent in the West, it is difficult to explain these measures as responses to particular abuses, as in the East. They are best seen as symbolic gestures against legislatively franchised privilege and legislative corruption. Thus, they are really eastern law carried to the West. Western populists remembering lotteries chiefly for the corruption and privilege that they represented in the East, prohibited them wherever they went.

Soon after statehood, the Western farm states enacted a series of statutes intended to add enforcement techniques to their initial gambling statutes. Public officials who failed to pursue and prosecute gambling offenders were subject to punishment. Witness immunity statutes were also added to the gambling prohibitions, and vagrancy laws were expanded to include the "common gambler." If nothing else, the vagrancy laws could be used to harass gamblers to leave town.

Finally, the Western farm states revised their laws to prohibit a new gambling phenomenon, commodities speculation. In states with strict gambling laws, commodity futures provided a legitimate forum for gamblers. Bucket shops were open to conduct what appeared to be *bona fide* futures transactions, but were in reality wagering contracts. Most states enacted bucket shop provisions to distinguish between authentic futures delivery contracts and illegal stock gambling.

Lotteries. States that outlawed gambling generally included all forms of lotteries in their prohibition. The universally accepted definition of a lottery in the West was any scheme for the distribution of money or property, among persons who have given or agreed to give, a valuable consideration for the chance, whether called a lottery or some other name. In every state, a lottery consisted of three key elements: *consideration* paid for the *chance* to win a prize. Other events characterized as a lottery might be bank night schemes, gift enterprises, and pinball machines.

In most states in the West and Midwest, and until this day, state constitutions have prohibited state-authorized lotteries more out of the fear of privilege and legislative corruption than out of a moral repugnance to lotteries per se.

By the twentieth century, however, any game that resembled a lottery was flatly prohibited, no matter how innocent. Pinball arguably was not a game of chance, and clearly not a form of speculation. It was literally only a nickel-and-dime business. Nor were bank nights and gift enterprises forms of speculation, but marketing techniques that were devised during the Depression to keep businessmen from going under. In fact, many of these businessmen were the same small-scale entrepreneurs that Jacksonians were in favor of protecting.

The Modern Era: A Trend toward Legalization

Western states historically imposed comparatively low taxes on their citizens. Indeed, low taxes became a staunch political tradition in the West. In times of fiscal crisis, such as the Great Depression and the recent recessions of the 1970s and 1980s, many Western states looked to legalized gambling as an alternative source of revenue. The Depression forced the establishment of pari-mutuel horse racing in six Western states: California, Oregon, South Dakota, Nebraska, Texas, and Washington. In other states that traditionally took firm positions against gambling, the populace often chose to pay higher taxes rather than to legalize gambling. In each case, courts ruled that the legislature was constitutionally barred from licensing any form of lottery. Recently, however, the Kansas constitution was amended to allow charitable Bingo. The charitable Bingo exception is common in the West and throughout the United States.

In recent years, there has been a movement toward a general decriminalization of gambling in a few prohibitionist states. In 1971, for example, the Washington legislature voted to authorize and license a number of gambling activities. Upon receipt of the bill, however, Governor Evans promptly vetoed it. In his view, the legislature had "opened the door to professional gambling in Washington." Further, he was not convinced that legalization was truly supported by the people. After three years of extensive caucusing, the legislature was able partly to override the governor's veto and to legalize licensed public card parlors.

By 1974, the politics of gambling had changed in Washington. Once fairly homogeneous, the population had become more diverse. The earlier consensus on the total prohibition of gambling was diluted by the arrival of immigrants whose ancestry was neither Jacksonian nor pioneer.

California, on the other hand, shows no sign of legalizing gambling. Although it suffers from some of the same fiscal problems as the large Eastern states, it has not turned to legalized gambling as a new source of revenue. Further, unlike some Eastern states, California has not had to legalize gambling to combat the involvement of organized crime. The Kefauver Committee Report noted that although Los Angeles and San Francisco have extensive illegal gambling, the state's gambling is not heavily infiltrated by organized crime of the Mafia type. According to U.S. Department of Justice estimates, less than a third of all Far West gambling is controlled by Mafia racketeers.[4]

Other Western states have been less hesitant to legalize gambling to raise revenue. Indeed, many of these states, such as Montana, Idaho, and Wyoming, were never resolutely in favor of prohibition. In 1965, Montana legalized pari-mutuel betting and created the Montana Horse Racing Commission, by which all participants in racing must be licensed. The state nets 1% of the gross receipts, while the track keeps 20%.

As early as 1937, Montana attempted to license certain games and "trade stimulators." For a $10 license fee, charitable organizations or businesses could provide cards and tables for playing Rummy, Whist, Bridge, Blackjack, Hearts, Dominoes, and Checkers. Also for a $10 license fee, businesses were authorized to operate trade-stimulating contests for the use of adult customers. As in Kansas, however, the courts later found this statute unconstitutional under the states' antilottery provision.

In 1972, Montana rewrote its constitution and omitted the antilottery clause. The new constitution specifically allows lotteries to be authorized by legislation, referendum, or initiative. The state has also decriminalized several forms of gaming. The Card and Games Act of 1974 provides that cities, towns, and counties may, for a fee, issue card game licenses to authorized vendors of liquor, beer, food, or other consumables. The 1974 act authorizes localities to issue licenses for Bingo and raffles.

Nevada: A Case Study

The Territorial Experience: 1827–1864. The story of Nevada's territorial history begins with a few exploratory treks by pioneer trappers (Jedidiah Smith and John C. Frémont) and religious groups in the third decade of the nineteenth century. The word "Nevada" itself is derived from a Spanish word meaning "snow capped" and was first applied to the mountains on its western border. The story of the Nevada territory ends with 15 years of gold fever, as town after town sprang up, bustled with life, and died according to the whim and luck of the prospectors. Politically and economically, this was a confusing era, full of both the divisiveness that sprang from conflicts between conservative Mormons and carefree gold-diggers, and the odd sense of community abandon that characterized the prospector, who willingly cast his lot with "Lady Luck."

The first substantial settlements in Nevada occurred shortly after the signing of the Treaty of Guadalupe Hidalgo in February, 1848, by which Mexico ceded the territory that included Nevada to the United States. Brigham Young and his faithful band of Mormons, who had established Salt Lake city only two years before, continued to expand westward and organized a government, which they called the "State of Deseret" in the Nevada Territory. Although the federal government did not recognize the new state, the Mormons continued to settle the area.

It was not until two years later, however, that the event that was to shape Nevada's early history came to pass. Gold had been discovered in California in 1849, and as hundreds of wagon trains began to pour through Nevada on their way to California, eager prospectors got out to test the soil. In 1850, a lone prospector climbed into a ravine near the California border and sifted a few specks of gold. Although it would be several years before the gold rush enveloped Nevada and its neighboring state, the discovery reverberated in Sacramento and other Pacific settlements and set the stage for the first important scenes in Nevada's social history.

The Permissive Period. Throughout the early 1850s, prospectors searched intensely for a big find in the Nevada Territory. By the spring of 1859, four finds near the California border had uncovered one of the biggest discoveries of the gold rush years: the Comstock Lode. The news ran through California papers in the summer of 1859, and within weeks the trails to Nevada swelled with prospectors, bringing with them a lifestyle that was to affect the state for generations.

Mining communities formed and grew to thousands within weeks: Gold Hill, Virginia City, Silver City, and others. Hotels, general stores, and dozens of the inevitable casino-bordello-saloons soon lined the streets. Even though gambling had not been prevalent in the straight-laced Mormon communities, it was now widespread. The prospectors of Nevada were veterans of the California gold rush, and the colossal uncertainties of their life made the hazard and the bet an integral part of the gold-mining lifestyle.

Impromptu government districts were established to guarantee land titles, and although the deeds were usually kept in a book of records behind the bar in the local saloon, they were generally accepted as legal by the California courts. Nonetheless, lawlessness and disorder reigned in the Nevada territory until 1861, when Congress, frightened by the secession of the Southern states and desperate for support from the Northern states, established the Territory of Nevada.

James Warren Nye, a native New York Republican and a political ally of President Abraham Lincoln, was appointed territorial governor. Nye had been Commissioner of Police in New York City and was a firm advocate of law and order. The wild lifestyle of the Nevada miners shocked him. He agreed with the Mormon conservatives from the outset, and in August, 1861, the first territorial elections were held. In his first speech to the representatives two months later, Nye left no doubt as to where he stood on the gambling issue. "Of all the seductive devices extant," he said, "I regard that of gambling as the worst." He continued: "It holds out allurement hard to be resisted. It captivates and ensnares the young, blunts all the moral sensibilities, and ends in utter ruin. The thousand monuments that are reared along this pathway of ruin, demand at your hands all the protection the law can give."

The First Sanctions Against Gambling. Following this lead, the legislature passed a broad statute banning all forms of gambling a month later. Violators were guilty of a felony and could be imprisoned for two years and fined $5,000. Even those betting on other people's innocent games were subject to six months in prison and a $500 fine. Witnesses who provided information to a grand or petit jury were not prosecuted. As a final incentive, District Attorneys received $100 for each conviction they could obtain.

Despite such attraction for enforcement, convictions under the act were virtually nonexistent. Gambling was as much a part of the Nevada lifestyle as were the mines, and no group of representatives in Carson City managed to change this phenomenon solely by the passage of legislation. Governor Nye sought federal help in support of his enforcement of the act, but Washington D.C., engaged in a civil war, was in no position to help the governor with a disobedience problem in the West.

Further, it appeared to Republican politicians that the election of

1864 might be very close, and they were eager to have another Republican state in their column, particularly if the election were thrown into the House of Representatives. Reversing its stand of less than a year before, Congress took only six weeks to pass the statehood bill and have it signed by the president. In July of 1864, the Nevada Constitution, its first and only basic charter, was written. The voters approved it in September, and in October President Lincoln declared Nevada a state, just in time for the November election.

The Formative Era: 1864–1910. Although Carson City was humming with political activity as Nevada entered its first decades of statehood, the real action of the new state's life was a few miles to the northeast on the slopes of Sun Mountain. There, the state's gold miners were busy devising methods to extract and refine the silver and gold of the Comstock. Their success meant that Comstock, gold mining, and the lifestyle that went with it were to dominate the history of Nevada for years to come.

A reversal of the original act occurred in 1869 when the state legislature made gaming legal in spite of the governor's veto. Many specific games were approved, and the first fees were imposed—half of these fees were retained by the counties, and the balance went to support the state.

One prohibition held up as it did in most other states—no lottery was authorized by Nevada nor would the sale of lottery tickets be allowed.

Between 1869 and 1907, many changes in regulations and fees were made, with the main concern being where and when gaming could be conducted and that games would be properly licensed and fees paid. Slot fees continued to go to the state and all other fees to the counties. In 1871 and 1881, the Nevada Benevolent Association was authorized to conduct raffles and gift concerts.

The Second Boom. For those with cash, gambling flourished until 1910, despite a serious depression that began in 1880 with the decline of the Comstock Lode. Nevada's gamblers still collected their chips in the back rooms of hundreds of small saloons throughout the state. In 1990, Jim Butler, an occasional miner, discovered new traces of gold and silver in Nevada's southwestern hills. Within months, the hundreds of prospectors who poured into the area matched Butler's discovery with their own, and Nevada was once again the object of a great gold rush. Tonopah and Goldfield became the new centers of mining activity, and with the miners came a revival of the rough-and-tumble lifestyle Nevada had known so well.

The Modern Era: 1910–1975. In 1909, there was a turnabout—total prohibition—all forms of gaming were again prohibited, the law to become effective on October 1, 1910. Violation was now a felony, and doors could be broken down to seize equipment. It was a repeat of the experience of the 1860s, during which gambling had, for four years, officially been illegal, although in fact it was widespread. Gamblers were still around; they were just more discreet. All that really happened was a loss of revenue from the lack of license and fee receipts. One of the reasons that Nevada's citizens tolerated the new gaming relaxation law so well was that virtually everyone assumed it would soon be repealed.

In 1915, upon the governor's recommendation, the legislature relaxed restrictions on gaming; social games could be played for drinks, cigars, or other prizes whose value did not exceed $2. Also permitted were games in which the deal changed after each hand. Operators were required to have licenses. During these years, the laws and their enforcement became less effective, and illegal operations increased and started taking business from the legal establishments. This caused a decrease in state and local license fees.

On January 16, 1920, the Eighteenth Amendment and the Volstead Act took effect, and Nevada, like the rest of the nation, was thrown into Prohibition. Prohibition did not engender respect for law enforcement anywhere, but in Nevada, where the laws against the consumption of liquor and gambling existed side by side, the effect was even more pronounced. Knowledge of the speakeasy password entitled a person to enjoy both vices—liquor and gambling—and disrespect for the law was rampant. By 1930, antigambling fervor was substantially exhausted. The only residents who strongly opposed gambling were apparently the same upper- and middle-class women who supported Prohibition, and their support among the citizenry was fading after two decades of experimentation. Talk of gambling legalization became widespread.

The true birth of Nevada's modern era of gaming began with the legalization of gambling in 1931. The "Wide Open Gambling Bill" occurred simultaneously with the passage of the six-week divorce law. Growth was slow during the 10 years following the Depression, and by 1941 growth had increased only 49% over the 1931–1932 level. However, between 1941 and 1944 gaming had increased 56%. The period 1942–1944 became the dividing point between Nevada's early gaming history and its modern era.

Through the mining camp days into the twentieth century, Nevada's casinos for the most part catered to the local gamblers. There was no effort to lure big-time gamblers from out of state. Reno and Washoe County were the leading areas, both in population and in the amount of gambling that took place. The construction of Hoover Dam (finished in 1935) caused some growth in Southern Nevada, but prior to World War II, Las Vegas had been little more than a water stop on the Union Pacific

Railroad and a respite for those traveling across the desert to southern California. Las Vegas at that time accounted for little more than 15 percent of Nevada gaming.

The turning point came at the end of World War II, when pent-up demand for enlargement would soon be answered with the long awaited availability of building materials.

In 1946, the Fabulous Flamingo, the first of the posh strip luxury casino hotels, burst on the scene. The many casinos on the strip shifted the dominant gaming from Reno and Washoe County to Las Vegas and Clark County. Also in 1946, new concepts of licensing and fees based on a percentage of gross win came into being. These fees were in addition to the earlier county and state fees.

In 1955, a major legislative change took place when the Nevada Gaming Control Board (with three members) was formed within the Nevada Tax Commission. The primary mission of this new agency was to inaugurate a policy that would eliminate the undesirable element in Nevada gaming and provide regulations for the licensing and operation of gaming.

In 1959, the current Nevada Gaming Control Act was enacted, creating the five-member Nevada Gaming Commission with absolute power to grant or deny any application for a gaming license. The commission also had the power to enact regulations and to act as the collection agency of all gaming taxes. The Gaming Control Board was removed from the Tax Commission and became the investigative and enforcement arm of the Gaming Commission. In 1961, a Gaming Policy Board (composed of the Governor, five members of the Gaming Commission, and three members of the Gaming Control Board) was formed. Its purpose was to discuss matters of gaming policy for the state.

Another major change occurred during the period 1967–1969. At first, corporate ownership of gaming establishments had been discouraged, and most ownership was through proprietorships and partnerships. This was sufficient as long as casinos were small, but some grew to 20 to 30 partners, and one had 50 partners. All of these had to be found suitable to be licensed. The corporate gaming laws that were enacted allowed companies to form Nevada corporations with a limited number of officers and directors who were "key employees." Howard Hughes was influential in these changes. He envisioned the future growth in southern Nevada gaming as being an increase in capability to handle larger volumes of business. Such corporations received funding from major money sources that could be identified as not empowered to influence gaming. This allowed the next major growth of Las Vegas hotels: the Las Vegas Hilton, Caesars Palace, the MGM, and numerous expansions of smaller casinos on the strip such as the Stardust, Frontier, Sands, Desert Inn, and others.

In 1971, the Gaming Control Board assumed all administrative functions for the Gaming Commission. The Gaming Policy Board became the Gaming Policy Committee, the membership of which changed to one member of the Gaming Commission and Gaming Control Board; two members of the general public; and two licensees. In 1977, one member of the State Assembly and one member of the State Senate were also added to the Policy Committee.

Regulation 6 became the "accounting control regulation" and was among the first regulations created by the new Gaming Commission.

In 1975, to protect the integrity of the industry, employee labor organizations became the subject of legislation that provided a mechanism to determine the suitability of union officials who represented gaming employees. This move grew out of a concern by state officials that organized crime might seek to gain another foothold in Nevada's gaming industry through union activity.

In 1979, it became possible for supervision to be appointed for casinos in distress because of the removal of operatives, and to keep from having to put people out of work.

In the 1990s, a new and current wave of expansion came upon the Las Vegas scene with the addition of the Mirage, Excalibur, Luxor, Treasure Island, and the MGM Casino Hotel and Theme Park.

As of this writing, there are 87,845 hotel rooms in place and an expected 7,043 additional rooms to come, some of which will replace the recently imploded Dunes, and others that will adorn the shore of the new Lake Las Vegas.

The success of this and future growth in Nevada gaming is based strongly on the premise that gaming is a major part of the entertainment world, and on the strong desire by the state to keep gaming as a major, healthy, viable, and productive industry, as evidenced by the following "Statement of Policy:"

> The State of Nevada Legislature hereby finds, and declares to be the Public Policy of the State, that:
>
> a. The gaming industry is vitally important to the economy of the State and the General Welfare of the inhabitants.
> b. The continued growth and success of gaming is dependent upon public confidence and trust that licensed gaming is conducted honestly and competitively, that the rights of the creditors of licensees are protected, and that gaming is free from criminal and corruptive elements.
> c. Public confidence and trust can only be maintained by strict regulation of all persons, locations, practices, associations and activities related to the operation of licensed gaming establishments and the manufacture or distribution of gambling equipment.

    d. All establishments where gaming is conducted and where gambling devices are operated, and manufacturers, sellers, and distributors of certain gambling devices and equipment must therefore be licensed, controlled, and assisted to protect the public health, safety, morals, good order, and general welfare of the inhabitants of the State to foster the stability and success of gaming and to preserve the competitive economy and policies of free competition of the State of Nevada.

2. No applicant for a license or other affirmative commission approval has any *right* to a license or the granting of the approval sought. Any license issued or other commission approval granted pursuant to the provisions of this chapter or Chapter 464 of NRS is a *revocable privilege*, and no holder acquires any vested right therein or thereunder.

CONCLUSION

In the past two hundred years, British and American gambling laws have undergone profound changes. Government policy, which was originally directed at the suppression of gambling, has developed to the point where gambling is now recognized as a legitimate recreational activity that needs only to be regulated to prevent excess and fraud. The success of new regulatory systems has recently led many state governments to legalize lotteries on a large scale, thus reversing a century-and-a-half old policy of suppression.

The philosopher George Santayana, in an oft-quoted dictum, observed that he who would not remember the past is doomed to relive its mistakes. It is with that observation in mind that this chapter has reviewed the development of gambling law from its earliest origins.

Having painted a picture both broad and detailed, we can reach specific conclusions. Specific suggestions for needed records, too, have been offered; it remains now only to make some general observations.

If history teaches any lesson, it is that each form of gambling must be examined on its own terms. The law has taken few "gambling positions." Instead, it has attempted to deal with public or private lotteries, wagering, and in specific locations, betting on sporting or other events, machine gambling, and casino-type operations. Reformers, too, ought to distinguish these types of gambling in discussions of reform.

The law has long recognized that different forms of gambling have different impacts on society. Only on a superficial level can our legal policies be considered contradictory. From a public policy viewpoint, gambling has never been thought to be inherently objectionable. Careful attention has always been placed on its social consequences. It has always been recognized, too, that its different forms have had different consequences. Questions must be asked about who operates it, who participates in it, levels of participation, methods of promotion, places of participation, and degrees of regulation.

A publicly run lottery, only mildly advertised and selling high-price tickets to the middle and upper classes to finance needed social improvements, is gambling in its most benign form. A private lottery, fraudulently milking the poor for the benefit of organized crime that serves as a source of public corruption and the capitalization of other criminal endeavors, is gambling in its most vicious form. Other combinations of these basic elements will, of course, produce forms of gambling having different mixtures of benefit and burden. The obvious point is that each new combination must be evaluated on its own terms. Sweeping generalizations should always be avoided.

It seems that our ability to control various forms of gambling through law enforcement varies. It is too often observed that gambling enforcement is inherently ineffective. Generally, this is said with only one form of gambling in mind, but the statement is uttered without qualification. History shows that gambling enforcement can be quite effective with the commitment of few resources against some of its public forms. The federal gambling-ship legislation was effective upon passage. Few enforcement efforts have been taken, yet the statute has been singularly successful. Similarly, overt casino or machine gambling can be controlled with a minimum of honest enforcement personnel. It is only when efforts are made to control clandestine private lotteries or sports wagering that the problems tend to outrun society's present level of enforcement resources. The formulation of new gambling policies, therefore, ought to proceed in full awareness of these distinctions and of enforcement limitation. Here, as elsewhere, people get what they are willing to pay for.

A comprehensive review of the development of the law of gambling also demonstrates the complexity of the legal policies that have grown up over the years. Comprehensive reform must take that complexity into consideration. Seldom can any issue be worked out by the consideration of only one body of law. The criminal law and its general policy of prohibition lies at the heart of society's legal attitudes toward the various forms of gambling, yet criminal law is supported by a complex series of parallel civil rules, few of which have been reduced to statutory form. Reform of the heart, therefore, may have unintended consequences in the extremities, unless careful attention is given to the civil law.

If the policy of the civil law is important, even more so is the policy of taxation. The single most important factor in the success of various efforts to substitute forms of public gambling for private illegal gambling is tax policy. Several general conclusions must be drawn. All of the evidence seems to indicate that there is no justification for the highly publicized expectation that the decriminalization of gambling will provide an important new source of revenue for public treasuries. Legalized gambling, too, probably cannot simultaneously serve the twin objectives of maximum gains in revenue and improved law enforcement through competition with illicit gambling. Finally, tax laws must be reformulated to recognize economic facts of life, so that taxation does not put lawful forms of gambling in uncompetitive positions with unlawful forms.

The relation of the law of other jurisdictions must be considered in the formulation and execution of new policies. The impact of the law of any one jurisdiction is a complex intermixture of criminal, civil, and tax policy. Equally so, the policy of neighbor states and, even more so, the policy of the federal government must be taken into account. Federal tax policy can frustrate the implementation of state efforts to work out new gambling policy choices. Indeed, unless it is possible to coordinate federal and state policy, it may not be possible to make new starts at the state level; it may even be unwise to try.

This conclusion began with reference to Santayana. It seems appropriate to end it with a reference to the dramatist George Bernard Shaw, who suggested that the only thing that history teaches is that history does not teach. The development of the law of gambling seems to have about it a tendency to return to where it began. A historian can only comment that it need not be so.

REFERENCES

1. H. Messick and B. Goldblatt. *The Only Game In Town.* New York: Thomas Y. Crowell Company, 1976.
2. Messick and Goldblatt.
3. *The Gamblers,* from the Old West Series. New York: Time/Life Books Inc., 1978.
4. Taken from *The Development of the Law of Gambling 1776–1976.* The National Institute of Law Enforcement and Criminal Justice Law Enforcement Assistance Administration, United States Department of Justice, Washington D.C., 1976.

Chapter 2

The Economics of Gaming

Since 1988, legalized casino-style gaming has been expanding rapidly in the United States and changing the face of the industry. Prior to 1989, Nevada and Atlantic City were the only U.S. jurisdictions with legalized casino gaming. Yet even with their reputation as North America's gambling meccas, casinos are more of a regional phenomena. For example, of the more than 22 million people who visit Las Vegas annually, nearly one-half are from the West and fully 30% travel from California, while just 10% are from the East.[1] On the East coast, one-fourth of all U.S. residents reside within 300 miles of Atlantic City. From this region Atlantic City gets over 75% of its visitors, the majority of whom live no more than 150 miles away.[2]

Since 1989 casino-style gaming has proliferated across the country on American Indian reservations, in limited-stakes casinos in South Dakota and Colorado, and on riverboats in Iowa, Illinois, Mississippi, and Louisiana. Further expansion of casino-style gaming will continue along regional lines, with the bulk of the visitors drawn from the areas surrounding the new jurisdictions.

This chapter examines the economics of the expansion of legalized gaming in the United States from a macroeconomic perspective, including factors driving this expansion, the impact on the economies of newly legalized jurisdictions such as Mississippi, and the impact on established jurisdictions such as Las Vegas.

THE EXPANSION OF LEGALIZED GAMING

In *Gambling and the Law*, I. Nelson Rose says that gambling in the United States is in its "third wave." The first wave started during the Colonial period and died out almost totally before the Civil War. The second wave started shortly after the Civil War, driven by the South's need to raise revenue to rebuild, and ended because of scandals, including the notorious Louisiana Lottery scandal of the 1890s. As a result of these scandals, voters became so disenchanted with gambling that they began to include antigambling language in their state constitutions. The third wave of legalized gaming began in the 1960s with the introduction of the New Hampshire sweepstakes in 1964. Since then a total of 36 states have introduced lotteries, which generated revenue of $11.5 billion in 1992.

Much of the motivation for the growth of legalized gaming manifests itself in the search by state governments to increase tax revenue and to extend the tax base in order to maintain existing programs. Lotteries traditionally have been the legalized gaming of choice for state governments, and to keep revenue growing lotteries have continued to turn to new games including multistate lotteries and "video" lotteries, in which participants play small-stakes games such as Poker, Keno, and Blackjack.

New games, however, have not kept lottery revenue growing as fast as the increasing reliance of states on this form of financing. This has led to a heightened interest in other forms of legalized gaming. Native American gaming has accelerated this process as states feel the loss of potential tax revenue to the tax-exempt Native American lands. Certainly, taxes on gaming revenue are seen as "painless" and "voluntary"—much easier for politicians to propose than other tax alternatives. There are, however, other fundamental changes that are helping drive the jurisdictional growth of gaming.

FACTORS CONTRIBUTING TO GAMING INDUSTRY GROWTH

Several factors point to the continued growth of gaming, but the overriding cause is the increase in disposable income associated with the move from an industrial economy to a service economy. Increasing productivity gives individuals more leisure time, and competition continues to keep the cost of manufactured goods down, leaving households with more disposable income. Disposable income has increased also because of demographic factors, including the arrival of the baby boom generation at their peak earnings age, the tendency of families to have fewer children to support, and the prevalence of double-income households. Moreover, an increasing proportion of household incomes is being spent on services, including leisure and entertainment, of which gambling is one part.

Casino gaming in particular will be a winner in this shift to a service economy, as over the years gaming has lost much of the moral stigma that it once had and is becoming more and more accepted as a form of entertainment. In addition, much of the population has not been exposed to casino gaming; thus, it has added cachet as a new entertainment and leisure product.

Increasing productivity in the manufacturing sector and industrialization of third-world countries make competition for manufacturing jobs keen. For example, Alabama recently granted approximately $200 million in tax abatements and other incentives to encourage Mercedes-Benz to locate 1,700 manufacturing jobs in that state. Jobs and disposable income are flowing out of the manufacturing sector into the generally untaxed service sector. Thus, states are finding their traditional sources of revenue based on a manufacturing economy under attack, and state budgets are feeling the pinch of flat or declining revenue. The legalization of various forms of gaming is an opportunity to capitalize on those trends.

When gaming is legalized in a particular jurisdiction, $200 million in incentives do not go along with it. Instead, gaming companies are expected to pay as much as 20 percent of their gross revenue in taxes. This is clearly a tax on leisure services that is unpopular in other forms of services. Additionally, a single casino can provide 700 to 1,500 jobs—jobs that are specific to that area and not directly in danger of export to other areas.

Once the legalization of casino-style gaming has started we look for the domino effect to take hold as more states realize the implications of the shift to a service economy and move to defend their jobs and broaden their tax base. For example, shortly after Iowa began riverboat gaming operations on the Mississippi River in 1991, Illinois introduced river boat gaming as well. After all, if Iowa has gaming and Illinois does not, a loss of potential revenue occurs when Illinois residents travel to Iowa. Unlike Iowa, however, riverboat gambling in Illinois has no betting limits or maximum chip buy-ins. This more liberal approach helps the competitiveness and profitability of operators there versus those in more restricted gaming venues.

The contagious desire to share in this "painless tax" from gambling continued with the state of Mississippi bettering the then-existing competition, allowing unlimited licensing and 24-hour dockside gaming as opposed to requiring the riverboats to cruise during the gaming sessions. This exemption translates into a tremendous cost and capital expenditure savings for gaming operators in Mississippi. Further, it allows for a land-based extension of the vessel, allowing the incorporation of hotels, restaurants, and other amenities into the overall casino development.

Not wishing to be left out, Louisiana has approved casino-style gaming on riverboats and certain forms of land-based gaming as well. Other states looking at legalized casino-style gaming include Texas, Pennsylvania, and Massachusetts.

This domino effect is also being driven by the growth of gaming on American Indian lands. In October 1988, the Federal Indian Gaming Regulatory Act was passed. The act provided that Native American tribes could conduct any form of gambling without restriction on tribal lands, if that form of gambling is legal within the state and an agreement, or compact, has been entered into between the state and the tribe.

Subsequent to passage, a series of legal decisions have been returned clarifying aspects and defining its power. The net effect of these decisions has been to clarify the types of games Native Americans have been allowed to offer and to make casino-style gaming more accessible to a greater segment of the U.S. population. Because states have no tax authority over operations on tribal lands, the state receives no direct tax revenue from Native American gaming operations. What follows, then, is not much different from a state's concern for its citizens and potential tax revenue being attracted to a legalized gaming jurisdiction in a neighboring state.

This "third wave" of legalized casino-style gambling is spreading rapidly across the country. It has been pushed by fundamental shifts in the economy as well as the need for states to raise additional tax revenue and compete with the spread of gaming on tribal lands and in neighboring states.

ECONOMIC IMPACT

The immediate economic impact of gaming in the emerging gaming jurisdictions is easy to see. Riverboat gaming revenue rose nearly 250% in 1993. Hundreds of millions of dollars in capital flowed into Mississippi with the opening of more than two dozen casinos opened in that state during 1993 and 1994. While the short-term effects of legalized gaming seem promising, the ultimate impact on the newly legalized gaming jurisdictions will depend on future competitive conditions, including the ability to attract tourism, tax structures, and the type of gambling allowed.

The success of the new gaming jurisdictions will depend upon tourism. The Nevada experience is an economy built not just on gaming but on tourism, with the bulk of the money flowing into the state from regions outside it. In the emerging gaming jurisdictions, with casinos placed near metropolitan areas and catering to a more local and regional clientele, the economic impact will not be as dramatic as hoped. Indeed, as opposed to manufacturing industries, "The multiplier effect in the casino industry is less pervasive. . . . If these new jurisdictions cannot offer gaming to patrons who come from outside the region, economic growth will be illusive at best."[3]

Casino-style gaming, focusing on local play, will probably not be the economic panacea that state legislators envision. These casinos will draw discretionary spending from other entertainment areas in the community such as theaters and restaurants. Only to the extent that they focus on local play to repatriate spending that goes outside of the community—to another gaming jurisdiction, for example—will they be successful.

The introduction of casino-style gaming is no guarantee that tourism will follow, either. Iowa was the first state to legalize riverboat gaming, albeit on a limited scale, when its first floating casino opened in April 1991. The number of casinos in Iowa peaked at five for a period of 14 months before two riverboats left for greener pastures in Mississippi after the opening of riverboat gaming in neighboring Illinois in September 1991. Riverboat casinos in Iowa now number three, and riverboat gaming revenue in Iowa fell 35%, from $70 million in 1992 to $45 million in 1993.

Having something more than gaming and the development of a tourism infrastructure will be critical for the new gaming jurisdictions to get the economic development they seek. However, as casino gaming spreads, increasing competition among new gaming jurisdictions will mute the economic impact of additional new properties.

Important to the development of a casino gaming and tourism industry is the tax structure. In late 1993, Mercedes-Benz chose to locate a manufacturing facility employing 1,700 workers in Alabama after the state granted approximately $200 million in tax abatements and other incentives. In contrast, when casino gaming is legalized, gaming operators are expected to pay as much as 20 percent of their revenue in taxes. In effect, the casino operators become partners with the state.

As a form of revenue enhancement, the taxation of casino gaming is highly effective. Discretionary spending flows from restaurants, malls, or savings, where the tax rate on the revenue may be 4% or 8%, or none at all, into casino gaming, where the tax rate is double or triple the sales tax rate. However, high tax rates can preclude investment in facilities and the development of tourist infrastructure. Operators cannot afford to turn over 15% or more of their revenue and support facilities like those seen in Las Vegas. Alternatively, an operator granted a limited monopoly for casino gaming can pay higher tax rates and afford to invest in facilities; with a limited monopoly, however, the operator has no incentive to do so. Nevada has boomed, in part, because the relatively low gaming taxes and the competitive market give operators the means and the incentive to invest in their facilities, construction of which can have a major impact on the local economy.

Finally, the type of gaming allowed, an outgrowth of the tax structure and the politics of getting gaming approved, has an impact on the development of a gaming and tourism industry. Types of gaming can be described by the size of the wager—small stakes generally being regarded as wagers of no more than $5 per play—or by the state licensing scheme—whether a limited number of licenses or a competitive scheme with licenses granted to all state-approved operators. Outside of Nevada, all new gaming jurisdictions have some form of limitation on wagers, on licensing, or on both.

Some of the most restrictive limitations for operators in new jurisdictions are on the size of wagers. South Dakota and Colorado, with their small-stakes land-based gaming, and Iowa's riverboat gaming all restrict wagers to less than $5 per play. This has the effect of increasing the cost for operators, or limiting their revenue potential, which thus tends to limit investment in facilities and amenities. The most successful of the small-stakes gaming jurisdictions appear to be the small mining towns of Colorado, because of their proximity to the metropolitan areas of Denver and Colorado Springs.

The other form of restriction is based on licensing. All the new riverboat jurisdictions have this to some extent, whether by number of licenses or by location. All the riverboat casinos are restricted to "navigable waters" within their respective states, which precludes casinos from going up just anywhere. All the new riverboat jurisdictions limit the total number of licenses allowed, except Missouri, which limits licenses to one per city except Kansas City and St. Louis, and Mississippi, which has competitive licensing with 20 casinos open in February 1994 and more on the way.

The early returns, from Mississippi with competitive licensing and Illinois with limited licensing, show the impact of the different licensing schemes. In 1992, Illinois had a full year of riverboat gaming with a maximum of five casinos open during the year, and it posted statewide gaming revenue of $226 million. Mississippi began riverboat casino operations in August 1992, eventually had five casinos in operation, and posted statewide gaming revenue of $122 million. In 1993, both jurisdictions grew rapidly. The growth of Mississippi far outstripped that of Illinois, however. In 1993, Mississippi gaming revenue increased nearly 550% to $790 million, while Illinois gaming revenue increased 168% to $606 million. At the end of December, 9 of the eventual 10 licensees were open in Illinois, while at the end of 1993, 17 casinos were open in Mississippi.

The competitive licensing of Mississippi and the lowest tax rate of any of the new gaming jurisdictions has brought a lot of capital to Mississippi, and that state has moved rapidly in the development of a gaming and tourism infrastructure. There can be no question that to date legalized gaming has had a positive impact to one degree or another on state and local economies. The ultimate effect, as gaming expands, will depend upon the ability to generate tourism, the tax rates imposed on the gaming operators, and the structure of gaming that is legalized in the various jurisdictions.

CONCLUSION

Since the late 1980s, a number of factors have conspired to drive the growth of legalized casino-style gaming in North America. The continuing shift from an industrial to a service economy, flat to declining tax revenue from traditional sources, and the acceptance of gaming as a form of entertainment is making the legalization of new forms of gaming appealing to state governments.

From gaming on Native American lands, to small-stakes casinos in the old mining towns of South Dakota and Colorado, to riverboats in the midwest, gaming is increasingly looked upon as a tool for economic development. Success is not assured, however, and it will depend on the ability of the casinos to increase tourism—a key component to economic development; on the tax structures imposed on casino operators; and on the restrictions that are placed on gaming by the implementing legislation.

Capital will continue to pour into current and future casino-style gaming jurisdictions. The industry will continue to grow for the foreseeable future because of the fundamental underlying factors and the many opportunities to bring casino-style gaming to people who have never before had that experience.

REFERENCES

1. *1990 Las Vegas Visitor Profile Study.* Las Vegas: Las Vegas Convention and Visitors Authority, Las Vegas, NV.
2. *Greater Atlantic City Tourism Marketing and Master Plan.* January 1990.
3. William N. Thompson. "Is Las Vegas Doomed to Become Another Detroit?", *Las Vegas Metropolitan Economic Indicators*, Vol. V (Spring 1992).

 *Part Two*

Casino Operations

Chapter

3

The Regulation and Control of Casino Gaming

Gaming control involves the adoption, interpretation, and enforcement of laws governing how or whether persons may offer or participate in gambling transactions. Laws are rules that a society establishes to govern its conduct. Gaming laws are the rules governing the conduct of gaming. Every industrialized country has some form of gaming law, even countries or states that prohibit it. Some places impose severe penalties for gambling infractions, while others have light penalties. Some allow only social or charitable games. These laws and the extent of their enforcement reflect how gambling is conducted. Enforcement is important because laws that are not enforced often result in widespread and socially accepted violations. Holland, for example, is known for its tolerance of individual behaviors—activities considered deviant in many societies, such as prostitution and drugs, are openly tolerated there, and gambling is no exception. For many years, all casino gaming was illegal, but law enforcement and prosecutors ignored the many illegal casinos that operated openly throughout the country. In many countries such as Holland, illegal gambling is more lucrative than legal gambling.

Underlying all reasoned laws is public policy[1]—that is, the reasons that the government is attempting to achieve certain goals by adopting a law. Public policy can be based on many considerations, moral, political, health, safety, social, and economic. Once a government sets policy goals, it must adopt specific laws to meet them. Government implements goals by adopting specific laws. For example, a law might state that parents must have their children immunized before the age of six, or face a civil or criminal fine. The severity of the punishment and the concentration on enforcement often reflect society's commitment to achieving the goal. To enforce these laws, the government may use existing law enforcement means, or create special agencies.

Four major facets of all gaming control systems are discussed. First is licensing, the process by which government grants persons the right or privilege to offer games to the public. Second is operational controls, the rules that government adopts to govern the conduct of the gaming operators and the games that they offer. Third is the setting of taxes imposed on the industry. Fourth is a system of accounting and audits that ensures that operators properly account for all revenues. Other areas that government regulation may address are price controls, patron disputes, building design, location, and aesthetics.

GAMBLING AND PUBLIC POLICY

A society's public policy regarding gaming usually falls into one of four general categories. The most restrictive is that gambling is an undesirable activity that government should not tolerate; the least restrictive is that gambling is an acceptable activity that its citizens and residents may engage in without government interference. Between these polar positions are others, including the position that gambling is inevitable and that therefore government should allow it, but restrict it so that it is not encouraged. Another common policy position is to allow gambling if its benefits outweigh its burdens.

Philosophical, theological, social, and economic arguments are offered to support each public policy position. For example, theological arguments generally support the position that gambling is undesirable. Theological and social/economic arguments are often similar in result, however, if not in analysis. The religious orientation of a society is a good predictor of whether that society will allow gambling. The secular laws of societies with a dominant religion tend to follow the teachings of that religion.

GAMBLING AS UNDESIRABLE

Theological Arguments

The most restrictive public policy position is that gambling is undesirable. While this position may have philosophic, economic, or social foundations, the religious orientation of a society is often paramount. Without a strong religious influence, the attitudes of a society usually concern questions of individual rights and the negative impact of gambling on society. A survey of the attitudes of the world's predominant religions is helpful in understanding this influence.[2]

Catholics. Gambling is more prevalent in Christian-dominated societies than in others. Not surprisingly, many Christian religions have the most liberal approach to it. For example, *The New Catholic Encyclopedia* states, "A person is entitled to dispose of his own property as he wills . . . so long as in doing so he does not render himself incapable of fulfilling duties incumbent upon him by reason of justice or charity. Gambling, therefore, though a luxury is not considered sinful except when the indulgence in it is inconsistent with duty."

This is not to imply that all Christian religions condone gambling. Still, with over a billion adherent worldwide, the Catholic Church's generally liberal attitude is significant.

Protestants. Many Protestant denominations believe that gambling is wrong for both theological and social/economic reasons. Still, no consensus exists among them. Some condemn gambling as sinful and wrong, while others leave decisions on gambling to the individual's conscience.[3] For example, the Church of England does not condemn gambling. In contrast, the American Baptist Convention adopted a resolution in 1959 stating, "The presence of widespread gambling is a symptom of economic decay and an indication that industrious, thrifty, and responsible living have [sic] failed . . ." The Southern Baptist Convention has consistently opposed gambling, according to a report written in 1976 for the Commission on the Review of the National Policy toward Gambling. This opposition has both theological and socio/economic arguments. The United Methodist Church also believes that all gambling is wrong, as does the Church of Jesus Christ of Latter-Day Saints (Mormons).

The basis for most Protestant theological arguments include the following:

1. *The work ethic.* Biblical teachings command Christians to use their talents and direct their efforts to productive vocations. Gambling is viewed as the antithesis of the work ethic, where gain is sought for no effort or productive service.
2. *The poverty ethic.* Christians should use their earnings for God's purposes, such as supporting one's family, relieving poverty, and supporting just causes. Gambling is a wrongful disposition of one's earnings.
3. *The obsession with money.* A Christian's devotion should be to God, not money. Greed, or devotion to money, is contrary to devotion to God. A typical theological argument is that gambling "vitiates love for God by exalting the worship of money" and "submits outcome to chance, therefore, subverting a trust in God's dependable provisions for human needs."
4. *The love of one's neighbor.* Gambling creates a much higher percentage of losers than winners. Gaming operators allow a system that exploits or steals from other humans for profit.
5. *The faith in God's plan.* Most Protestant denominations believe that God has a plan based on love and justice. Their members are asked to work productively in an ordered society. They believe that gambling shows a lack of faith in God's plan and instead a trust in luck.

Judaism. The Jewish religion has no strong pronouncement against gambling *per se.* Jewish teachings frown on the habitual or professional gambler as a noncontributor to the good of society, but has no similar condemnation for the occasional gambler who otherwise meets his or her societal obligations. Israel, the only Jewish state, does not permit casino gambling.

Islam. The Koran, Islam's holy scriptures, condemns gambling as Satan's work. Its teachings view gambling as taking without compensation. There is an exception for horse racing because betting on this event encourages training for holy wars.

Most Moslem nations prohibit gambling, including Saudi Arabia, Syria, Pakistan, and Indonesia. A notable exception is Turkey, which, not surprisingly, has a secular government and close ties to Western nations. Egypt has casinos, but does not allow its own citizens to gamble.

Hindu. The Hindu religion views gamblers as impure and incapable of finding the truth. India and Burma, both with predominantly Hindu populations, do not allow casinos.

Buddhism. Buddhism, the dominant religion of Eastern Asia, views gambling as an activity that should be avoided. The Buddha includes gambling as one of the evils that will lead man to ruin. Japan does not allow casino gambling, but does allow betting on boat, horse, and bicycle races.

Social and Economic Arguments

Beyond theological arguments, many view gambling as undesirable as a matter of social or economic policy. The prevalent view is that gambling is a deleterious profession; that is, a vocation that has no utility and produces no public good. Other social and economic reasons offered for banning gambling include the following:

1. *It leads to compulsive or problem gambling.* The belief that gambling creates or encourages destructive, pathological, or problem behavior that results in financial ruin to a significant number of people.
2. *It diverts money from productive businesses.* The belief that society benefits if its citizens invest their money in the creation and promotion of productive businesses that provide services and create products, and that spending money on gambling does neither.
3. *It lowers the standard of living.* The belief that persons without disposable income use their money to gamble rather than to buy essential goods and services, such as health care and food. This lowers the standard of living among the poor.

4. *It contributes to crime.* The belief that gambling creates crime because people will steal to support a compulsive gambling habit; organized crime is attracted to gambling because it is a cash industry and can be used to exploit people. Besides direct increases in crime, some assert that gambling leads to increases in prostitution and drug use. This belief is based on the proposition that persons who gamble also tend to partake in other vices.

5. *It increases the cost of law enforcement.* The belief that the increase in crime resulting from gambling increases the cost of law enforcement.

6. *It furthers police corruption.* The belief that organized crime will attempt to corrupt police to achieve special privileges.

7. *It necessarily damages the individual.* The belief that gambling is based on the operator always maintaining a theoretical advantage, so the gambler, by design, is likely to suffer financially.

8. *It corrupts athletics*[4]. The belief that people who bet on sports may attempt to bribe athletes to fix games. This destroys the purpose of amateur athletics and corrupts professional athletics.

GAMBLING AS AN INEVITABLE VICE

A second policy position is that gambling is an inevitable vice. Proponents of this view believe that people are going to gamble regardless of legality, and that if government permits gambling, it can (1) prevent excessive gambling, (2) keep undesirable elements out of the industry, and (3) ensure that the casino provides fair and honest games.

Another argument relies on comparison of the benefits and costs to society between illegal and legal gambling. Many perceived benefits of criminalizing gambling were mentioned in the discussion of "undesirable" policy. The costs of making gambling illegal often address the best use of government resources to control the deviant behavior of its citizens. Gambling is often seen as harmful only to the person who engages in it; that is, it is a victimless crime. This contrasts with crimes such as murder, rape, theft, and other serious deviant behavior. By making gambling legal, limited law enforcement resources, such as police, judges, prosecutors, and prisons can concentrate on these serious deviant behaviors. "Victimless" deviant behavior can then be permitted, but controlled and not encouraged, through regulation.[5]

Making gambling illegal also imposes other costs on society that government-controlled gambling may eliminate. For example,

1. Criminals will protect their illegal gambling monopolies with violence.
2. Illegal gambling profits and winnings will go untaxed.
3. Persons indebted to criminal gambling organizations may resort to crime to pay their debts because criminals are not likely to recognize discharges of the debts by the legal system.

4. Persons convicted of gaming crimes will be socially stigmatized.
5. The populace will lose respect for a government that is unable to enforce unpopular laws.[6]

GAMBLING AS A SAVIOR

Governments may dislike gambling, but allow it to achieve some governmental goals. Proponents of this view assert that while gambling is undesirable, its negative impact is less serious than what would occur if tourism declined or if the government did not have tax revenues to provide other needed services. In other words, they see gambling as the lesser of two undesirable alternatives.

The problems attributed to gambling are seen as less substantial or subject to alleviation by the gambling tax revenues. Gambling is seen as creating positive economic benefits. The presence of casinos and ancillary businesses may increase tourism, employment, restaurants, and accommodations previously deficient or nonexistent. These increases may lead to creating new residents or retaining existing ones. Whether any other goals are achieved, gambling at least may generate needed taxes.

The Atlantic City experiment was based on the concept that gambling is not meant to be an end, but to be a means to fulfill worthwhile goals.[7] The premise for the experiment was that government is uneasy with, and hostile to, the gaming industry but accepts it with the view that it must (1) achieve the worthwhile goals, (2) minimize social and governmental costs, and (3) be strictly controlled.[8]

This policy toward the gaming industry creates conflicts. For example, in New Jersey gaming was intended to revitalize Atlantic City, increase tourism, and be "the catalyst needed to stimulate construction, provide new jobs, and generate new tax revenues."[9] The extent to which such goals are achievable is directly linked to the success of the industry, and success is most likely to be achieved by increased revenues through marketing and promotion. On the other hand, government hoped to protect the gambler from exploitation by preventing the casinos from stimulating demand for the casino product, so it restricted the casinos from marketing and promotion. Thus, the process requires an attempt to meet contradictory goals through compromise that usually frustrates one or both goals. This is illustrated in the discussion on the granting of gaming credit later.

GAMBLING AS AN ACCEPTABLE ACTIVITY

The view that gambling can be an accepted activity has different origins. Some believe that government should not interfere with a person's choice on whether to engage in an activity that does not victimize others. Others view all life as containing elements of risk, and so do not believe that reasons exist to single out gambling for prohibition. Still others view gambling as having positive social values, maintaining that gambling

1. Serves as a social adhesive for the working class.[10]
2. Provides a form of adult play.[11]
3. Contributes to male bonding.[12]
4. Provides enjoyment to elderly citizens and others who would otherwise have no entertainment outlets.[13]

POLICY GOALS

After a society adopts a public policy toward gambling, it adopts a general approach to implement it. Implementation involves both the adoption of laws and their enforcement.

A society's implementation of gambling policy is often a better reflection of its citizens' attitudes toward gambling than are the legislature's attitudes in adopting the law. For example, in the United States, betting on individual sporting events is legal only in Nevada. Yet, estimates are that in 1993, Americans wagered over 50 billion dollars on sporting events in states other than Nevada. While the government may believe that citizens should not wager on sports, many Americans do not share this view and are willing to break the law to make these wagers.

The combination of laws and enforcement usually results in defining one of five distinct policy goals. The most restrictive is for government to pass and enforce laws to eradicate gambling from society. The least restrictive is for government both to allow gambling and to provide government structures to ensure its survival against external threats.

Eradication

The most restrictive approach is to eradicate gambling. This requires the legislature to adopt laws that prohibit gambling *and* the criminal justice system to enforce those laws with the goal of eradication. This goal is not achievable unless the laws provide penalties that either prevent the offenders from engaging in the activity, usually through incarceration, or that have sufficiently severe penalties to provide a deterrent. Also, important is that the police and prosecutors have sufficient resources and motivation to enforce the laws.

Decriminalization

Decriminalization occurs when either laws or enforcement fail to achieve the goal of deterring an illegal activity. While the laws may prohibit an activity, the police or prosecutors do not adequately enforce them. This may occur because of a lack of resources, philosophical differences on the value of the law or through corruption. The magnitude of illegal gambling in many countries, including Holland and the United States, reflects decriminalization of gambling in many places where it is illegal.[14]

Gambler Protection Model

Some governments allow casino gambling, but attempt to regulate the industry to minimize undesirable social consequences. Central to this approach is the notion that casinos should not exploit the public by encouraging them to gamble or exploit gamblers by encouraging them to gamble beyond their means or wager more than they would without encouragement to achieve this goal. These societies may adopt laws that prevent casinos from advertising, offering entertainment, sponsoring junkets, or conducting other activities that stimulate interest in casino gaming.

Great Britain offers the purest form of gambler protection. A casino applicant can only obtain a license if it proves that the area where it proposes a casino has a substantial unstimulated demand for one. The proponents of the British system believe that allowing casinos to stimulate demand for casino gaming is undesirable. They reason that legalized gaming creates social burdens, particularly compulsive gambling, and stimulates gaming among lower-income residents. They assert that compulsive gambling can devastate families and individuals. Likewise, encouraging gambling among the lower classes may result in nondiscretionary dollars going to gaming instead of food, clothing, education, and health care. As a result, either the standard of living goes down or the government must provide additional services. Consequently, Great Britain prevents casinos from stimulating demand for their products.

Rev. Gordon Moody, former Secretary of the Churches' Council on Gambling (U.K.), describes the model as one that is "legalized and arranged for gamblers."[15] He argues that (1) the model should not involve the government taking gambling taxes except as levied on any other transaction, (2) government should not legalize forms of gambling that it believes provide the highest returns for the operators, and (3) government should ensure that operators do not exploit the gamblers to increase the *handle*, the amount of money flowing through the industry. In the unstimulated demand model, government can adopt gaming regulations that hinder industry growth, and enforce such regulations strictly even if it decreases operator and government revenues.[16]

Government Neutral Model

Charitable gaming is common in many American states and in other countries where commercial casino gambling is prohibited. Often government approaches the licensing of charitable gaming no more intensely than the licensing of other businesses. Yet the sums generated by this form of gambling are often significant. For example, in Minnesota the pull-tab industry generates about $1.26 billion in handle each year.[17] In Australia, slot machines in social and sports clubs garner equally impressive revenues. In New South Wales alone, slot machines in registered clubs generate revenues of over $1.4 billion (Australian). The net revenues go to support the clubs, which can be established for any lawful athletic, social, or political purposes. In both instances, regulatory scrutiny of the gaming industry is not significantly more intense than that for many other industries under government authority.

This model does not reflect a moral or socio/economic bias against gambling, at least for charitable causes. Nor does it recognize that the government has any special obligations to protect the industry.

This Government Neutral model may distinguish gambling transactions based on monetary amounts. Governments often impose greater restrictions on business activities based not on the activity but on the monetary amounts involved. For example, local offering of stock in a company of less than $1 million may undergo less government scrutiny than $100 million in a national or international offering. Commercial real estate brokers may undergo more rigorous licensing than residential real estate agents. Likewise, the Government Neutral Model may apply lesser standards to smaller transactions, and more heavily regulate larger transactions. For example, governments may allow private parties or charities to offer prizes only to a certain monetary limit every year, or require different licenses based on net revenues generated in a given year.

Government may also decide that small-stakes gambling is harmless but that gamblers need protection from the high-stakes variety. It may apply a Government Neutral Model to forms of low-stakes gambling and a Government Protection Model to high-stakes gambling, or ban high-stakes gambling altogether. In Mississippi, for example, licenses to conduct low-stakes bingo games are routinely granted with little regulatory scrutiny, while applicants wishing to operate high-stakes games must undergo more rigorous licensing and follow stringent regulations. In South Carolina, tavern owners can easily obtain licenses to operate low-stakes video gambling devices, but high-stakes gambling is prohibited.

Government Protection Model

Where the Gambler Protection Model supports regulation for the gambler, the Government Protection Model provides regulation to protect the gaming industry and the economic interests of the state. An analogy is to the restrictions that a bank may put on a business to which it lends money. If the bank lends a few hundred dollars to a borrower, a simple promissory note might suffice; if it lends millions of dollars, the loan papers might be hundreds of pages long. In both cases, the bank wants to see the business succeed, but it also puts more restrictions on the borrower when the bank's interest is greater. The Government Protection Model is often found where the government has a heavy reliance on the industry to meet tax expectations.

Often commentators are confused by how a government can claim that gambling is a moral and acceptable activity, but still have an extraordinary regulatory apparatus. The basis for regulation is not the government's perception that gambling is immoral or produces undesirable social effects, but instead that if outside parties view the activity as such, the industry as a whole will suffer. These parties include federal government, capital markets, and voters.

Government's primary role in the Government Protection Model is to protect the industry from threats to its existence.[18] Gaming is different from most other industries because it is perceived by many as a vice. Its very existence may be tenuous, as public perception of the benefits and burdens may change and influence the legality of the activity. Besides its fragile legal existence, the casino industry faces eradication if the gambling public perceives it as dishonest or associated with organized crime. This threat may come from (1) a federal government that can make gambling illegal on a local level, (2) voters or legislators who can change the law, or (3) gamblers who choose not to patronize casinos that are perceived as dishonest. As a growth industry, casinos also need the support of capital markets, such as banks and stock exchanges, and access to these markets is often contingent upon the favorable perception of the gaming industry by these institutions.

Government's response in the Government Protection Model is to protect the industry by providing a mechanism to ensure the national government, the voting public, capital markets, and actual and potential gamblers that the industry is both free of criminals and honest. These mechanisms are stringent licensing, detection, and strict enforcement of transgressions by casino operators that violate the perception of honesty and freedom from criminal elements.

Operators realize that this protection is effective only if provided by government. Convincing others that the industry is honest and free of criminals by self-regulation is difficult, if not impossible. Therefore, operators are willing to subject themselves to losses of freedoms, risk, and expense as the price of maintaining both the reality of control and the desired public perception. Often this price is high. To achieve the desired results, government creates a burdensome licensing process, costly accounting and reporting systems, and disciplinary procedures that could result in severe fines or license revocation.

In the United States, Nevada was the only state with legal casino gaming between 1931 and 1978. Its casinos are allowed to stimulate demand. Nevada began regulating gaming in the late 1950s, with the primary purpose of keeping criminals out of the industry. The initial reason for regulation was fear that the federal government would outlaw the casinos if organized crime could use Nevada-based operations to finance or conceal profits from other illegal activities.[19] Other rationales for keeping the criminal element out of the gaming industry were subsequently offered, including that (1) the perception that the industry is dishonest would impair its development;[20] (2) preventing criminal influence would ensure the honesty of the games;[21] and (3) keeping the criminal element out would ensure proper accounting for tax revenues.[22] From the premise that the State should keep criminals out of the gaming industry, an entire system of regulatory control evolved.

Government's second role in the Government Protection Model is to promote and defend the gaming industry. This requires it to take an active interest in convincing the outside world that the regulatory system has successfully excluded organized crime, and is protecting the honesty of the games. When the industry is attacked, government staunchly defends it against its critics.

A final role that government plays in the Government Protection Model is to provide a means for solving the industry's problems. For example, no single casino may be capable of testing equipment or games sold by distributors to ensure that they cannot be manipulated or cheated to the casino's or the gambler's detriment. Equipping and maintaining a lab and trained personnel would be too costly for a single operation, so government, through collective funding from casino taxes, may finance and operate a games laboratory to provide this service. Another example is expert law enforcement to detect and apprehend individuals who cheat the casinos. This may require intelligence, agents trained in cheating detection, and special laws to address the peculiarities of the gaming industry.

The Government Protection Model does not attempt to discourage or encourage the industry's stimulating demand for the casino product. It presumes that the gaming industry will use its resources to maximize revenues, including marketing to encourage participation.

Nor does the model concede the gaming industry any more influence over the regulatory process than any other model does. Government often creates agencies whose goals are to promote and support a particular industry or its participants. For example, worker's compensation programs are designed to assist workers who are injured on the job. Often, these programs provide monetary rehabilitation and placement services for injured or disabled workers; yet the workers rarely are seen as having the ability to influence the system. If the gaming industry is able to gain significant influence over the regulatory process, this is despite the system not because of it. In contrast to the Gambler Protection Model, regulations are a balance of regulatory and economic consideration. Likewise, enforcement is distinctly regulatory as opposed to prosecutorial.[23]

Moreover, because this system is most likely associated with a gaming industry whose tax revenues are important, if not critical, to the government, stronger methods to ensure against "capture" are often applied.[24] When the National Commission on the Study of Gambling reviewed the Nevada regulatory system, it did so with a critical eye. Because tax revenues from gambling made up about half of the state budget, the commission was influenced by the perception that the state regulators might yield to every request of the industry, but it found otherwise. "Serious questions arise as to whether a state that relies so heavily on a single industry for its revenue needs is truly capable of regulating that industry properly." The Commission concluded, "The Nevada control structures have stood the tests of time and, often, bitter experience . . ." Methods to combat the perception of "capture" are discussed later.

Hybrid Policy Goals

Hybrid models exist that borrow elements of the Government Protection and Gambler Protection Models. Often, underlying these hybrids is public policy that views gambling as a savior—in other words, the financial reward from gambling is believed to be more important than the potential harm. These hybrid systems try to realize the revenues from gambling, but eliminate the harms, particularly to the citizens. Puerto Rico, for example, allows casinos to stimulate demand outside its borders to attract tourism, but seeks to protect Puerto Rican residents by prohibiting casinos from stimulating demand within the Commonwealth by advertising. Other jurisdictions allow casinos to stimulate demand outside their borders, but prohibit their own population from engaging in gaming. They might adopt a Government Neutral or Government Protection Model as applied to nonresidents, but attempt to eradicate the activity by their residents.

CONSEQUENCES OF REGULATING LEGAL GAMING

Obviously, policymakers hope that the adoption and enforcement of gaming laws will meet their intended goals. For example, in the Gambler Protection Model, government attempts to ensure that the gaming industry does not stimulate demand for its product. Often, however, the adoption and enforcement of gaming laws may have unintended consequences—many times economic ones, including costs incurred by the government and the industry in complying with the laws or the economic impact of the laws on the casino market.

Each country that allows casino gaming has some regulation. Two basic regulatory types are economic and social. The former is usually an attempt to rectify imperfections in a free market for the public benefit to ensure that consumers receive quality service at prices indicative of a competitive market. Industries typically perceived to have market imperfections are those with relatively large fixed costs (for example, shipping), where the existence of several large firms would entail the wasteful duplication of costly capital facilities (electricity or gas), or where there is a finite supply to be distributed (radio or television airwaves). Examples of such regulatory agencies include the Interstate Commerce Commission, the Federal Energy Regulatory Commission, and the Federal Communications Commission.

Absent government interference, the gambling industry is not usually subject to natural market imperfections.[25] With relatively little cash outlay, a person can operate a gambling game. A table and three cards is enough to play three-card monte, and a pair of dice and an alley are sufficient to play craps.

Government involvement in gaming is based either on social regulation; that is, the impact of the industry's product upon society or on government protection against external threats. Social regulation usually concerns public health or safety. Examples include the Occupational Safety and Health Administration (protecting against occupational injuries and illnesses), the Consumer Products Safety Commission (unsafe consumer products), and the Environmental Protection Agency. Under the Gambler Protection Model, gaming control involves protecting the public from the non-health-related detriments of a perceived vice.

Economic Impact

Regulation of an industry for social or political reasons will have economic impact. This can be direct (for example, explicit regulation meant to have economic impact) or indirect (for example, not necessarily intended but resulting from regulation). Regulations can have indirect economic impact by creating barriers to entry, imposing regulatory costs, inhibiting or preventing innovation and change, or prohibiting or restricting advertising or marketing. Regulations intended to have economic consequences include taxation, price setting, and licensing criteria that require potential competitors to make minimum capital investments.

A government might create a government-operated monopoly if it desires. But, where private enterprise operates gaming, no external considerations exist to prevent or require a competitive economy.

In most jurisdictions, gambling is not subject to market imperfections. Of all factors necessary to support a Free Market Model, a key is the absence of barriers to entry. These barriers can take on a number of different forms, including

- Extreme or significant capital requirements resulting from scale effects.
- The existence of patents or copyrights.
- Scarcity of, or control over, a necessary resource.
- Excessive skill or knowledge requirements.
- Social, cultural, or religious taboos.
- Absolute cost advantages (for example, advantages possessed by established firms that are able to sustain a lower average total cost than new entrants, irrespective of size of output).
- Large initial capital requirements.
- Product differentiation, either natural or artificial, such as ad advertising.
- Retaliation or preemptive actions.
- Vertical integration, (for example, requiring entry at two or more levels).
- Governmental restraints.

Barriers discourage entry into an industry by potential competitors, and thus allow the established firms to earn supernormal profits.

How a market becomes a monopoly, an oligopoly, or competitive depends upon explicit regulation (for example, state law may dictate that there be only one casino or 15 riverboat casinos). Sometimes natural occurrences shape markets. For example, the island of Tinian can physically hold, at best, only a few casinos. More often, the law will not dictate the number of casinos, but will influence whether a given market becomes a monopoly, an oligopoly, or competitive. One example is where only a few sites in a state qualify under the criteria of where an operator may place a casino; another is where the government requires substantial investment to qualify for a license. This may make investment attractive for the first entrant who can make monopoly profits and, perhaps, even a few other entrants. At some point, however, competitors will not be willing to enter the market because the potential profits do not justify the capital costs.

Regulatory Costs. Regulatory costs are a mixture of fixed and variable costs that the casinos attempt to pass on to gamblers through higher costs. In the gaming business, the pricing of the gaming experience is not as simple as in other businesses, where the price of the product goes up if the cost of producing it increases. Casinos provide games for gamblers to play. They make money by winning it from gamblers, and the amount won results from the slight advantage the casino has in the odds of the game—sometimes as little as 1% in craps and blackjack. To make more money in a given transaction, the casino must raise its "prices," usually by increasing its odds at the gaming tables and slots. As the costs rise, however, demand for the product decreases. If all competitors have the same fixed regulatory costs, they must compete on a different basis. Because casinos must pay more to comply with regulations, the cost of doing business in New Jersey is higher than in Nevada, and Nevada is higher than other places. So, all other things being equal, Nevada's casinos can offer better odds to gamblers than New Jersey's and still make the same income from a given game. In vying for foreign trade, better odds means price-sensitive Asian gamblers will choose Nevada over Atlantic City. The higher the regulatory costs, the smaller the market for the casino product will become.

CONSIDERATIONS IN DEVELOPMENT OF A REGULATORY SYSTEM

Form of Ownership

Either private operators or the government can operate legal casinos. Proponents of private ownership assert that government does not have the expertise to enter the gaming industry. The Commission on the Review of the National Policy Toward Gambling discovered several substantial practical difficulties in government taking direct responsibility for operations, noting that the state would have to actively promote an entertainment business.[26] Other concerns were that

1. Government has no experience in casino business.
2. Government would have difficulty retaining qualified management because of the differences between public- and private-sector salaries.
3. Even if government could fund qualified management, it would be difficult to retain them.[27]
4. Government funds would have to be invested and put at risk to build and operate the casino.

Another concern is that casinos do not always win, and if the casino loses, government funds would be at risk.[28] Still others believe that the public's trust in government would be impaired if the government ran casinos for profit.

Proponents of government ownership disagree. They perceive private operators as a threat to the integrity of the casinos. Having public ownership and operation helps eliminate the possibility that greed will overcome regulatory policies of preventing excessive gambling and ensuring the honesty and fairness of the games. It also reduces the need for, and cost of, regulatory enforcement. Other arguments for government-run casinos are that (1) 100% of net profits will go to the public coffers, (2) criminals are more easily excluded, and (3) the public will have confidence in the casino's integrity.

Number of Casinos

Competitive markets do not limit the number of entrants. If demand for gambling increases, so does the supply of casino games. The gaming industry expands supply either by increasing the number of games at existing casinos or by building new casinos. Governments, however, rarely allow the market to determine the number of casinos or games. Nevada and Mississippi are rare exceptions, both allowing virtually unrestricted growth.[29]

More common are direct or indirect government restrictions on the number of casinos. The Gambler Protection Model dictates that the government only allow casinos to meet the unstimulated demand of the populace. Therefore, while there are no absolute restrictions on the number of casinos, as in England, applicants for a new casino license must prove that a substantial unstimulated demand exists within the community where the proposed casino is to be built.

In hybrid models, where gambling is a means to achieve other goals, the concept of using casino gambling to increase tourism and provide economic benefits to a community may dictate a limited number of casinos. These limitations are often seen as minimizing the negative impact on the community by providing the most secure regulated environment; producing economies of scale in single casinos; or containing casino impact, including partial integration of the casino into the architectural and aesthetic aspects of the city.[30]

Another factor that may influence government to limit the number of casinos is regulatory capacity and competence. This factor has equal application in the Gambler Protection and the Government Protection Models. Both rely on strict regulation to achieve their goals, and this regulation requires personnel, equipment, and expertise sufficient to regulate the number of casinos permitted. Governments may limit the number of casinos to a number that can be effectively regulated.

Who Should Regulate the Industry?

BENEFITS OF ADMINISTRATIVE AGENCIES

Gaming law in most jurisdictions is administrative law, and administrative law is a hybrid. In American jurisprudence, government has legislative, judicial, and executive branches. The legislative branch makes the law, the judicial branch interprets it, and the executive branch enforces it. However, in administrative agencies, these functions merge. The rationale is that an administrative agency with multiple powers and expertise is more efficient and can respond more quickly to industry problems and needs, free of political pressure.

For example, Nevada's gaming regulation features a two-tier administrative structure. The State Gaming Control Board enforces gaming laws, conducts investigations, and prosecutes offenders, which are traditionally executive functions. The Board also resolves customer disputes and makes recommendations on licensing matters, which are quasi-judicial functions. Finally, it adopts standards for gaming devices, which is a legislative function. The other agency, the Nevada Gaming Commission, issues and revokes licenses, which is a judicial function. It also adopts regulations, which is a legislative function. Nevada is somewhat unusual for a two-agency system in that the Gaming Control Board (the enforcement wing) also has extensive quasi-judicial powers. In other words, in many situations, the prosecutor and the judge are the same. In Nevada, operators must tread lightly in their dealings with the enforcement wing because the enforcers stand, in many cases, as the judge; that is, the ultimate decisionmaker.

Other jurisdictions take different approaches. In some, there is an actual adversarial relationship between the enforcement agency and the licensee—almost like a prosecutor and defense counsel. Both present their cases to a neutral trier of fact, usually a gaming commission, which decides to issue licenses or to take other action. New Jersey is an example of the adversarial relationship. Still other jurisdictions have opted to have only an enforcement agency, and let judges issue licenses and resolve disputes.

The notion of the regulatory agency as a guardian of the public interest is an extension of a legal view of regulation dating to the late nineteenth century.[31]

In 1938, Dean James Landis asserted that regulatory agencies should have "an assemblage of rights normally exercisable by government as a whole" to make decisions as problems arise.[32] The policy goals of the agency should be loosely defined by the legislature with responsibility for carrying them out delegated to the agency that has expertise in the area.

Accordingly, "the assumed predicates were a body of technology relevant to the solution of problems in the field and a consequent self-sufficiency or autonomy, implying immunity from the political process."[33]

CRITICISMS OF ADMINISTRATIVE AGENCIES: THE CAPTURE THEORY

Proponents of the Capture Theory argue that regulatory agencies are eventually "captured" by the industry that they regulate. While many versions of the Capture Model are found, the notion is commonly associated with George Stigler, whose central thesis is that ". . . regulation is acquired by the industry and is designed and operated primarily for its benefit."[34] This acquisition, argues Stigler, comes about because the industry can utilize the regulatory machinery to (1) acquire cash subsidies, (2) limit entry, (3) gain control over complements and substitutes, and (4) assist in price-fixing schemes.[35]

Other economists explored the capture notion before Stigler. In 1954, John Kenneth Galbraith wrote the following in his work on the Great Depression in reference to the Securities and Exchange Commission:

> [R]egulatory bodies, like the people who comprise them, have a marked life cycle. In youth they are vigorous, aggressive, evangelistic, and even intolerant. Later they mellow, and in old age—after a matter of ten or fifteen years—they become, with some exceptions, either an arm of the industry they are regulating, or senile.[36]

Galbraith's work was followed in 1955 by political scientist Marver Bernstein's work, *Regulating Business by Independent Commission*, which also viewed the regulatory experience as a process. Bernstein contended that the regulatory commission possesses a life cycle comprising periods of gestation, youth, maturity, and decline.

In the gestation period, some group attempts to impose upon the legislature a commission establishing law to remedy some perceived public wrong. Once established, the regulatory agency moves into its youth, a period of exuberance tempered only by uncertainty as to how it is supposed to behave. This period yields to that of maturity, characterized by heavy judicialization, a narrowing of the viewpoint of the agency, a dependence upon precedent, and an increasing backlog focusing more and more of the agencies' attention on yesterday.[37] The old-age period of Bernstein's model is characterized by a deepening of the entrapment by the industry and a high degree of bureaucratic senility on the part of the agency.[38]

THE MULTIPLE INTEREST THEORY

Economist Sam Peltzman expanded on the work of Stigler. He theorized that while the regulated attempt to influence the regulatory process, "no single economic interest captures a regulatory body."[39]

Peltzman proposed that a regulatory equilibrium exists where politicians act in a way that maximizes political returns. Because politicians are elected, they will follow whatever course of action will most likely ensure re-election. In other words, politicians attempt to regulate an industry such that the overall value of serving the regulated, the public, and other interest groups maximizes the political benefits. Louis Jaffe also espoused a politically-based analysis of administrative agencies. He noted that:

> The elements of this political process are common to all potential lawmaking activity—the intensity of a given problem, the degree to which it is felt throughout an organized and stable constituency, and the representation (or lack thereof) of varying interests within and without the lawmaking body.[40]

Nevertheless, interest analysis is not a simple comparison of consumer versus producer or, in the casino industry, between the casino and the patron. Any given regulatory process involves multiple interest groups, including organized labor, suppliers, and professionals. Moreover, within each group may exist opposite interests.[41]

Assessing the Power of Interested Parties

Interest analysis assumes that interest groups or their members will use influence to steer the course of regulation to their economic favor. Therefore, under interest analysis, a major determinate of resulting regulation is the extent of the influence exercisable and exercised by each interested party.

Many factors may determine the power of an interested party to assert influence over the regulatory process. First is the size of the regulated occupation. In states where gaming is of critical importance to the economy, the industry has greater ability to hold political power. Beyond influencing voters by political contributions or direct appeal, members and groups in a large gaming industry have the resources to hire lobbyists, to create and fund cohesive trade associations, and to mobilize.

Second is the strength of competing interested parties. This competition may occur in two ways. One way is between groups attempting to use regulation to create a transfer of wealth and groups wanting regulation for social gains. This is often a battle between consumers who want regulation only to cure market imperfections and other interested parties who want to create inefficiencies so as to acquire wealth from the consumer. The other way may be between the groups attempting to use regulation to transfer wealth for their own benefit.

If the public are the consumers but lack sophistication or information, they are unlikely to be organized or have collective abilities to assert political power. Consumers, or the public, tend to obtain sophistication unless an issue becomes salient to their lives. Where the public is not the consumer, its interest may change from concerns over the cost of the product to receiving a share of the wealth through taxing the industry on windfall profits.

Third is whether the jurisdiction has a competitive political party system. Jurisdictions that are not dominated by a single political party tend to be less influenced by a single interest group.

Fourth is the extent to which the regulatory system has sufficient safeguards to prevent interest-group influence. They range from the obvious—for example, regulators should be prohibited from being employed by, or receiving valuable gifts from, the regulated—to the subtle—ensuring input from all interest groups on regulatory changes.

Figure 3.1 shows the conflicting interest groups that can affect the regulatory process.

Gaming Industry Associations. Industry associations are the most effective tool for the industry to promote its interests. Gaming industry associations comprise members of the casino industry. From a political prospective, industry associations can pool their resources and influences behind particular political candidates, they can hire effective lobbyists, and they can speak with a unified voice on issues.

Gaming Industry Members. Having many firms in an industry facilitates good regulation because it reduces the likelihood that any given firm has economic significance. Thus, removing that firm will not create a major market disturbance to either the industry or labor.

A single-industry member may be able to exercise significant influence over a regulatory agency where that member holds either significant economic or political power. In such a situation, the industry member, or a sub-group of industry members, may seek to influence regulations that benefit it, or the small group, at the expense of other industry members.

The Public. The public may have many interests in the gaming industry: as consumers, as workers, or as residents in a community with casinos. As an interest group, the public may have as their primary goal keeping the tax burden on the casinos and tourism.

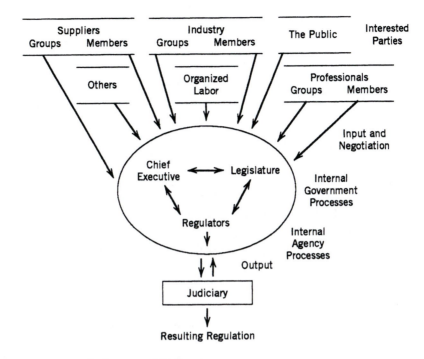

Figure 3.1   The Interested Parties

Both the focus and the strength of the public as an interest group can be significantly altered where the gaming industry's patrons are primarily nonresidents; that is, nonvoters.[42] In this situation, the politicians face little political risk by processing legislation or regulation that involves transfers of wealth from the nonvoters (that is, consumers) to its residents by subsidizing their taxes or by allowing the industry to maximize profits.

Another example is where the pressure for legalizing small-stakes games is coming from the public. They want gambling not as a source of government revenue, but for recreational purposes.

Professionals. Professionals, particularly attorneys, often serve as the interface between the regulators and the regulated. Attorneys can serve a vital role in the regulatory process because of their expertise in both law and specific regulation. Moreover, they often have a longer and more stable relationship with the regulators, and so can expedite and mediate solutions to problems between the regulated (that is, their clients) and the regulators in the most efficient manner.

Organized Labor. Casino gaming is labor intensive. Casino employees may attempt to influence regulation to achieve higher wages, better benefits, job security, or better working conditions.

Suppliers. Suppliers of both gaming and nongaming goods and services may attempt to influence regulation to create barriers to entry or to mandate use of their products. For example, local suppliers benefit if regulation mandates preference for local goods. Existing licensed suppliers benefit by requiring supplier licensing.

The Judiciary. A group that may influence the process by oversight is the judiciary. Professors Landes and Posner assert that the judiciary is important in the process because it can provide stability to the equilibrium between the various interest groups by supporting the laws as adopted by the legislature in the manner anticipated by the parties.[43]

Political Activity and Cooling Off

Both the Gambler Protection and Government Protection Models seek to prevent undue influence over, or capture of, the regulators by the regulated. In the Gambler Protection Model, the fear is that the casinos will attempt to influence the regulatory system to help increase their profits. The practical vehicle would be to modify or repeal regulations that protect the gambler by preventing the operator from advertising or otherwise stimulating demand. Likewise, the design of the Government Protection Model attempts to protect the industry from external threats and other situations that would harm the industry. It is designed to control the industry economically. Capture theorists argue that the industry would attempt to "capture" the regulators to manipulate the market economically by limiting entry and assisting in price-fixing schemes.

Two avenues by which the industry may attempt to influence, or capture, regulators are the political process and the promise of private employment after government service.

No system of government is perfect, and electing government officials by popular vote is no exception, particularly where the size of a candidate's election fund plays a prominent role in deciding election outcome. The political process can affect gaming regulation if political contributions can influence—or if the public believes they can influence—the granting of licenses. This is most threatening if elected officials are the license grantors. One common solution is to delegate the licensing process to administrative agencies. This envisions that, aside from the appointment, elected officials should play no role in the regulatory process.

Further independence can be achieved by (1) requiring persons from different political parties to be appointed, (2) providing fixed terms for appointees, (3) requiring confirmation by the legislative branch, (4) requiring background checks of potential appointees, (5) enforcing conflict-of-interest rules that prevent appointment of persons with specified ties to the industry, and (6) requiring all regulators to provide financial disclosures. The purpose is to isolate the regulators from political influence.

New Jersey has a policy of prohibiting casinos from contributing to political campaigns. The purpose of the ban is to isolate the industry from the political process. However, the problem of undue influence on the political process is already addressed by state limits on the amount of campaign contributions. To further extend it to a total ban against contributions may disenfranchise the entire industry by denying the casinos a reasonable opportunity to support the candidate of choice. New Jersey also prohibits casino employees from running for, or holding, political office. However, it may seem extreme to deny a person the right to participate in government simply because of his or her chosen profession.

Another measure is "cooling-off" periods, which prevent regulators from leaving their positions to take gaming industry jobs. The purpose is to avoid the appearance that the casino industry can influence a regulator by holding out the possibility of post–government-service employment.

For example, under Nevada law, casinos may not employ former gaming regulators and certain of their staff for one year following the last day of a person's service on the Board or Commission. A company involved in the gaming industry may not employ a former nonclerical staff member for one year following the last day of employment if that person (1) had principal duties that included formulating policy contained in the gaming regulations, (2) conducted an audit or investigation of the prospective employer within the last year, or (3) had knowledge of the trade secrets of a direct competitor as a result of his or her government service.

Two problems occur with "cooling-off" periods. First, knowing that one cannot use skills acquired while working for the government in the private sector makes the government job less appealing. This is not as much of a problem as it was ten years ago since, with the proliferation of gaming, former gaming agents from one jurisdiction can find lucrative jobs in other jurisdictions. Another possible solution is to make government employment as attractive as private employment; for example, by offering much better salary and benefits than the gaming agents and regulators are now receiving. A second problem is scope. The cooling-off periods often do not prevent professionals, such as accountants or lawyers, from representing casinos before their agency immediately after leaving government employment. A solution would be to extend the cooling off period to prevent a former regulator who is an attorney from representing applicants shortly after resigning.

Another problem in many states where casino gaming is now legal is the concept of "juice," which means that an applicant will be given preferential or special consideration unrelated to his or her merits by hiring a particular consultant, attorney, or accountant who has close ties with government officials. Conversely, this applicant can delay or prohibit a competitor from obtaining a license. Regulators should be most appalled by claims that someone has juice. Juice implies corruption because for it to work, the regulators must necessarily violate their duties or responsibilities to the state. Professionals who appear before the regulators should be angered by such claims because they suggest that applicants should choose their representatives *not* based on experience, knowledge, intelligence, or work ethic.

Other methods are used to prevent capture. These include

- Prohibiting applicants and their attorneys from communicating with board and commission members regarding the merits of their applications except in public hearings. This avoids the perception that "deals" are made in the back room, which is wrong and should be avoided.
- Prohibiting gaming licensees and persons who appear before the regulators from serving in any capacity, a director, advisor, or fund-raiser, with the campaigns for those public offices that regulate gaming or appoint the regulators. This would avoid the appearance that a person who is close to the government officials regulates the industry, or who appoints or advises the regulators can influence their decisions.
- Preventing casinos from giving any [complimentaries] to regulators and staff.

LICENSING

All established governments that allow casino gambling impose some form of licensing. Differences between jurisdictions are based on four factors: breadth, depth, criteria, and standards of the licensing process. Breadth means the extent to which a government requires persons or entities associated with the gaming industry to go to obtain a license. For example, Germany requires only the operator of a casino to obtain a license, whereas New Jersey requires virtually all persons having any business with the casino to do so. This includes persons who supply glass for the front of slot machines and nongaming service companies that regularly do business with a casino. Depth means the extent to which government requires persons within a licensable entity to undergo an individual investigation. Criteria are those matters that the government considers in granting licenses. England, for example, requires an applicant to prove that the area in which it wants to open a casino has an unsatisfied and unstimulated demand for casino gambling. This criterion results from England's broader policy objective that casinos should only fulfill the populace's unstimulated demand for gaming opportunities. Standards are the minimum attributes that applicants must have to qualify for licensing.

Breadth

Casinos do not operate in a vacuum. They must contract with, and rely on, many other entities and persons to carry on business, among them employees, contractors, and suppliers of many types of goods and services, including gaming equipment. A governmental concern is that licensing not become a mere coat of respectability for operators while allowing unsuitable persons to profit from casino operations through other means.

Breadth of licensing is intended to prevent unsuitable persons from

1. Using a surrogate that qualifies for a license to serve as the owner/operator.
2. Attempting to influence operations through control of some goods or services critical to the casino.
3. Attempting to blackmail or pressure management or owners.
4. Gaining influence through the ability to control unions.[44]

As an example, suppose a casino operator has a valid license. An unsuitable associate has a hidden interest in the operation, but licensing prevents the associate from directly taking a portion of the net profits. The associate's challenge is to obtain his or her share of the profits without attracting the attention of the gaming regulators. Methods used include selling goods or services to the casino at prices far beyond market price, charging exorbitant "finder's" fees for arranging financing for the casino, and removing money from the win before it is counted.

If government views hidden interest as potentially detrimental to its public policy, then some level of licensing beyond the operator is usually implemented. Typical systems involve a combination of "tiered" licensing and accounting controls. Tiered licensing involves categorizing every group of individuals or entities associated with the gaming industry into two or more tiers. Each tier is then subject to some level of licensing scrutiny. A hypothetical tiering is presented here.

Placing a group in a particular tier is usually based upon a consideration of two factors. The first factor is the need to maintain a level of regulatory control over a particular group, which may vary between jurisdictions. For example, if organized crime has strong influence over labor, this may justify moving suppliers of a particular product or the construction trade

Tier	Type	Requirements
1	Operators Owners Persons entitled to profits Suppliers of gaming devices	Full licensing scrutiny, including independent investigation.
2	Manufacturers of gaming devices Key casino personnel	Licensing and routine review of intelligence files and police checks.
3	Manufacturers of associated equipment	Registration with the gaming authorities.
	Other casino personnel, junket representatives, landlords, lenders, labor organizations, gaming schools	Routine police and intelligence review may be done. Gaming authorities retain right to require licensing of any of these entities.
4	Suppliers of noncasino goods and services	No registration. Gaming authorities retain right to require licensing.
	Nongaming employees, persons doing business on the premises of a casino	
5	All others	No registration. Gaming authorities may ban persons from entering a casino and prohibit casinos from dealing with him or her.

into a higher tier with greater scrutiny. Similarly, if the nature of legal gaming within the jurisdiction will not produce large revenues, the likelihood of attracting criminals is less and may justify less scrutiny. The second factor is capability and budget. Placing all groups in a mandatory licensing tier with full investigation will require substantial commitment by the regulatory agency in terms of trained personnel to conduct the investigations even if there is only a single casino in the jurisdiction. Unless the jurisdiction has a large, well-trained staff and the budget to conduct the investigations, it should place groups in the tiers on a priority basis. Usually, the top priority is owners and operators, followed by persons sharing in profits, distributors, manufacturers, and key employees. Other considerations include the desire to license all necessary entities quickly to begin realizing revenues, questions of whether politically or legally a particular group can be subject to licensing, and whether the cost of licensing a group outweighs its benefit to the state.

Depth

Once a group that must obtain a license is identified, governments must decide who within that group needs to undergo an investigation. Suppose operators must go through full investigation and licensing. If the operator is an individual, that decision is obvious. More commonly, however, casino owners and operators are corporations or partnerships. The structure for corporations differs between countries, but usually involves officers, directors, and shareholders. Shareholders are persons or entities that hold shares in a company. Shares entitle their holders to control of the corporation through voting for the board of directors to receive earnings through current or accumulated dividends that are declared by the board of directors and to pro rata distribution of assets upon liquidation.[45]

Depth of licensing for corporations concerns which officers, directors, and shareholders must undergo licensing scrutiny. Similar considerations are needed for other business formations, such as general and limited partnerships, trusts, joint ventures, limited liability companies, and joint stock associations.

Criteria

Regulators can consider many criteria in assessing an application for a gaming license. These criteria can be either fixed or discretionary. Fixed criteria are quantifiable in that an applicant either meets them or does not. Discretionary criteria are minimum qualifications that are not subject to quantification, but are based on the discretion of the gaming regulators.

Examples of fixed criteria include the following:

1. The person has not been convicted of a felony (South Dakota).
2. The person has not been convicted of any crime involving gambling, prostitution, or sale of alcohol to a minor (Mississippi).
3. Sixty percent of company capital must be owned by Portuguese citizens (Portugal).[46]
4. There must be a minimum capital investment of 1.5 million ECU (Spain).
5. There must be a five-star hotel with a minimum bed capacity of 1,000 to 1,500 beds (Turkey).
6. There must be a contract with a municipal government for a building in a community that has thermal waters (spas) or is seaside (France).
7. The person must be of good character, honesty, and integrity (Tinian).
8. The applicant must have the organizational and financial ability to conduct casino operations (Puerto Rico).
9. There must be an existing substantial demand for a casino among potential gamblers (The Bahamas).

10. The applicant must have, or be able to obtain, the services of persons with experience in managing and operating a casino (Queensland).
11. The person must be capable and judged likely to comply with the gaming laws (Great Britain).
12. The casino must be in a vessel that fits in with Iowa's riverboat history (Iowa).
13. The casino must be in Central City, Blackhawk, or Cripple Creek (Colorado).

Standards

Given discretion either to grant or to deny a license, the regulatory body must assess the evidence in a given application against some standards. These can be defined or left to the intuition of the regulators. For example, regulators may be given a statutory directive to deny an application if they have any reason to believe that the person does not meet any criteria. This standard would result in fewer licenses being approved than one that requires regulators to grant a license based on a preponderance of the evidence. That is, if the regulators weigh the evidence for and against the applicant, the decision to grant a license will be based on which has more weight. For example, suppose a person was convicted of theft, while a college student 20 years ago, and a licensing criteria is honesty. Obviously, theft involves dishonesty, so the theft is some evidence of the person's dishonesty. Under the "any evidence standard," the applicant would be denied a license. Suppose further that the applicant has led an exemplary life since a conviction for "taking a sleeping-bear cement mascot from a motel's lawn as a college prank." Under the "preponderance standard," he would probably obtain a license.

POTENTIAL ECONOMIC CONSEQUENCES OF LICENSING

The licensing system employed by a state will influence the number of competitors. In a perfect competitive system, competitors enter the market if the existing entrants are making extraordinary profits. How quickly or easily they enter is greatly influenced by licensing. Obviously, existing competitors will have an advantage if the licensing process creates an enormous barrier.

Licensing can create barriers to entry in four major ways. First, it can add uncertainty and risk to the decision on whether to enter a market if regulators regularly deny licenses to applicants. All other things being equal, a company will devote its resources to a market where it is more likely to obtain a license. Second, the length of time that a licensing investigation takes may create a barrier. Companies that want to enter a market do so based on the current economics of that market. If licensing takes a substantial amount of time, the company must forecast the economics for when it may obtain its license, which adds risk to the decision to enter. Third, a potential entrant will consider the cost of licensing in order to decide if its money will generate a higher return in this market or business as opposed to another. Fourth, the licensing process may cause social stigma and embarrassment to a potential entrant. This may discourage some companies, especially diversified companies where embarrassing news could hurt its other businesses.

Governments should understand that the laws promoting barriers to entry affect competitive markets and have economic costs. Monopoly and oligopoly markets result in higher cost to the consumer and lower output. In the casino industry, lower output means higher net profits on lower gross revenues; it also means lower employment and fewer games and devices.

OPERATIONS

Restrictions on the Games: Type, Mix, and Rules

Casino operators can offer the gaming public an extensive number and variety of casino games and devices. A person can find over two dozen varieties of blackjack in casinos worldwide, which can involve, among other things, whether (1) the dealer uses one or as many as six decks, (2) the dealer must hit or stand on a 17, (3) all cards are dealt face up or face down, and (4) under what circumstances the gambler may double-down, surrender, or split the hand. Blackjack is only one game. Currently, Nevada has approved about 35 table games and about 200 gaming devices that casinos may offer.

Restrictions on the type and rules of games and devices are tied to the ability of the government to effectively monitor play to prevent cheating and skimming, and to ensure proper accounting. Control over the games and devices is easier, is less expensive, and requires fewer staff if fewer types of games are permitted, and the rules are set by statute or regulation.

A good example is the apprehension of persons who cheat at blackjack. A card marker can alter the backs of cards, and figure out the value of the dealer's hole card in this game. Knowledge of the hole card assures the gambler of an advantage over the casino. Blackjack cheaters are so skillful that a novice can be told that a deck contains a marked card and be unable to identify the markings, while the card cheat can read the marking from across a room. Another method of cheating is "card crimping." This is the act of deforming a card, often by bending the corners, to make the point value readable to the crimper from the back and face of the card.[47] Other cheats will hold out one card from a discarded hand, and substitute it for another card during play. Suppose the gambler can hold out a jack from a discarded hand. If the dealer deals him a three down and a face card, the cheat can switch the three for the face card. All of these methods of cheating can be minimized by requiring that all cards be dealt to gamblers face up, and prohibiting the gamblers from touching the cards.

Like other industries, the gaming industry is evolving—the casinos of today are significantly different from those of twenty years ago. Catwalks in the ceilings from which security could look down to observe play have been replaced by sophisticated pan-tilt and zoom video cameras. In place of old mechanical slot machines are new microprocessor-controlled machines with 256,000 color monitors. Most casinos now have coin changers, and some are even cashless. Gambler-tracking systems give the new casino operator immediate information on a gambler's play. Even some games have changed. Video poker has replaced the reel slot machine as the game of choice among slot gamblers in many casinos. Table games, such as pai gow poker, red dog, and others, are new, and variations of existing games such as gambler's choice 21, double-down stud, and Caribbean stud, are common in some casinos.

The casino industry is no different from any other industry in that operators need to implement innovations to stay competitive. An athletic shoe made of canvas and hard rubber might have been a best seller in the 1960s, but would garner few sales in today's world of light-weight nylon, pumps, and other innovations. Likewise, the preferred games of 30 years ago are less popular today. If a casino cannot adapt to changes in gambler demand for new or different games, it may lose gamblers to casinos that can offer the desired products.

Operating Hours

Most jurisdictions restrict the hours that casinos may operate. In the Gambler Protection Model, closing the casino may inhibit excessive gambling by giving the player an opportunity to get away from the casino atmosphere to reflect on the nature and extent of his gambling.

Another reason to limit hours may relate to regulatory and public safety issues. Operating casinos for extended periods requires the government to provide more service for the entire period. This requires more police and regulatory staff, and government may decide that the cost of these services does not justify marginal tax revenues for the lower revenue segments of the day.

Alcohol

Alcohol is a drug that can lead to intoxication when used. Intoxication is a state of toxic poisoning characterized by an impaired physical and mental condition commonly known as drunkenness or inebriety. The Gambler Protection Model would prohibit the service of alcohol by casinos to persons who are gambling. The rationale is that serving alcohol, particularly on a complimentary basis, is an inducement to gamble and may result in the person playing with impaired judgment.[48]

Absent a total prohibition, the government can place other restrictions on the service of alcohol. For example, in New Jersey a gambler must specifically request a drink. A common prohibition is that casinos cannot allow visibly intoxicated persons to gamble.

Intoxication as a defense against the enforcement of a debt is not new. A gaming debt is no different from most other debts. The only unusual aspect is that it results from a gaming contract. A wager between the casino and the gambler is a contract because it involves a set of promises for the breach of which the law gives a remedy. The promises are, on the casino's part, that if the gambler wins, the casino will pay according to the rules of the game; on the gambler's part, that he or she will pay the amount of the bet if he or she loses. A gaming contract, therefore, is merely a type of contract arising out of a gaming transaction.

To be bound by a contract, the gambler must have the capacity to incur the debt. The general rule is that a person has the capacity to incur contractual obligations unless special circumstances exist. Gamblers have argued incapacity based on severe intoxication. Doubt exists in many states whether incapacity due to intoxication is a recognized defense.

The Government Neutral (or the Government Protection) Model, usually takes consistent approaches to both gambling and alcohol consumption (that is, that those are individual choices). A basic tenet of individualism is that persons are accountable for the consequences of their own actions. If someone wants to climb a mountain and gets hurt, it is not the mountain's fault for being there.

Advertising

Whether to allow casinos to advertise is a policy decision based on the potential negative impact of gaming on a community. Proponents of the ban argue that advertising encourages people who would otherwise not gamble to use nondiscretionary funds for gaming purposes. Instead of buying books, appliances, or food, they spend their money on slot machines. Thus, society as a whole will suffer because the general standard of living will decrease. Some states, however, confuse their goals and policies. On one hand, they want casinos to provide jobs and taxes; but on the other hand, they wish to discourage gambling by banning advertising.

Banning casino advertising, but allowing casino gaming, can be consistent. In societies that permit legal gaming and have rational policies underlying their regulatory structure, two distinct systems exist.

Adopting a Gambler Protection Model is acceptable public policy if government understands the potential consequences of such a decision. A component of the Unstimulated Demand Model is the ban on advertising. In a competitive market, consumers can only make rational decisions on where to spend their money if they have information about the rates charged and the products offered by competitors. A most common method of acquiring such information is through advertising. Advertising is often an imperfect source of information, but it may be better than no information at all. Casinos frequently advertise straight pricing information that consumers will find of the greatest value. For example, some casinos advertise that their blackjack games have single decks or that their craps games offer ten-times odds.

A ban on advertising disrupts a competitive market. Often, this disruption helps established firms, but it can also hurt the entire industry. In a closed market, the ban may benefit existing casinos as it prevents consumers from making rational decisions on where to bet, and may promote oligopoly prices. If the market is close to another market that allows advertising, a ban may be counter-productive because the other market can use advertising to draw price-conscious consumers. In all instances, a ban on advertising burdens the gambler, who has a greater difficulty in obtaining pricing information.

Entrance Requirements

Three types of entrance requirements are common. The Bahamas is typical of jurisdictions that believe gambling is socially undesirable, but necessary to promote tourism. Under Bahamian law, citizens and ordinary residents cannot gamble in their casinos. Short of prohibiting residents from playing, governments can place various restrictions on who can gamble. The most common are age restrictions. Usually persons under the age of 18[49] in some places, and 21[50] in others, cannot enter the casino.

Jurisdictions that follow the Gambler Protection Model often have restrictions designed to protect the gambler from impulse gambling. The most notable is Great Britain's waiting period. Only members or their guests may gamble in British casinos. A person must make application in person at the casino, and must wait at least 48 hours before being admitted as a member and being allowed to gamble.[51]

Another common requirement is strict dress codes in the casino. For example, Turkish casinos require male patrons to wear coats and ties. Other places have similar requirements regarding the formality of dress. Such codes are justified on many grounds. Some policymakers in poorer countries believe that gambling should be discouraged among its poorer residents. Since this group is less likely to have formal attire, they are less likely to gamble. Also, requiring formal attire requires greater deliberation before playing, thus reducing impulse gambling. Finally, a dress code is viewed as a means to support an image of propriety in the casino atmosphere.

Admission fees are common in many places. These are usually inexpensive, and are used to generate revenues. In some places, however, they are sufficiently high to inhibit the casual bettor.

Other requirements prohibit casinos from allowing entrance or play by

1. Persons designated by regulators. These are usually career criminals, those who have stolen from casinos or patrons, or members or associates of organized crime.[52]
2. Those whose families object to the person gambling (Turkey).
3. Military personnel in uniform (France).
4. Regulators and their staff.
5. Visibly intoxicated persons (Nevada).
6. Casino employees (Bahamas).

Credit Play

Credit play is the policy of allowing persons to gamble on credit by signing credit instruments that the casino can negotiate through normal banking channels or enforce through the courts. Public policy debates over whether casinos should be allowed to grant credit address collection methods, effect on gamblers, and competitiveness. Three principal arguments against casino credit are that allowing credit (1) will allow casinos to engage in undesirable methods of collection, (2) may result in casinos skimming funds by writing off gaming debts or not reporting paid debts, and (3)will result in gamblers losing more than they can afford.

The first concern is more often associated with illegal than with legal gambling. The former, by definition, is operated by criminals. Because of their willingness to ignore criminal statutes and engage in illegal gambling, they also have little regard for other laws, including debt collection procedures. In contrast, legal gaming operators often undergo rigorous licensing examinations, including whether they conduct their businesses in strict compliance with all laws. The public may confuse illegal gaming operators with legal ones. The perception of organized crime accomplices collecting gaming debts is confused with the professional and ethical enforcement of credit found in virtually all places where gambling is regulated. Engaging in any illegal collection practices would jeopardize a gaming operator's license. [Laws governing abusive collection practices often give substantial rights to debtors.] In recent times, no Nevada or New Jersey gaming operator has been charged with any crimes related to debt collection, nor has any been successfully sued for such.

Good regulation can also prevent the skimming of funds through the credit process. Casinos can abuse the credit process in two ways. Most states tax gross gaming revenues, which are all sums that the casino retains as winning or won less all sums that it pays out as losses. This allows the first method of skimming in which a person in association with a casino can obtain cash or chips by opening a credit line, not gamble, and convert the chips to cash. The casino, in turn, makes no collection effort, and writes the debt off. The net effect is that the funds go to a third party, and the casino pays no taxes. In the second method, a casino employee or owner can collect a debt from a patron, not report its collection, and have the debt shown as uncollectible.

Regulation and proper enforcement may address both situations. Licensees must maintain extensive records on all credit gamblers, and must follow detailed internal controls in issuing and collecting gaming credit. These procedures ensure that one or two employees cannot work with a third party to defraud the casino. Enforcement procedures allow the regulators to verify the accuracy of the information contained in the records.

The final issue concerns whether the extension of credit encourages persons to gamble beyond their means.

Jurisdictions adopting the Gambler Protection model often prohibit all forms of gambling credit. For example, in Germany, gamblers may only gamble with cash or cash equivalents, such as traveler's checks. Other jurisdictions that have Gambler Protection Models limit the extension of credit. Laws may fix the amount of credit that casinos may extend to a gambler. New Jersey employs a different system. Its casinos may accept checks, which are a form of credit because the casino must rely on the gambler's financial standing to ensure that the bank will pay the check when presented for payment. New Jersey requires that the casino present the check within a certain number of days depending on the check amount. Small checks must be presented within a few days. This system is based on the belief that gamblers will not spend more than the available cash in their checking accounts if they know the casino must present the check for payment within a short period.

The Government Protection and Government Neutral Models place no limits on credit unless gambling on credit is perceived different from gambling with cash.

Good long-range casino planning dictates that the casinos not allow gamblers to lose more than they can afford. Casinos want to retain a gambler's business over many years, and they do this by keeping gamblers within their means. If a gambler exceeds his or her capabilities, the casino risks the loss of that gambler's business and the likelihood of collection. Nevertheless, some casinos and gamblers do abuse the credit process. Gamblers often do so by obtaining credit at many casinos, the cumulative effect of which is to exceed their means. Casinos try to avoid this by using credit reporting services, but are not always successful. If a jurisdiction finds that some casinos are recklessly granting credit, regulations capping the percentage of credit that can be written off as uncollectible may limit the problem.

Banning credit can have a substantial economic effect if an area's casino industry competes for gamblers against another jurisdiction that allows credit. Many gamblers who gamble well within their means prefer credit so that they do not need to carry large amounts of currency. They are more likely to gamble in jurisdictions that allow credit than in those that do not. Moreover, the federal government created an artificial demand for credit play by adopting cash-reporting requirements. Under federal law, casinos must file reports on gamblers who lose more than $10,000 in cash, but need not make similar reports for gamblers who gamble on credit and pay with a check. Persons who are offended by government intrusion into their personal spending habits also prefer to gamble on credit.

Accounting

Accounting regulations control and protect the flow of revenues generated by gaming activities. Government has two principal objectives in controlling the revenue streams of private casinos. First, accounting regulations can inhibit nonlicensed persons from sharing in casino revenues. This ensures that unsuitable persons are not evading the licensing process through "hidden interests." Second, depending on its tax rate, the government can have a minor or major interest in ensuring that all revenues are properly accounted for and taxed. This prevents "skimming" (where the owners receive revenues but do not pay taxes on them) and employee theft or embezzlement.

Casino accounting is more difficult than accounting in most businesses, where each transaction is recorded. For example, a grocery store keeps records of each item sold. Even other cash businesses, such as money exchanges or banks, record all individual transactions. In the casino, it is impractical to record each bet made, so governments and casinos must rely on accounting by aggregate.[53] The accuracy of this type of accounting must necessarily rely on accurate and secure handling of all casino transactions and collecting, transferring, and paying cash; granting and recording credit; and exchanging, collecting, and disbursing gaming chips and tokens.[54]

Accounting controls can take various forms from actual governmental participation in the accounting process to mere reporting. Governments may impose any of the following requirements: (1) governmental participation; (2) governmental audits; (3) independent audits; (4) minimum internal controls; (5) recordkeeping requirements; and (6) reporting requirements.

Governmental Participation

Governments can best ensure that all revenues are properly accounted for by being actively involved in the accounting process.

Where gaming is restricted to gaming devices only, on-line monitoring systems give government accountants the opportunity to monitor play as it occurs. Louisiana uses an on-line system to monitor slot machine activity at private "truck stop" casinos with up to 50 games and taverns and other locations with no more than 3 games. On-line systems also are commonly used in government-operated video lottery terminals, which are similar to slot machines.

In a casino table-game environment, this would require that government agents be present and participate in every transaction that involves the transfer of money, credit, or monetary equivalents, such as chips. Surveillance would require that government personnel be present to record and review surveillance tapes. As one can imagine, this system would be financially impractical in most jurisdictions unless a jurisdiction had a single large casino or some other unique characteristic.

Short of full government participation, in some jurisdictions government participates in certain aspects of the accounting process. New Jersey, for example, has government offices on the casino premises. In Louisiana, the landbased gaming devices are electronically linked to state police headquarters, and allow on-line monitoring of all gambling activity. This is possible in locations that allow gaming devices only.

Governmental Audits. If there is no governmental participation, a cost-efficient method of ensuring proper cash controls is through the audit process. This requires that the government retain a trained and competent staff to conduct the audits with sufficient regularity to be a deterrent to illegal or poor practices. Typical audit objectives are to ensure that the unlicensed casino (1) is not paying or allowing unlicensed persons to receive gaming revenues; (2) has adequate internal control procedures; (3) is following its internal control procedures for the handling of cash and transactions; (4) is properly reporting its revenues; and (5) is paying all taxes and fees.

Government audits of the casinos often are unannounced and irregular. Staff auditors may conduct long, detailed reviews or spot checks of compliance with certain regulations or procedures.

Outside Audits. Another method of meeting governmental accounting objectives is to require casinos to undergo annual audits by independent outside accounting firms. The government may have these firms conduct an audit of the casino's financial statement and a review of the casino's compliance with its internal control submission.

Internal Control Procedures

Internal control procedures are the procedures a casino implements to govern its business. They are generally written instructions on how employees and management must handle a particular situation. Internal control procedures govern virtually every aspect of the casino business. For example, they address how a blackjack dealer deals, collects, and pays wagers. They also may dictate who can announce gaming credit and how cage employees must grant this credit. The goals of internal controls are to reasonably ensure that

- Financial records are accurate and reliable.
- Assets are safeguarded with recorded accountability for assets compared to actual assets at reasonable intervals.
- Transactions are performed and assets accessed only according to management authorization.
- The casino maintains proper segregation of functions, duties, and responsibilities.

Government may dictate internal controls through the adoption of detailed regulations, or it may allow each casino to devise its own set of internal controls that meet set standards.

Recordkeeping. Most governments require casinos to maintain detailed records of all transactions. This facilitates the audit process either by the government or by independent auditors, and allows for government investigations into the casinos' activities.

Reporting. Besides independent audits, governments usually require the casinos to provide many types of periodic reports. These are most commonly tax returns, but other reports that governments may require include employee lists, loans, equipment purchases, junket agent and junket lists, bad debts, involvement in foreign gaming, and significant contracts.

Compliance Committees. Another vehicle that government can use to ensure proper accounting and regulatory compliance is a compliance committee. Regulatory agencies often dictate the membership criteria, but such committees usually include one or more outside members. These committees must meet periodically to review the casinos' compliance with all gaming laws. They also may be empowered to conduct investigations and provide advice to the casinos.

REGULATORY PRICE CONTROLS

In most industries, regulatory price controls mean that the government sets prices for services. For example, a state public service commission may set basic telephone rates at $9 per month. In the casino industry, government sets rates by dictating the odds of the games.

Price-setting disrupts a competitive market. Often, it helps established firms because it eliminates competitive pricing. If the industry's market is only locals, price-setting may be good for casinos that do not have to compete based on price, and if the price set is above market price. This is bad for gamblers, however, who will not get the best deal. If the market is national or regional, price-setting may harm both the gamblers and the casinos. A problem in these jurisdictions is that serious gamblers do not like the rigidity of fixed odds. They prefer to go to casinos that compete based on odds because they get a better deal. Gamblers only benefit from price-setting in systems, such as monopolies, where the casino could and would give worse odds if the law did not mandate lower odds.

Similar consideration is regulatory flexibility in adapting to market conditions. In other words, does the casino have business discretion to change game rules, procedures, and game mix, and to introduce new games? If it does, the industry can adopt new trends and technologies very quickly. Businesses that can adapt quickly have the better chance of surviving.

TAXATION

Casinos exist in three types of markets: monopolistic, oligopolistic, and competitive. Windsor, Ontario, is an example of a monopoly since the province has announced that only one casino will be allowed there. It may not always be a monopoly, however, because Detroit, which is adjacent to Windsor and accessible by bridge, may have legal casinos in the future. In the Monopoly Model, the taxes that casinos pay the state can be much higher in most circumstances. Thus, the casino usually will set odds more favorable to the house than it would in a competitive market. This pricing is a function of how many games the casino can offer before the cost of adding one additional game exceeds the revenues that can be derived from that game. The difference between when this point is reached in monopoly and competitive markets is that in a perfect competitive market the marginal revenue curve is the same as the demand curve. In a monopoly, the marginal revenue curve intersects the marginal cost curve at a lower output and a higher price. The effect is that the monopoly casino provides fewer games at higher odds, or institutes other costs to maximize profits.

Because a monopoly casino's margins are much higher (that is, the price of the goods less the cost of goods), it can afford to pay higher taxes. For example, Splash, in Tunica, Mississippi, was the only casino in the Memphis area. It charged patrons to park and enter the casino, but it still had four-hour waiting lines just for admission. Other casino operators were attracted to the area, and eventually obtained the licenses to open. No longer a monopoly, Splash had to alter its pricing structure—fewer, if any, patrons were now willing to pay an admission not charged by its competitors. Because of few entrants, the Memphis area is not a perfect competitive market. Instead, it mirrors an oligopoly where the profit-maximizing price is somewhere between those of the perfect competitive and monopoly markets.

When setting a tax structure, government dictates output. In the casino industry, output equates to the number of games and devices that the casinos offer the public, and the number of games and devices offered drive other areas, such as the number of employees, capital investment, and ancillary and complementary industries. All industries have demand curves for their product. Usually, the higher the cost, the lower the product demand. Taxation can be either a fixed or variable cost, but in either case it increases the cost of the product. The more that the government taxes casino gaming, the lower the demand for it. Conceivably, the government could tax the industry so heavily that gamblers would go to other jurisdictions, or gamble with illegal operators.

REFERENCES

1. Not all laws are well reasoned. Some result from corruption and others by accident. Sometimes legislative bodies pass a law believing that they are dictating conduct of one sort, but the courts interpret their laws differently than intended. The alternate interpretation results in effects to a society that were not intended or consistent with that society's public policy.
2. For a more in-depth treatment of the subject, see William N. Thompson. *Legalized Gambling*, Santa Barbara, CA: ABC-CLIO, 1994.
3. C. Bahmueller. *State Policy and the Ethics of Gambling*, p. 745.
4. *Sports Betting and College Athletics*, p. 311.
5. Bernard Polders. *The Gambling Papers*, pp. 207–208.
6. P. Helsing. *Gambling—The Issues and Policy Decisions Involved in the Trend toward Legalization—A Statement of the Current and Chronism of Benign Prohibition*, p. 773.
7. Bruce Ranson. "Public Policy and Gambling in New Jersey," *Gambling and Public Policy*, 1992.
8. Id.
9. R. Benjamin Cohen. "The New Jersey Casino Control Act: Creation of a Regulatory System," *Seton Hall Legislative Journal*, pp. 1, 3, 1982.
10. R. McKibben. *Working Class Gambling in Britain 1880–1939: Past and Present*, 1979. Cited in G. Smith, "The 'To Do' Over What to Do about Sports Gambling: Sanitizing a Tainted Activity," *Gambling and Public Policy*, Vol. 21.
11. V. Abt, G. Smith, and E. Christensen. *Business of Risk*, 1985. Cited in G. Smith, "The 'To Do' Over What to Do about Sports Gambling: Sanitizing a Tainted Activity," *Gambling and Public Policy*, Vol. 21.

12. J. Rosecrance. "The Social World of Sports Betting," *Arena Review,* Vol. 2, pp. 15–24, 1987. Cited in G. Smith, "The 'To Do' Over What to Do about Sports Gambling: Sanitizing a Tainted Activity," *Gambling and Public Policy,* Vol. 21.

13. T. Martinez. *The Gambling Scene: Why People Gamble,* 1983. Cited in G. Smith, "The 'To Do' Over What to Do about Sports Gambling: Sanitizing a Tainted Activity," *Gambling and Public Policy,* Vol. 21.

14. William N. Thompson and J. Kent Pinney. "The Mismarketing of Dutch Casinos," *Journal of Gambling Studies,* Vol. 6, pp. 205–221, Fall 1990.

15. Rev. Gordon Moody. "Legalized Gambling: For or Against Gamblers," *The Gambling Papers, Proceedings of the Fifth National Conference of Gambling and Risk Taking,* 1982.

16. J. Skolnick and J. Dombrink. "The Limits of Gaming Control," 12 Conn. L. Rev. 762, 772, 1980.

17. Telephone conversation with the Minnesota Lawful Gambling Board, May 24, 1994. Net Profits from pull tabs were $235 million. This industry has grown from a total handle of $111 million in 1985.

18. Another goal that often accompanies the protection of the industry is the protection of the state's principal interest in tax revenues. This is accomplished by stringent accounting, audit, and reporting requirements.

19. Eugene M. Christiansen. "The Role of Government in Commercial Gambling," *The Gambling Studies: Proceedings of the Sixth National Conference on Gambling and Risk Taking,* p. 128, 1985.

20. Richard Lehne. *Casino Policy,* Rutgers University Press, 1986, p. 45.

21. Alfred N. King. "Public Gaming and Public Trust," 12 Conn. L. Rev. 740, 1980.

22. Richard I. Aaron. "Maintaining Financial Integrity of the Casino Through Licensing Regulation," *The Gambling Papers: Proceedings of the Fifth National Conference on Gambling and Risk Taking,* 127, 1982.

23. J. Skolnick and J. Dombrink. "The Limits of Gaming Control," 12 Conn. L. Rev. 762, 773, 1980.

24. In the protection model, the government is attempting to protect its economic stake in the gaming industry. This defined goal is not necessarily inconsistent with the broader goals of the industry; it promotes industry growth. Besides the issue of whether government should promote gambling, the goal is not necessarily inconsistent with notions of good government. Strict licensing, accounting and audit oversight, and enforcement of the gaming regulations are similar to the methods used in the "unstimulated" demand model. The "capture" theory, however, is based on a benign government collusion with the industry. Specifically, the industry will use the regulatory machinery to its own benefit, usually to limit entry or assist in a price-fixing scheme.

25. A notable exception would be where physical or workforce attributes limit the number of possible casinos. Tinian, a small island near Guam, is a good example. The island has an indigenous population of only 300. This is insufficient to staff even one large hotel/casino. Even if workers were imported, the size of the island and its ability to provide infrastructure would limit the number of casinos to a few at best.

26. Commission on the Review of the National Policy Toward Gambling, *Gambling in America*, p. 102, 1976.

27. W. T. O'Donnell. "A Chief Executive's Views on the Necessity for Comprehensive State Control and Regulation in the United States Gaming Industry," 12 Conn. L. Rev. 727, 730, 1980.

28. Alfred King. "Public Gaming and Public Trust," 12 Conn. L. Rev. 740, 760, n. 116, 1982.

29. Nevada requires that persons wishing to open casinos in Las Vegas or Reno with 15 or more slot machines must also build hotels with at least 200 rooms and certain other amenities. This is similar to inducements used by the Province of Saskatchewan to build hotel rooms in isolated areas by holding out the possibility of obtaining a privileged liquor license. Mississippi requires the casino to be built over a river.

30. J. McMillan. "The Impact of Casinos in Australian Cities," *Gambling and Public Policy*, p. 87.

31. *Mun v. Illinois*, 1877.

32. J. Landis. *The Administrative Process*, 1938.

33. L. L. Jaffe. "The Illusion of the Ideal Administration," *Harvard Law Review*, Vol. 86 (no. 1183), 1973. The "public interest" theory has been criticized as naive and ineffective. According to one critic, the theory is based on two debatable assumptions: First, that the agency will use only relevant and value-free concepts; second, that the agency is insulated from the political process. To others, the concept of the "public interest" presents additional problems. The term *public interest* is somewhat vague, not unlike the terms *general welfare* and *common good*, which also creep into regulatory enactments. Even allowing for this vagueness, if the public interest is the driving force behind regulatory intervention in the market, one would expect to see greater regulation in those industries experiencing greater market failure or imperfection. There is, however, no positive empirical link between regulation and those industries in which significant externalities are present; in situations in which consumers repeatedly underinvest in information; or where firms are heavily concentrated. Furthermore, the actual experiences of regulatory agencies brought to print by such authors as Kolko and Bernstein document regulatory activity outside of the notion of the public interest. Lastly, many of the federal agencies founded upon the public interest model proved more detrimental to the market than beneficial. Dean Landis used two agencies as exam-

ples of his model, the Federal Trade Commission and the Interstate Commerce Commission, both of which proved to be, at best, ineffective, and, at worst, destructive of the industry that they regulated.

In spite of its significant criticism, most modern-day writers still implicitly adhere to it by writing from the vantage point of the "public-spirited" regulator or concerned modern citizen. Rarely, are there works in economics, especially at the textbook level, that give insight and advice to the firm or industry on how to thwart, capture, or tamper with regulations. A notable exception is Chapter 1 of Owen and Braeutigam, *The Regulation Game* (1978).

34. George Stigler. *The Citizen and the State.* Chicago: University of Chicago Press, 1975, p. 114.

35. The acquisition of cash subsidies, Stigler's first reason for industry to demand regulation, is tenuous because it would tend to excite entry by new firms. Cash subsidies would only be sought by an industry having control over entry or if the subsidies could be earmarked for existing firms. Although Stigler appears to come to this realization (p. 116), this same general argument holds for his contention that an industry demands regulation to control complements and substitutes, and to assist in price-fixing schemes.

36. John Kenneth Galbraith. *The Great Crash.* Boston: Houghton Mifflin, 1954, p. 172.

37. Marver Bernstein. *Regulating Business by Independent Commission* Princeton N.J.: Princeton University Press, 1955, p. 90.

38. To its critics, the capture notion poses certain problems as a general theory. First, a regulatory body frequently oversees several different competing industries, such as is the case with the Interstate Commerce Commission. In these instances, the capture theory stands as too simple an explanation. Second, the theory focuses solely on the role of the regulated in compromising the regulators and ignores other external forces in the process. Therefore, it fails to explain the thousands of court cases between the regulated industries and their regulators within a capture content. Moreover, if the capture theory were an accurate depiction of the real world, there would be thousands fewer lawyers in the United States. Likewise, the capture model fails to explain the industrial lobbying effort against regulations that have been evident since the mid to latter seventies.

39. Sam Peltzman. "The Economic Theory of Regulation after a Decade of Deregulation," In *9 Brookings Papers on Economic Activity,* edited by M.N. Barry and C. Winston. Washington D.C.: Brookings Institute, 1989.

40. C. WRS. Jaffe. "The Illusion of the Ideal Administration," *Harvard Law Review,* Vol. 86 (no. 1183), 1973.

41. See, for example, J.M. Buchanan and G. Tullock. "Prollujer's Profits and Political Response: Direct Controls Versus Taxes," *American Economic Review,* March 1975.

42. See R. Tollison. "Regulatory and Interest Groups." in *Regulation, Economic Theory and History,* p. 69. Ann Arbor: University of Michigan Press, 1991.

43. W. M. Landes and R. A. Posner. "The Independent Judiciary in an Interest Group Perspective," *Journal of Law and Economics* (December 1975), pp. 875–901.

44. Lester B. Snyder. "Regulation of Legalized Gambling, An Inside View," 12 Conn. L. Rev. 665, 714, 1980.

45. H. Henn and J. ALexander. *Corporations.* Horn Book Series, 1983, p. 396.

46. A. Cabot, W. Thompson, and A. Tottenham, (Eds.). *International Casino Law* (2nd ed.), 1993.

47. Nev. Rev. Stat. §465.083 ("It is unlawful for any person, whether he is an owner or employee of or a gambler in an establishment, to cheat at any gambling game.") See also, Nev. Rev. Stat. §465.015, and *Sheriff v. Martin* [1983].

48. R. Lehne. *Casino Policy,* p. 47, 1986.

49. Jurisdictions that require gamblers to be at least 18 years old include Argentina, Tasmania, Queensland, Mauritius, Paraguay, Spain, Great Britain, France, and Puerto Rico. The age restriction in British Columbia is 19 years old.

50. Jurisdictions that require gamblers to be at least 21 years old include Nevada, New Jersey, South Dakota, Mississippi, and other U.S. jurisdictions. Turkey requires gamblers to be at least 25 years old.

51. N. Fagan and N. Kent-Lemon. "Great Britain," in *International Casino Law* (2nd ed.), 1993, pp. 312–313.

52. Nevada, New Jersey, Tasmania, and Tinian regulators maintain such lists.

53. M. Santaniello. "Casino Gambling: The Elements of Effective Control", 6 *Seton Hall Legislative Journal,* pp. 25–27, 1982.

54. Id.

Chapter

4

Casino Organizational Structures

INTRODUCTION BY ARTE NATHAN, VICE PRESIDENT OF HUMAN RESOURCES, MIRAGE RESORTS

The gaming industry has experienced a tremendous evolution in the past 40 years. Isolated in Nevada and the Caribbean in the 1950s and 1960s, it expanded to New Jersey in 1978, and in the mid-1990s it began to proliferate in many other states and countries in the form of riverboats, Native American casinos, and land-based development projects. This growth brought with it an increased involvement with regulators, new business partners, the investment industry, unions, and new communities, all of which were keenly interested in the business plans of the growth-oriented gaming companies. Inevitably, the human resources strategies were one indication of the organizational and professional viability of these new companies.

The human resources changes brought about by this evolution have been significant. Historically, at-will employment policies and minimal training were the norm; human resources departments primarily coordinated payroll distribution and the maintenance of personnel files. Today, sophisticated hiring, training, fair treatment and recognition policies serve as support mechanisms within the business plans of successful gaming companies. The human resources development strategies now being used by casinos include the following.

Targeted selection. With an emphasis on friendliness and service, employees are initially screened for outgoing personalities, commitment to quality service, and stability. In the past, the "dummy up and deal" mentality was prevalent; today's customers expect casino employees to meet them with friendliness and a desire to exceed their expectations.

Effective training. All hourly employees are trained to know what their job tasks are, why those tasks are performed, and how best to perform them before they are allowed to start work. This training is conducted by trained department personnel, who use structured training guides developed for each job classification. The gaming customer today is a sophisticated traveler who expects quality service—the kind that only a well-prepared employee can provide.

Successful gaming companies are teaching management and task skills to their line managers and executives. Basic skills include legal responsibilities, conflict resolution, and delegation. Leadership skills are also important and include motivation, speech making, and business writing. Annual in-service training provides managers with the tools to effectively lead their employees.

Fair treatment. The most successful companies are staffed by employees who like where they work, and nothing satisfies employees more than being treated fairly.

Recognition. Performance should be reviewed on a continual basis; supervisors should note and comment when performance is good and help employees improve when performance is below acceptable standards.

These are just a few of the strategies that effective human resource departments are employing to meet the business demands of the gaming industry. While these strategies reflect traditional human resource values, they are new to the gaming industry and in step with its current needs.

In the final analysis, the product sold by gaming companies is service; the rooms, food, and slot machines are equal, but the service sets one company apart from the others. As more people experience gaming in facilities close to their homes, the service will determine whether they become satisfied, repeat customers. The professional gaming companies—the ones that have well-developed human resources programs—will take the greatest advantage of this growth.

To attempt to provide an overview of casino organizational structures, it is important to note that there is no uniformly used structure. The number and type of games played, the technology utilized by the operation, and individual managerial philosophies will dictate the scope and size of each organizational chart. For instance, a major hotel/casino in Las Vegas or Atlantic City will have many more employees and a taller structure than a gaming riverboat found in Mississippi. Thus, although some state gaming regulations do dictate the minimum number of employees required to perform various gaming functions as well as their reporting relationships, generally, the formality and the dynamics of casino organizational structures vary.

Perhaps the most consistency can be found through an examination of job titles and employee functions associated with a *typical* gaming operation. With this in mind, this chapter will present an analysis of the organizational structure and employees that may be found in a full-scale casino operation offering a full range of table games, slots, and other forms of casino entertainment.

GENERAL AND ADMINISTRATIVE

At the top of a casino organizational structure is the general and administrative staff as delineated in Figure 4.1. The chief executive officer may be referred to as the casino manager, director of casino operations or president of casino operations depending on the size of the operation and job title preferences. This person is responsible for the successful operation of all gaming components and has discretionary authority to "run the business." Although this sounds like omnipotent and unfettered power, there are certain restrictions. Gaming regulations and operational internal control procedures may restrict access to "sensitive" areas of the casino (that is, eye-in-the-sky surveillance, the soft count room, etc.) in order to prevent collusion, money laundering, or evidence tampering. In these cases, even the top administrative casino personnel may not have the authority/power to enter these areas, and in fact the establishment will face licensing problems if deviations from these standards occur.

A summary of the essential or daily job functions of a casino manager includes a review of daily gaming reports and related statistics, among them:

- *Win/loss.* Casinos will compile a daily manager's report in conjunction with the master game report, known in gaming jargon as the "stiff sheet" (See Chapter 7), which provides a review of the win or loss of each casino game or gaming area with related percentages. Also included in the report will be a month-to-date analysis and year-to-date analysis with comparative figures such as last-month-to-date and last-year-to-date.
- *Handle.* The gross volume or amount "handled" by the house/casino.

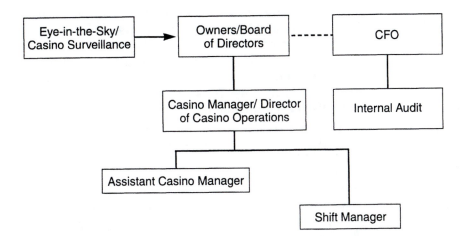

Figure 4.1 Casino General and Administrative Organizational Chart

- *Drop*. The total money taken in by the casino via currency/tokens/chips in table drop boxes. Casinos refer to a "soft drop" and a "hard drop." The soft drop is the currency or paper money received from table gaming activities, while the hard drop is the coin or tokens received via slot machines. Each of these drops is counted by separate teams in larger casinos, with a notable exception: The soft count team not only may count the currency from the table games, they may also be assigned to count the currency generated from bill validators found on numerous contemporary slot machines.
- *Hold*. Often referred to as the "PC/percentage," this is the *amount held* by the casino from the drop, while PC is reported as a percentage. The hold percentage is usually computed by dividing the win by the drop.

Additional duties of a casino manager encompass the selection and rules of games, casino layout/design modifications to increase maximum play, coordination with the credit manager in the extension of customer credit when the amounts are exceptionally high, and ensuring adherence to internal control procedures as required by a government gaming regulatory body and standards established by the accounting department. The casino manager usually acts as the final authority in customer disputes and can initiate investigations into alleged gaming misconduct by customers or employees. All gaming department heads report to the casino manager, and the property's marketing strategy as well as policies, rules, and procedures for operational success are likewise conveyed to these department heads.

Many casinos now offer special events, usually through a special events/marketing department, such as boxing matches, golf tournaments, and poker tournaments, and the casino manager not only is involved in the planning but also assesses the success of each program. Budgeting and forecasting are included in the job description. This executive must do a review of "comps" (complimentaries extended to casino players) to make sure these are in accordance with customer play.

Perhaps the single largest responsibility for today's casino manager is establishing an environment that will create an enjoyable experience for guests and employees. The industry has witnessed a metamorphosis of the business from a smoke-filled gambling hall to casino entertainment and gaming attractions. Top executives have realized that competition dictates that a quality product be offered to guests, provided by employees who are willing to enhance each customer's visit because each employee is made to feel special by management. Therefore, the casino manager of the 1990s must understand employee motivation, human relations and communication skills, team-building concepts, and participative management. The days of telling employees to "dummy up and deal" or "we didn't hire you to think" most certainly are over.

Traditionally, casino managers rose through the ranks, often starting as Blackjack or dice dealers and then being promoted to a floorperson, pit manager, shift manager, and assistant casino manager. Two trends have recently emerged. First, as gaming continues to proliferate across the United States and internationally, a number of gaming companies have experienced a dramatic shortage of qualified gaming managers. To meet this human resources challenge, management development programs have been created within these companies to create fast-track advancement plans. The Promus Corporation, Harrah's gaming entertainment division, has established two concepts to meet its needs: The President's Associate Program and the William F. Harrah Institute of Casino Entertainment.

The President's Associate Program identifies/recruits MBAs who have previous work experience (usually nongaming) and places them in a general management development program involving courses and seminars in gaming, with eventual placement at a casino property. The William F. Harrah Institute of Casino Entertainment places current Promus managers without a gaming background in an intensified series of gaming seminars and training courses. These individuals are subsequently phased into various gaming operations. The Mirage Hotel/Casino offers a Management Associate Program (MAP), in which college graduates undertake a 1-1/2-year casino training program and then are placed in gaming management positions.

The second trend in the business focuses on the number of casino workers who are returning to the classroom to secure a four-year or two-year degree.

The message is clear: Upward mobility in today's casino organizational structure is being predicated on education.

The assistant casino manager, as the job title suggests, works with the casino manager and may in fact perform many of the day-to-day routine duties, allowing the casino manager to focus on long-range planning.

Casinos operate with three shift managers: one for the day shift, one for the swing shift, and one for the graveyard/late shift. Shift managers become the authoritative source in the absence of the casino manager or assistant casino manager. They are analogous to field marshals, directly overseeing the table games and gaming pit operations (a pit refers to the physical configuration/location of the Twenty-One and Craps tables, etc.). Many of the day-to-day gaming activities are handled by shift managers without the involvement of the casino manager. Obviously, shift managers must be extremely knowledgeable in all aspects of gaming and exercise extraordinary business judgment and customer skills.

Figure 4.1 shows two components that offer a check and balance on the casino manager. The internal auditor and the eye-in-the-sky (also known as casino surveillance) operate independently from the casino manager, with the former position reporting to the controller or chief financial officer, and the eye-in-the-sky likewise reporting to the owner(s).

The internal auditor reviews staffing and standard operating procedures used in the casino to make sure all prescribed accounting and internal control policies are being followed. He or she is given the task of writing a formal plan that will create a clear audit trail for gaming regulators. The internal auditor is also given the responsibility for training all employees affected by the currency transaction provisions of the Bank Secrecy Act and guaranteeing compliance with this federal law as applicable to financial institutions and gaming operations.

Surveillance (the eye-in-the-sky) maintains camera surveillance over gaming operations in the casino. Operating from a highly secured surveillance room, this department uses state-of-the-art wide-angle lenses and zoom cameras to focus on employees and guests, watching for cheating scams, slot manipulations, and other illegal acts in the casino. When suspected cheaters are spotted, surveillance contacts gaming enforcement regulators, who work with surveillance and casino security guards to catch the perpetrator in the act. Surveillance videotapes are then used as evidence in court to convict the apprehended culprits.

BLACKJACK/TWENTY-ONE

Figure 4.2 illustrates the typical organizational chart for the operation of Blackjack/Twenty-One games. Casinos often have several Twenty-One pits, and one pit manager or pit boss is assigned to each. Pit managers complete the daily/weekly work schedules and supervise the floorpersons. Critical to their job performance is the careful monitoring of all gaming activities within their respective pits, making sure all game rules, wagers, and payoffs are in accordance with prescribed internal control procedures. These managers may be approached for credit by a player, or by a floorperson on behalf of a player, and a pit boss will confirm the player's credit eligibility through the cage or refer the player to the credit manager.

Markers/IOUs, known as rim credit, can be issued by pit managers; pit managers also have the authority to issue comps based on a computer-generated report, floorperson ratings, and other predetermined criteria.

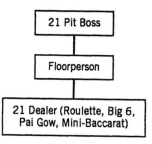

Figure 4.2 Blackjack/Twenty-One Organizational Chart

Unresolved customer disputes are referred to the pit boss, who also has the right to request surveillance scrutiny of suspected cheaters. Pit Bosses have the authority to remove decks of cards from a game and maintain control over unused and unissued decks of cards (some casinos will only allow a shift manager to make this decision).

Pit managers generally have 7 to 10 years of gaming experience and historically have used this position to train for promotions to shift managers.

Anyone who has observed a Twenty-One pit has probably noticed supervisors in business attire moving from game to game, closely monitoring the gaming action. These are floorpersons, who are responsible for maintaining the integrity of the game, ensuring that the dealer is operating in accordance with prescribed procedures, and watching for improper game variances. Normally, floorpersons observe or supervise four games, although some casinos will reduce this number with high-stake table games.

One of the primary functions of a floorperson is to track player betting habits and rate player action. Floorpersons use four criteria when rating a player:

1. Buy-in amount to the game
2. Duration of play
3. Average bet
4. Largest bet

Using this criteria, the floorperson completes a rating card or inputs the information in a computerized rating system that calculates the value of the player. Calculated ratings are issued on a point or dollar value, and players will receive or be denied complimentary services based on these ratings. Some operators have used surveillance department tapes to help determine accurate rating systems.

Requests for markers or credit play are initially directed to floorpersons, and these are the first people contacted by a dealer when a player dispute arises. Their duties also include verifying chip amounts brought to the table by hotel security to replenish a depleted table inventory. These "fills" are counted by the dealer and verified by the floorperson in the presence of the security officer. The dealer and floorperson will sign a fill slip attesting to the accuracy of the count and the fill amount. The same procedure is followed when chips are removed from a table, except then a credit slip is used. Floorpersons issue approved new decks of cards and remove used decks. Used decks are systematically tracked and controlled by the casino to prevent the reintroduction of cards from these decks into games. A tracking form is used with each deck that must be initialed or signed by the dealer and floorperson.

Miscellaneous duties may include signaling for a cocktail server for a guest and contacting a casino porter to dispose of accumulated trash or spillage. Floorpersons may have limited comping authority.

The ideal floorperson needs to be knowledgeable not only in the game of Blackjack but also in Roulette, the Big 6, Mini-Baccarat, and Pai Gow Poker, since a Twenty-One pit may include all of these games. As a rule of thumb, a minimum of three years' experience in dealing multiple games is required prior to promotion to floorperson. As is the case with all public contact employees, floorpersons must possess excellent customer relation skills and be able to work with a team of employees to ensure a positive experience for guests and coworkers.

The final employee shown in Figure 4.2 is the dealer. The title "blackjack dealer" is somewhat of a misnomer. Contemporary casino dealers must be able—and often are required—to deal Roulette, the Big 6 (or "Wheel-of-Fortune"), Pai Gow Poker, and Mini-Baccarat. During training, dealers also learn how to deal Craps, which enhances their value to casinos. Dealers must pass a dealing audition demonstrating hand dexterity and payoff accuracy in order to be hired.

The primary function of a Blackjack dealer is to deal the game of Twenty-One from a single deck or multiple decks that are either hand-held or dealt from a shoe. Some gaming operations have established a "per-hand-per-hour" minimum for dealers as a basis for assessing productivity (*i.e.*, 60 to 72 rounds per hour or one hand every 73 seconds). Gaming experts disagree on the exact number, and many argue that using this quantitative criterion alone overlooks the qualitative, customer-relations factor that must be included in any productivity assessment system. Nevertheless, the average number of hands per hour is critically important to casinos, since it relates to increased revenues. To meet this challenge, many operators have turned to automated deck shufflers, eliminating or significantly reducing the dealer's shuffling function and thus increasing the speed of the game. Some gaming executives estimate that a 10–20% increase in hands can be realized through the use of automatic continuous shufflers.

A list of a Blackjack dealer's duties also includes selling casino chips to players for currency and inserting the currency with the use of a plastic paddle into a slit found on the top of the Twenty-One layout that causes the currency to fall into a metal drop box attached to the bottom of each gaming table. Copies of fill and credit slips are likewise deposited into these drop boxes. Dealers explain the rules of the game, including how players motion for additional cards as desired, when and if "insurance" can be purchased (that is, when the dealer's up card is an ace); when players may double-down and/or split pairs. Some house rules additionally permit players to "surrender" a hand to reduce the amount of their original wager. During the game, the dealer will present a reshuffled deck to a player to allow him or her to cut the deck.

Most casinos pay dealers minimum wage or a moderate hourly wage, since these employees can earn considerable amounts from tips (also called "tokes") given by players as a direct gratuity or through hands played by the player for the dealer. Twenty-One as well as Craps dealers form their own tip committees and distribute collected amounts in various ways:

- Shift by shift.
- Employees working within each pit.
- Table by table—dice dealers have used this method most frequently, and some casinos are now experimenting with this method for Twenty-One dealers.
- Twenty-four-hour basis—Baccarat dealers working all three shifts have opted to split all tokes collected over 24 hours.
- Each dealer keeps his/her own tips.

Finally, Twenty-One dealers must be ambassadors of goodwill toward customers and be able to promote positive customer relations. This is often quite difficult in the industry when dealing with a player who has lost a considerable amount of money.

Collectively, all gaming employees share two common job functions: identifying players who have overindulged and appear to be under the influence, and realizing when they are dealing with compulsive/addictive gamblers. There is a new-found social responsibility in the gaming and casino entertainment industry, and many times customers need to be protected from themselves by employees.

CRAPS/DICE

The terms "Craps" and "Dice" are used interchangeably. Crap games, like Twenty-One, were the mainstay of casinos for years. However, with the increased revenue production of slots, many casinos have reduced the number of Crap games, thereby reducing space allocations for them.

As with Twenty-One, Crap tables are configured into a pit and managed by a dice pit boss or dice pit manager (see Figure 4.3).

Dice Pit Managers have essentially the same duty as their Twenty-One counterparts: maintaining the integrity of the game. However, the game of dice is much more complicated than Twenty-One because of the wagering variations allowed. Dice floorpersons observe two crap tables and rate players' action, watch to make sure dealer payoffs are correct, refer requests for credit to the credit manager, and oversee fills and credits.

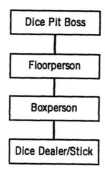

Figure 4.3   Craps/Dice Organizational Chart

Limited comping authority is given to these employees and, as is always the case, supervisors must maintain excellent customer and employee relations.

The boxperson is a supervisor unique to the game of dice. Noticeable by his/her business attire and *seated* at the game, arms draped over the crap table, this person is the frontline manager of each Crap game. Boxpersons maintain stacks of casino chips directly in front of them and receive all currency wagered by guests. They are responsible for dropping all currency into the drop boxes attached to the bottom of each Crap table. Boxperson duties include watching the dice, which includes how the dice are handled and tossed by the "shooter" as well as employees; inspecting any dice that are tossed or dropped from the table; and issuing new dice as deemed necessary. Wagering payoffs are scrutinized for accuracy by the dealers and to prevent past-posting, that is, placing a bet on a number after the number has been recorded by the toss of the dice. Extreme attention to the game is required, and many times this employee's serious demeanor is mistakenly interpreted. It should be noted that recent changes in human resources management have witnessed combination jobs in the dice pit, with the boxperson carrying the title of box/dealer. Finally, it is not unusual to find two boxpersons working a game with extreme amounts of business or "high rollers."

Three dealers are employed at each Crap table, and a fourth dealer works relief, thereby creating a four-person team. As with Twenty-One dealers, dice dealers work a standard eight-hour shift, but in both games dealers are given frequent breaks because of the intensity of the games. Dealers may work 45 minutes with a 15-minute break, 40 minutes with a 20-minute break, or a similar variation. Large casinos provide a dealer's room where these employees can get a snack, watch television, or rest while waiting for the continuation of their shift.

Two of the dice dealers flank the boxperson and are responsible for accepting player wagers, collecting loss wagers, and paying off winning bets placed on their portion of the table. The third dealer, referred to as the "stick person," operates a croupier stick, which is used to deliver the dice to the shooting player and to retrieve thrown dice. Note that the game is designed to avoid dice handling by employees. The stick person calls the game, announcing new shooters and dice totals that have been tossed, and generally creating an exciting atmosphere. He or she also handles wagers and payoffs in the middle of the Crap table. Dealers can significantly affect the amount of wagering at a dice game, and many times casinos will motivate dealers to "talk up" proposition bets that have more favorable odds for the house. As with Twenty-One dealers, dice dealers rely on tips for the vast majority of their income and collect gratuities via tip-pooling arrangements previously discussed.

SLOTS

Figure 4.4 represents a variety of employees who may be found in a large casino's slot organizational structure.

Slot machines were once thought to be a necessary evil, a diversion, something to keep the spouse happy while the real money was being wagered at the Twenty-One, Baccarat, or Crap tables. Today, in many

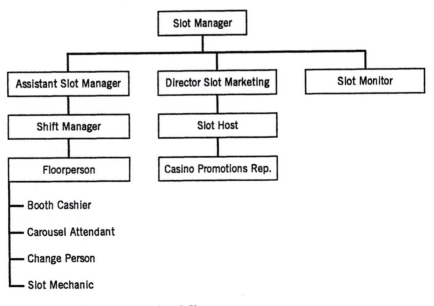

Figure 4.4 Slots Organizational Chart

gaming jurisdictions slots have become the leader in at least two areas: gaming revenue and technology.

Most recent gaming revenue figures from the state of Nevada indicate that 60+% of all gaming revenue is being generated by slot operations. This has resulted in a wider variety, diversification, and number of slots on casino floors, often at the expense of Twenty-One and Crap tables. Slots, secondly, have emerged as leaders in technological changes and game enhancement. Electromechanical slots have been replaced by computerized models with high-resolution graphics and EPROM computer chips that regulate random payoffs per preset programs. Modern machines feature bill validators or currency acceptors, and several operations use coinless or cashless machines, obviating the need for coins or currency. Touch-screen technology and multiple game screens also represent cutting-edge changes in slot manufacturing. Thus, the slot department has become a vital component in gaming operations, and its employees play an integral part in the success of the business.

The slot department is headed by a slot manager or director of slot operations. This person analyzes daily slot revenues and is responsible for maximizing the layout, types, and denominations of machines on the casino floor. Slot marketing and promotions are coordinated with this manager, and the success of each program is thoroughly scrutinized.

Comping policies for slot players are determined by the slot manager, who also establishes personnel policies and staffing requirements. Total departmental staffing depends on the number of slots, the square footage and physical layout of the casino, the number of automatic change dispensers and machines with bill validators, whether a slot club is offered, and service expectations of slot customers.

As noted in Figure 4.4, an assistant slot manager works in association with the slot manager. Day-to-day operations such as scheduling, employee disciplinary situations, and miscellaneous activities indigenous to the slot department are often handled by this employee.

Each shift is headed by a shift manager, who circulates on the casino floor, ensuring a smooth and efficient operation. This manager constantly evaluates employee performance and verifies adherence to internal control procedures. Disputes with payouts are brought to the shift manager prior to being referred to the head of the department. Larger casinos may employ an assistant shift manager.

The slot floorperson monitors the operation of slot machines, makes sure change persons are circulating throughout the casino, and participates in the payment of "handpay" jackpots. Handpay jackpots exceed the slot machine's coin hopper capacity (that is, 1,200 to 1,500 coins in a quarter video poker machine) and are verified by the slot floorperson. Slot jackpots won in the United States exceeding $1,200 require a tax declaration form, which is also handled by the slot floorperson. When all the coins in a slot machine's hopper are dispensed, the floorperson does a hopper fill in conjunction with either casino security and/or a change person or shift manager.

Casinos allow floorpersons to attempt to fix minor slot machine malfunctions and specify a machine out of order if there is a major problem. Guests who have cashed out an unusually large number of coins frequently ask floorpersons for assistance carrying their winnings to the coin cashier window. Floorpersons also review and audit all slot booth cashier and change-person money banks, noting any shortages or overages.

Slot booth cashiers can be observed throughout a casino working from within a wooden and glass configuration known as a *slot booth*. These cashiers sell rolls or racks of coins and casino tokens in exchange for currency. Customers wishing to redeem coins won from slot machines give their winnings to the booth cashier, who dumps the coins in an automatic counter or jet sorter and pays the customer per the amount registered on the counter's win meter. Cashier's may issue the currency for handpay jackpots to floorpersons and exchange cash given to change persons for additional rolls of coin, and some announce customer jackpots over the public address system as a form of internal marketing.

Casinos arrange special-attraction slot machines in a round or rectangular configuration known as a *carousel* and utilize a carousel attendant to dispense change and draw attention to these machines. Carousels are designed so that the attendant will be elevated within the configuration, which allows this employee to move quickly and freely from machine to machine while keeping an eye on the entire bank. Carousel attendants' duties can best be described as a combination change person, booth cashier, and promoter.

The final coin-dispensing employee in the slot department is the changeperson. Using a change belt or a slot cart that holds rolls of coins, the changeperson circulates throughout the casino selling coin to slot patrons. Changepersons either solicit sales by shouting "Change," or are called over and stopped by a slot player, or react to the change light (the "candle" or "lamp") on top of a machine, which has been activated by a player waiting for change. The advent of automated change dispensers, bill acceptors on slot machines, and coinless/cashless machines has resulted in the reduction of change personnel in casino operations. Nevertheless, although technology has brought increased services to guests and the reduction of payroll, casino operators have realized that guests still require and desire personalized treatment. Thus, the industry has witnessed a recent change to the slot department organizational charts: slot clubs.

Slot clubs are analogous to airline frequent flier concepts. Slot players either enroll themselves in the club with a slot club attendant or are approached on the casino floor by a slot host. Players who enroll are given a computerized card that can be inserted into any slot machine. An electronic message on the machine welcomes the player by name and the computerized slot-tracking system records points for the player based on amounts wagered and duration of play. Points are then redeemed by players for gifts or cash depending on the casino's policy. Slot clubs come under the supervision of the director of slot marketing, who is responsible for designing additional slot promotions. These might include slot tournaments or shuttles to and from the casino for local slot players.

Slot tournaments involve invitations to frequent or preferred slot customers with a special bank of slot machines reserved for tournament play. Players play these machines, and the highest points totals/credits scored result in cash awards or prizes.

As previously mentioned, slot machines periodically malfunction and require the services of another slot department employee: the slot mechanic. This employee normally is trained at a special school or by the manufacturer of the various slot machines. The job is critical to the operation, since inoperative machines with prolonged downtimes can significantly impact slot revenues. Additional duties include cleaning the interiors of the machines, installing new machines, and assisting in the movement of machines as directed by the slot manager.

One final employee found in the slot department is the slot monitor. This employee is employed only in highly computerized operations and monitors ongoing slot play, noting machines getting high-volume play and dispatching slot hosts to meet and greet players. Malfunctions are recorded and reported to slot mechanics, and other deviations are quickly detected and addressed. The slot monitor generates computer reports for each machine which reveal the amount of play, coins in, coins out, major jackpots, and player preference. These reports are used by the slot manager to alter the floor layout, moving less played machines into higher-traffic areas or removing machines that do not test well.

Coins and currency collected by slot machines are removed by a slot drop team; these employees are part of the accounting department of the casino. Slot machines retain coins in two receptacles: the hopper and the drop buckets. The slot drop team removes the drop buckets from the bottom of the machines and transports the coins to a hard count room, where they are counted through the use of automated coin counters and wrappers. Collected currency is counted by the soft count team in the casino cage or separated from the hard count by the hard count team.

BACCARAT

Employees working in the Baccarat room or pit of a casino are shown in Figure 4.5.

Baccarat carries the distinction of being the most elegant game in the casino. Its employees dress in tuxedos or formal attire and perform their

Figure 4.5 Baccarat Organizational Chart

duties in an extremely ornate Baccarat room. Baccarat players wager significant amounts of money and expect the royal treatment.

The Baccarat manager oversees the wagering and operation of the game. Like all gaming executives, this employee reviews game percentages, noting wins and losses and betting trends. Baccarat managers have or develop a list of high rollers and must maintain excellent customer relations with their clientele.

Larger casinos use Baccarat shift and pit managers and floorpersons in much the same manner as other previously discussed employees with the same job titles.

Baccarat dealers deal the game from a shoe, announcing each dealt card. Customers may then bet with the house or their own hand. The dealer collects lost wagers and pays off winning hands. Because of the ambiance of the game, a well-trained dealer deals with flair, stimulating wagering from players and creating excitement for onlookers.

A Baccarat shill is an employee who sits at the Baccarat table and gambles with house money to create activity in the baccarat pit.

KENO

Keno is a game played much like Bingo. Keno boards with numbers from 1 to 80 can be viewed on walls throughout the casino, and players wager on the 20 numbers that are randomly drawn with each game. The total number of selections appearing on the board determines the amount of the player's winnings per game.

The gaming revenue center is headed by a keno manager, who is responsible for the daily operations. The keno manager determines jackpot limits, payoff tables, and keno board locations, and monitors the number of games per day to maintain maximum profit structures. Generally, this person does the interviewing and hiring for the department and dictates the type of internal and external marketing to be done for promotional purposes. A keno manager will likely have eight to ten years of keno experience and must have strong customer relations and analytical skills.

Mega-resorts often employ an assistant keno manager, but medium and smaller-size casinos utilize shift managers as assistants. Shift managers act in the capacity of the keno manager when this person is off the property. Routine functions include computing percentages of games, maintaining game records (drop, win, etc.), handling unresolved customer disputes, verifying winning ticket payoffs, and opening and closing each game. The shift manager directly supervises keno employees working at the main keno counter.

Some keno departments employ second and third persons, best described as quasi-supervisory personnel or assistants to the shift manager. Supervisors oversee the submission of all tickets both by keno writers and keno runners, and they control the tempo of the game. Smaller operations use keno writers as a "second person," maximizing job efficiency.

Keno writers, as the name suggests, "write" keno tickets for players who submit their plays at the main keno counter. If the casino has a non-computerized operation, the writer receives the ticket from the player, with the number of selections and the amount of the wager marked by the customer. The writer then uses a house ticket to duplicate the wager, giving the player a validated ticket that can be used to verify a winning combination of numbers. Computerized systems allow the writer to place customers' tickets in a machine that reads the numbers and issues a validated ticket. Keno writers are also responsible for paying winning tickets, first making sure the ticket corresponds with the appropriate game and number sequence. Computerized systems have a program that prints out a list of winning tickets for each game, which simplifies the task of the keno writer as well as the keno runner. Jackpots over a predesignated amount will be referred to the shift manager for payment.

Keno runners are utilized to maximize play throughout the casino. They circulate throughout the casino, restaurants, and other designated public areas, securing tickets and wagers from customers and taking these to the keno writers at the main keno counter for processing. Verified winning tickets are paid by the runner, thus allowing the guest to remain in the restaurant, at the gaming table, or at a slot machine. Runners are an example of ultimate customer service, who, if properly employed, can promote the keno game, restock keno tickets and markers at table setups, provide good public relations, and encourage repeat plays on wagered tickets, all of which significantly affect the revenue generated.

POKER/CARD ROOM

Casino Poker-room operations are unique, since the casino dealer is *not* playing against the player. Rather, the casino is responsible for controlling the deck and dealing cards to players, who wager against each other. See Figure 4.6.

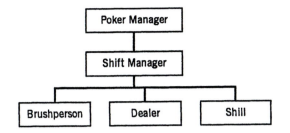

Figure 4.6 Poker Department Organizational Chart

The card room is supervised by a poker room manager, who manages all operations of the games, sets and oversees the game rules, and, in conjunction with the casino marketing department, organizes special invitation Poker tournaments. Managers must have complete knowledge of all types of Poker and possess strong customer relation skills.

As is the case with all departments discussed, Poker has shift managers who run the room in the absence of the manager.

One of the more unique job titles in a casino operation is "brushperson." This employee stands at the front of the card room and solicits players for the game. The brushperson normally performs the additional function of dealer. Many brushpersons keep a log of players waiting for a seat at one of the games and will announce the next person's name over the public address system.

Poker rooms, like Baccarat rooms, employ shills, who sit at the poker tables to encourage players to join the game. Shills may be cross-trained as dealers or brushpersons. Unlike other Poker room employees, proposition players—they cannot keep their gambling winnings or raise or call bets during the game.

BINGO

Bingo is commonly found at major casino operations. This gaming department comes under the supervision of a bingo manager, who administers bingo game procedures, jackpots, payouts, and bingo room personnel. Promotions and marketing are directed by the manager, who coordinates programs with the casino marketing department. See Figure 4.7.

Working with the bingo manager are shift managers and bingo agents/callers/cashiers. Duties of these employees include

- Calling bingo games over the public address system.
- Selling tickets to customers.

Figure 4.7   Bingo Department Organizational Chart

- Circulating throughout the bingo room selling additional tickets between games and helping customers during the games.
- Cashing winning tickets.
- Promoting a positive image for the bingo department and the casino.

RACE AND SPORTS BOOKS

Casinos are constantly looking for new sources of revenue or additional forms of casino entertainment. Race and Sports Book operations are relatively recent additions to the casino floor space and offer not only a new source of revenue but also one of the most exciting forms of customer entertainment.

Race books offer wagering odds on horse track races and, in some cases, dog tracks. Races at all major tracks are featured on boards with posted odds for each horse in each race.

Sports Books feature odds on college and professional basketball and football games, major league baseball, national hockey league games, and major sporting events, such as boxing matches, the Superbowl, and the World Series. Bettors can wager on daily games or place "future bets" on upcoming sporting events. Race and Sports Books found at Caesars Palace or the Las Vegas Hilton have dedicated significant floor space to this gaming revenue center and have taken the lead in featured technology. These rooms use motion-picture–size screens to televise multiple games; use computerized, electronic reader boards to provide odds and informational updates on games in progress; host parties and promotions on special days (that is, Superbowl Sunday); feature sports celebrities making personal appearances; and set the odds nationally for most collegiate and professional games.

Casinos may split the managerial responsibilities between a Race Book Manager and a Sports Book manager or combine the job (see Figure 4.8). The remainder of the staff consists of an assistant manager(s), shift managers, writers, and cashiers who accept customer wagers and pay

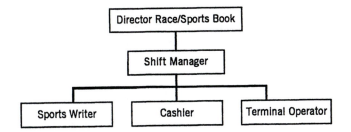

Figure 4.8 Race & Sports Book Department Organizational Chart

winning tickets. Additional duties include posting scoring updates on the reader boards, explaining wagering procedures (e.g., football parlay tickets), and creating good customer relations.

CASINO MARKETING/SPECIAL EVENTS

In this chapter, a number of references have been made to the need for marketing the various games offered by the casino. Casinos accomplish this either through the efforts of each gaming department head or in conjunction with a specialized department known as casino marketing/special events (see Figure 4.9).

This department plans, coordinates, and implements marketing and advertising concepts for the games and plans events such as golf tournaments, boxing matches, tennis matches, and any special event that will attract large numbers of people and gamblers.

A director of casino marketing heads the marketing segment. Because of the popularity of slots, this executive may focus entirely on slot promotions or spend the vast majority of time on slot advertisements. Support staff within this department include a director of customer development, customer development representatives, VIP service representatives, and casino hosts. The director of customer development is responsible for developing and implementing programs to attract key casino players. he

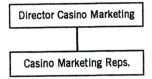

Figure 4.9 Casino Marketing Department Organizational Chart

or she also (1) processes credit applications and handles room reservation requests, (2) provides player rating reports and recommends comp status to the casino manager, (3) interacts with casino hosts to ensure that invited guests are being given first-class treatment, and (4) helps with markers due and payable by invited guests. If the director of customer development is exclusively assigned to the slot department, he or she works on slot promotions and membership enrollment in a slot club.

Customer development representatives handle most of the clerical and logistical details for the director of customer development. Their duties may consist of contracting preapproved players and listing details for upcoming casino events, coordinating all requests for room reservations, maintaining computer reports on players, telemarketing promotions, acting as greeters either at the airport or at the casino for VIPs, and working with casino hosts to help maintain top customer service standards. VIP service representatives are often found at the front desk of a hotel/casino, attending to the needs of casino VIPs upon arrival and initial check-in. Many casinos have a special VIP lounge adjacent to the front desk where the players can be registered, welcomed, and given a gift. These employees may be compared to front desk concierges and mainly serve to make invited casino guests feel extremely pampered and welcomed. If the customer development department is dedicated exclusively to slot operations, casino hosts may provide the same services for other preferred customers. The primary functions of a casino host are soliciting and booking major players for the casino, handling their rooming accommodations, maintaining contact with players while they are in-house, helping with marker collections, and creating a true sense of casino entertainment for these very important guests.

CAGE

Our final casino department is the casino cage. As the front desk of a hotel is the hub of activity, the casino cage can be described as the nerve center for casino operations, since all financial transactions eventually filter through this department. Also, perhaps more than any department in the casino, the cage must adhere to currency transaction reporting requirements dictated by the Bank Secrecy Act.

Cage operations come under the jurisdiction of the director of financial operations (or controller of chief financial officer). Daily operations are maintained by a cage manager. Cage shift managers run the three shifts and control internal operational procedures. The most visible person to the general public is the cage cashier, who sells casino chips and tokens to casino guests, redeems chips for currency, cashes traveler and personal checks and money orders, and, in some instances, sells coin to and receives coin from slot players. Cashiers have control over safety deposit boxes and rent these to players for the safekeeping of valuables. These employees frequently handle all types of guest questions, ranging from casino procedures to locations of restaurants.

Each casino maintains a main bank for the casino bankroll, and a main bank cashier serves as a teller to supply the cage and other cash distribution with currency fills, and accepts incoming cash that will be stored in the casino's vault and eventually deposited in the bank. Coin cage cashiers keep track of jackpots and fills as well as the amount of money collected by each shift in the slot department. They verify and count cash collected in a slot booths and from changepersons and distribute cash for slot jackpots. They also make change or handle transactions for hotel stores and retail shops as well as hotel restaurants. Moreover, banks for slot booths and other hotel cashiers are issued from this subdepartment, and these employees may issue the tax forms required when large slot jackpots are won.

Monies won at the casinos' table games are brought to the casino cage in drop boxes by security guards, where the boxes are emptied and counted by a soft count team. This team consists of three or four employees who are observed by a representative from the casino or accounting department. Currency and chips from each game are counted separately and recorded on the master game report, or the "stiff sheet," and this information is forwarded to the casino manager and controller's office for analysis and distribution to other gaming department heads.

Although pit clerks physically perform their duties in the table game pits, they are considered part of the cage organizational structure. Essentially, pit clerks act as informational liaisons between the gaming pits and the cage. Primary duties consist of securing credit information on players, inputing player rating criteria into the computer, accurately recording and balancing player markers and credit transactions, and handling phone conversations between the pit and the cage.

Credit and markers extended to casino players are eventually controlled and issued by a credit manager. This employee, working with credit clerks, researches the financial background of customers through contacts with listed lending institutions or central credit and determines the available credit line. On the other end of the spectrum is the collection manager, who is responsible for collecting markers and credit extensions. Quite often terms for payment of large markers are arranged with players (for example, 60 or 90 days). Credit clerks handle the clerical and administrative duties associated with marker collections.

The casino cage organizational chart (Figure 4.10) shows one other subdivision known as the coin room. This department collects coin from slot machines and delivers it to a main coin room, where the money is sorted,

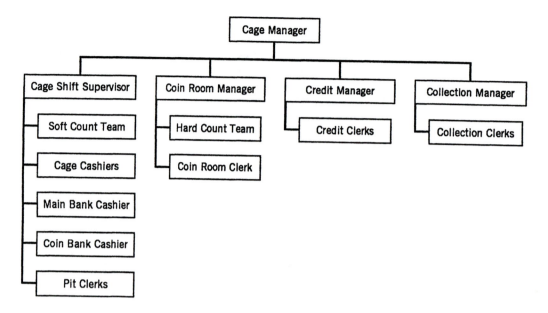

Figure 4.10   Cage Department Organizational Chart

coined, and wrapped for deposit at a bank or recirculation into the casino. This "hard count" process is heavily dependent on technology and coin sorting/counting equipment that expedites this money accounting process.

MISCELLANEOUS EMPLOYEES

Other employees found in a casino organizational chart include the following.

Security guards. These employees, in addition to maintaining law and order in the casino, assist with table fills and chip credits, transport drop boxes to the soft count room, maintain a physical presence by the casino cage to discourage robbery attempts, and control general access to the cage. Today's security guards may not wear the traditional police officer's uniform or carry a weapon. Rather, their presence has taken on a subtle demeanor, as many wear sport coats or blazers and "blend in with the crowd."

Cocktail servers. Casinos have traditionally provided complimentary drinks to players and utilize cocktail servers to provide this service. Tips for servers can be extremely lucrative, and a cocktail server's job in a dice pit or high-table-limit game can be one of the better employment positions in a casino.

CONCLUSION

The organizational structure for a large casino operation requires multiple layers and talented individuals in order to be successful. As with any organization, employees involved in the process must feel like they are important and are appreciated by management. In the high-pressure and rapid pace of the gaming and casino industry, quite often employees and management rush through their days "taking care of business." If a casino is to be successful over the long run, it not only must organize employees as depicted in this chapter, but must also never forget that employees are the most valuable asset available to management and must be consistently recognized for their hard work and efforts.

This chapter provides a general model for a casino organizational structure, and readers are reminded that this structure can and will vary according to individual operational needs and size. The one common denominator with all casino organizational structures is the need for a systematic approach to employment and deployment of human resources.

5

Hotel/Casino Food and Beverage Operations

Remember your last vacation? What was the most common topic discussed? Chances are, you were always thinking or talking about last night's dinner, today's breakfast, or what you wanted to have for lunch. In short, food and beverage was your constant companion; if you were not consuming it, you were talking about it. Gaming may be sweeping the country, but visitors spend more time and energy talking about where, when, and what they want to eat and drink.

Food and beverage has a major impact on our lives—They control a great deal of our activity. Gaming executives know this and try to use it to their advantage. While guests certainly want to be overwhelmed by gaming attractions, hotel and casino environments, and other forms of leisure and entertainment, the quality, availability, and perceived value of food and beverage offered by a particular property will have a great influence on guest satisfaction and company profitability.

FOOD AND BEVERAGE DEPARTMENT OBJECTIVES

The gaming property's food and beverage department objectives parallel those found in any other type of restaurant operation. Anyone involved in food and beverage management and service hopes to meet or exceed customer expectations while simultaneously earning a fair profit. However, the gaming executive normally employs different means to these ends.

While the typical restaurant manager strives to earn a profit on the sale of food and beverages, most gaming executives are more concerned with enhancing gaming revenue and, if necessary, will absorb a loss in the food and beverage department so long as gaming revenue is enhanced adequately. It is quite common, for instance, for a casino to offer reduced-price, or comped, food and/or beverages to gaming customers, because if they are happy and continue playing, over the long run the profits earned from these guests will be much greater than the losses absorbed by the food and beverage department.

Most gaming properties are willing to sacrifice some profit or sustain losses in food and beverage in order to attract and retain gaming customers. Usually, the more "low end" the customer base served, the greater the loss can be. For example, a food and beverage department serving a cost-conscious market may plan for as much as a 35% loss.

Most hotel/casinos seek to achieve three major food and beverage department objectives: (1) enhance the gaming revenue; (2) provide maximum guest convenience; and (3) attract a large volume of gaming guests.

Enhance Gaming Revenue

There is a significant positive correlation between the value perception guests have of a property's food and beverage offerings and its gaming revenue and profits. An old axiom in the casino business states that if you "Feed them, they will gamble." Attractive food and beverage outlets will entice gaming guests. For instance, some gaming executives feel that as many as 80% of guests visiting a hotel/casino's buffet will gamble before leaving the property.

Guest Convenience

When guests visit a hotel/casino, management wants them to spend as much time as possible in gaming activities. If a food or beverage outlet is inconveniently located or is too time-consuming for the guest to seek out and patronize, gaming activity will be adversely affected. In this case, the property risks two negative guest reactions: One, guests will have less time to gamble; two, some guests may decide to leave the property and visit competitors that have more user-friendly food and beverage services.

Attract Gaming Guests

Hotel/casinos typically offer similar gaming attractions. They also tend to house similar sleeping room amenities and various forms of nongaming entertainment. Therefore, one of the few distinctions a property can offer is a unique food and beverage service.

It is not unusual for a hotel/casino to experience a dramatic increase in customer counts after it adds or remodels a food or beverage outlet. Gaming guests tend to flock to properties that offer high-value food and beverage service. They will also be discouraged from visiting competing properties. High customer counts usually generate increased gaming revenue.

FOOD AND BEVERAGE OUTLETS

A hotel/casino usually needs several food and beverage outlets if it wants to achieve the major objectives mentioned above. Food and beverage must be plentiful, convenient, and value-laden. Properties tend to offer a wide variety of outlets in order to appeal to the greatest number of potential gaming guests.

Buffet

Breakfast, lunch, and dinner buffets are very popular in the hotel/casino. These outlets usually charge one price for an all-you-can-eat meal.

Out-of-town visitors particularly like these buffets because they are unique and are not normally available back home. A popular buffet will attract many guests, most of whom will gamble.

The buffet is one of the hotel/casino's major marketing tools. Experience shows that if it is presented properly, it will have a high value perception among guests. To the typical guest, the buffet is the biggest distinction a property has to offer. It is not unusual for guests to base their visits solely on the type and quality of the buffet offered and its accompanying price tag.

Room Service

Some hotel/casinos would rather eliminate room service because it tends to reduce the amount of time guests can spend in the casino. However, most properties offer room service because it is an expected amenity. Some guests would be upset if it were unavailable.

Most properties offer room service 24 hours a day. A few prefer to limit their hours of operation, since not only does it tend to keep guests in the room and not on the casino floor, it is also an extremely expensive form of food and beverage service.

To make up for the increased operating expense, some hotels limit the menu selections. This allows the property to price room service offerings competitively and tends to speed service, thereby returning patrons to the casino more quickly.

Snack Bar

The typical hotel/casino houses several snack bars operating on various time schedules during the day or night. If nothing else, most hotel/casinos have a conveniently located snack bar—or kiosk, if space is scarce—near the Race and Sports Book operation. Gaming guests at the book hate to leave the premises or go too far away to get something to eat or drink. Many of them will seek and patronize the books that make it easy for them to spend the majority of their time handicapping, betting, viewing races and sports events, and socializing with other players.

Snack bars today usually run the gamut from sweet shops and small delis to nationally branded fast-food operations located throughout the property or in a food court. Snack bars offer today's guests a familiar option. Many guests are used to eating at a Burger King or Taco Bell, and some are more comfortable there than in a property's table-service restaurant. These units offer low-priced menu options and very quick and convenient service. Management and guests appreciate these characteristics.

Some hotel/casinos offer several nationally branded fast-food operations as an alternative room service option. This strategy allows the property to price the room-service menu items high enough to cover most, if not all, direct costs for those guests who demand the traditional amenity, while simultaneously allowing other guests to "brown bag" it in their rooms. This can be a win–win situation, in that management controls its costs and guests have several value options available.

Coffee Shop

The hotel/casino will always have a 24-hour coffee shop. Gaming guests arrive and depart at all hours of the day and night; many of them are on different time zones; and they all have different needs. For example, some want breakfast at 8 P.M.; others want lunch at 6:00 A.M. The well-stocked coffee shop can handle almost any request; if it cannot, the competitor next door will.

Some properties use their coffee shops to handle room service. This can be a more economical way to operate this amenity than opening a separate room service kitchen.

Gourmet Room

A hotel/casino will usually have some type of gourmet room, normally open five to six hours per day. Advertised hours are traditionally 6 to 11 P.M. However, the room is prepared to stay open to accommodate "high rollers" (that is, guests who enjoy several comp privileges because they are willing to gamble a large amount of money). High rollers are sometimes referred to as "best customers."

The gourmet room is a very costly but very necessary amenity, because management usually uses it to entertain lavishly its high rollers. The best players (those who have a high "rating") are offered this luxury level of food and beverage service at no charge. The hotel or casino courting high rollers must have one or more luxury restaurants or it cannot compete for these players.

Specialty Restaurant

The typical hotel/casino will have at least one specialty, or theme, restaurant. The larger properties will often have three or more. It is not unusual to find steak, seafood, Italian, Mexican, and Oriental restaurants in the mega-hotel/casino.

Some specialty restaurants may take the place of a gourmet room. For instance, a nationally branded restaurant (such as Spago or the Coyote Cafe) will usually satisfy high rollers. If nothing else, it provides more food and beverage variety and keeps them in the property longer.

Catering

Catering is a common amenity in the typical hotel/casino. In some properties there is a separate catering department that handles most catering needs. Unusual requirements, such as late-arriving high rollers who request last-minute catered functions, are typically handled by the room service department. This organizational structure is more efficient because the regular catering crew does not have to be on the clock 24 hours a day.

Showroom

Most hotel/casinos have one or more showrooms and/or lounges that provide entertainment. Unlike the typical lounge, the large showroom usually has a more formal seating policy and more limited hours of operation. The showroom also may have food service along with beverage service, though more and more properties are eliminating food and offering limited beverage service only.

Food service in the standard showroom can be inefficient and too costly for most properties. Some gaming guests miss the old days when almost every hotel/casino had a dinner show at 7:30 and a cocktail show at 11. However, today's typical gaming customer does not seem to mind the drinks-only shows.

Main Bar

The typical hotel/casino will have several main bars throughout the property, with at least one open 24 hours a day. Guests can sit at these bars and watch their drinks being prepared. As a general rule, food is not offered at these bars, though there are usually some complimentary dry snacks available.

Portable Bar

A portable bar is one that can be moved at will or operated intermittently for special events (it is sometimes referred to as a "banquet" bar). It is typically used for catering functions and hospitality suites, but may also be used in operations that set up minicasinos in the property to cater to high rollers. For example, a small, intimate Baccarat room will usually have a gourmet buffet table and portable bar set up at no charge to guests.

Lounge

Lounges are similar to main bars, the major difference being that guests are usually served only at tables. In some lounges, there may be a combination of main bar and table service, though in most cases lounge patrons receive table service from cocktail servers who retrieve finished drinks from a service bar located outside the guests' view.

Lounges also differ from most main bars, in that they typically offer some form of entertainment. A main bar may have, for example, a small bandstand, but usually entertainment is housed in a lounge where seating is more plentiful and the seating policy can be controlled by management.

Casino Service Bar

A main bar or service bar located in a lounge area usually doubles as a casino service bar. Actually, the casino service bar is a way of defining a particular type of beverage service rather than a specific type of bar.

The casino service bar is used to record comp drinks served to players. For instance, if a bartender prepares drinks for cash-paying guests in the lounge, he or she will ring up the sale on the cash-paid key of the register. But if he or she prepares comp drinks for players in the slot machine areas, those sales will be rung up on the comp key for control purposes. Comp sales are also tracked so the hotel/casino can pay the government sales and/or entertainment taxes that should have been collected from guests.

COMPS

Comps and reduced prices are mainstays of the food and beverage department's marketing plan. It is thought that in the typical hotel/casino, one-sixth of its food sales and one-third of its beverage sales are comped.

A hotel casino must have liberal pricing policies if it wants to achieve its food and beverage department objectives. Comps, competitive prices, and high perceived values are necessary to attract and retain gaming guests.

A hotel/casino's food and beverage department is usually not considered a profit center. Its function is mainly to support gaming, and it is usually expected to lose a bit of money. This strategy was developed many years ago and is followed to some degree by most hotel/casinos.

The loss-leader philosophy suggests that a customer usually has a set budget when he or she visits a hotel/casino, and that this budget must be used to cover transportation, food, room, beverage, gaming, and incidental charges. If the customer has, say, $500 to spend, and if the hotel/casino charges $200 for nongaming activities, he or she will have $300 to lose in the casino. But if the hotel/casino charges only $100 for nongaming activities, the customer has $400 to lose. In the long run, this customer will leave $500 at the hotel/casino, one way or another. It is thought, though, that a guest will perceive a greater value if the bulk of his or her budget was spent on gaming.

This philosophy survives today, albeit in several variations. For example, some hotel/casinos may reduce their food and beverage price subsidies but retain free self-parking, valet parking, entertainment, and souvenirs. Other properties may use creative advertising to distract guests from the total prices they must pay for food and beverage. For instance, a hotel/casino may advertise a $3.95, all-you-can-eat buffet, but tack on an extra charge for soft drinks. The property may also reduce food costs at the buffet by issuing a ticket to guests, with which they get only one serving of meat, seafood, or other specialty items, but can freely consume the other foods.

These creative revisions of the original philosophy came about because the basic comp policies were abused in many hotel/casinos. Managers were handing out comps indiscriminately to friends and relatives who were not gaming guests and therefore, could not justify receiving them.

Comp policies are also revised occasionally because guests are not restricted to one hotel/casino—they can take their gaming dollars across the street. Consequently, the guest with the $500 total budget will not necessarily drop it all in one place.

Hotel/casinos have become more careful when doling out comps and reduced prices. For instance, many properties today use electronic "tracking" systems to record players' average bets, average playing time, and so forth. This allows management to determine more precisely the types and amounts of comps players should receive.

While hotel/casinos tend to adopt more discriminating comp policies, it is still unusual for a property to create true profit centers in the food and beverage department. As a general rule, food and beverage prices are subsidized to some degree.

There are only a few instances where hotel/casinos attempt to charge full prices for food and beverage. These situations occur whenever management can identify guests who stay at the property but do not gamble. For example, some conventioneers do not gamble, but love staying at properties where rooms, food, and beverage are economically priced. If management is faced with such customers, it may ask them to pay higher room rates and full prices for hospitality suites and catering functions. In extreme cases, management may ignore these guests and not seek their patronage.

Some people feel that it is unwise to penalize conventioneers, or any other nongaming customers, because they may come back later on holiday and patronize the properties that welcomed them when they did not gamble. Statistics show that a large segment of the gaming market was initially introduced to this form of entertainment when on a business trip or convention and that follow-up vacations were planned as a result of this initial experience. The property charging full prices at that time may be unable to compete for this subsequent business.

Hotel/casinos that lease space to tenant restaurants may have no control over their pricing policies. Consequently, these restaurants may charge full prices for their products and services. However, most hotel/casinos offer preferred operators generous lease terms and conditions as well as high-traffic locations to ensure that menu prices will be value-oriented.

Types of Comps

Conceivably, the number and types of comps used by hotel/casinos are limited only by management's imagination. As a general rule, though, there are four basic categories.

Beverage (B). Beverage is the most common comp offered. Usually, all players are eligible for free drinks while they are playing, but properties will usually pour different quality liquors depending on the type of player served. For example, when ordering a rum and coke, a slot machine player playing a $5 slot machine may qualify for a premium brand, whereas a guest playing a quarter slot machine may receive only a well brand.

Food (F). Food is a comp usually found in the typical hotel/casino, though it is not nearly as common as the beverage comp. One of the reasons most hotel/casinos have several food outlets is that doing so allows them to tailor the food comp according to the quality of the player receiving it. For example, a high roller will qualify for comps at all food outlets, whereas a lower-rated player may qualify only for a buffet comp.

Room (R). Comp rooms are usually offered only to high rollers. Since the typical comp room is a suite or similar type of accommodation, the player receiving this comp usually is the highest- or next-highest-rated player in the hotel/casino's rating system.

During slow periods, a hotel/casino may be willing to offer reduced-price packages in order to attract visitor volume. For instance, a property may piece together three days, two nights, two drink tickets, two tickets at the comedy club, and two breakfast buffets, and offer this package at a special bargain price. While technically not a comp, the end result is the same: The increased visitor volume usually translates into more guest play and increased gaming revenue and profits.

Transportation (T). Only the hotel/casino's highest-rated players will qualify for expensive free transportation from their homes to the property. Management has no qualms about paying a player's first-class air fare and all accompanying ground transportation charges if the player is willing to risk a considerable gaming budget and spend at least four to six hours per day playing table games, or six to eight hours per day playing slot machines.

Players living in communities surrounding hotel/casinos may obtain free transportation from those properties that own shuttle buses specifically used to swing by scheduled locations (for example, an apartment house lobby) to pick up and drop off passengers who, it is hoped, are willing to gamble.

Some bus tour operators join hands with hotel/casinos to reimburse riders traveling to these properties. For instance, a bus tour operator in an adjacent town may put together a package with a particular hotel/casino, whereby the tour operator charges the passengers a token amount to ride the bus and the property reimburses them with chips or other scrip that can be used only in the property's casino. Along with this reimbursement, most properties will also toss in a free buffet meal.

Other Comps. There are other "freebies" hotel/casinos can offer, though generally these are not as abundant as the four listed above. Usually these other comps are promotions offered periodically, typically during slow periods. For instance, a property with a theme park attached may offer comp visits to certain players. Some properties may offer a player a few extra chips at buy-in time (for example, if you purchase $50 worth of quarters for the slot machines, you may receive an extra slot token or two at no charge). Some hotel/casinos may offer one free pull on a gigantic slot machine as a promotion—visitors walking through the casino can try their luck at winning a car, a vacation, or a satin jacket emblazoned with the property's logo. Some properties may offer a free drink or a free pull (or free spin on a Wheel of Fortune) to patrons who cash their pay checks at the hotel/casino cashier cage.

Calculating Comps

As a general rule, the typical hotel/casino is willing to comp guests up to one-half of the amount it expects to win from them. For instance, if management expects to win $100 from a player, it may "give back" as much as $50.

Casino hosts, usually in conjunction with other managers, normally calculate the comps the property will offer its players. Hosts are the property's "ambassadors," who attract players and cultivate their business. Casino hosts typically specialize; for instance, some work only in the slot machine area as slot hosts.

The casino host uses a combination of computer record keeping and gut feelings to calculate the comps he or she will offer players. In other words, calculating comps is both high tech—the computerization of a player's gaming activity—and low tech—the casino host's educated judgment.

As an example, assume that a guest is playing a $1 slot machine and is wagering approximately $500 per hour. If this player plays two hours, he or she is placing at risk about $1,000. Since the property can set the win percentage it wants from a machine, the casino host has a good idea of the amount of money this player is most likely to lose during the two-hour period. If the property sets a 3% win ratio (that is, its $1 slot machine has a 97% "payout"), it expects to win $30 from this guest. Therefore, according to the industry's most common rule of thumb, the casino host may comp this player up to $15 worth of goods and/or services, regardless of how much he or she actually wins or loses. The fact that this player is willing to risk $1,000 tells management that, sooner or later, it will grind out its 3% win.

Rating Players for Comp Privileges

The hotel/casino must rate its players for comp privileges. The higher a player's rating, the more comps he or she will receive. Usually the lowest-rated players will qualify for free drinks while they play, as well as, perhaps, some trinkets such as baseball caps, T-shirts, or glassware. The highest-rated players have RFBT comp privileges—that is, free room, food, beverage, and transportation. In some cases, the very high rollers may also receive comp privileges at neighboring attractions; for example, if there is a heavyweight boxing title bout in town, a hotel/casino may pick up the tab for this event for its special players.

Player rating is an inexact science. Generally speaking, when a hotel/casino evaluates a player, it considers the person's (1) credit line; (2) average wager; (3) amount of playing time; and (4) "theoretical" win. It is important to keep in mind, though, that each hotel/casino views these criteria differently. For instance, a player with a $15,000 credit line may rate an RFB comp at a major property, whereas he or she may rate a RFBT comp at a smaller one.

Consider how a hotel/casino with a slot club could rate its slot players for comp privileges. A slot club issues guests computerized pocket cards to insert in slot machines while they are playing. This card keeps track of their play and awards points based on the amount of money wagered. As players earn points, they can redeem them for various prizes, such as free dinners, shows, or T-shirts.

The computerized cards issued to guests can also be used to earn points at table games. For instance, a player can give the card to the floor supervisor at the dice tables, who adds points to it based on the amount of money wagered.

A hotel/casino does not necessarily have to have a slot club system to rate its players. In fact, the typical property uses the slot club technology to rate the lower and middle players, relying primarily on management judgment to rate the high rollers.

Furthermore, a property could conceivably rely strictly on management judgments and floor supervisors' powers of observation to rate all players for comp privileges. In this case, a hotel/casino may have four ratings for its slot players. The best rating is given to the player who purchases a rack of silver dollars ($100) and keeps playing them until they are all gone. The second-best rating is assigned to the player who purchases a rack of silver dollars, goes through the rack one time, and cashes in what's left. He or she then buys another rack and goes through it the same way, repeating the cycle several times. The third rating is used to identify the player who buys several racks but primarily "churns" the money (that is, keeps cashing in and repurchasing racks but plays very little). The last rating is given to the player who buys a lot of racks but churns the money without placing a wager, instead cashing the racks at other change stations in the casino. This player always has a lot of silver dollars and gives the impression of playing quite a bit; however, he or she is merely recycling the money while having a few free drinks. Under this system, only the first and second ratings qualify for more than the standard beverage comp.

FOOD AND BEVERAGE PRODUCTION AND SERVICE

The basic operating activities performed by the hotel/casino food and beverage department are similar to those executed in any other type of restaurant establishment. However, there are a few differences that management must be aware of in order to achieve department objectives.

For one thing, management cannot afford stockouts of food and beverage. Patrons expect an abundance of products as well as a wide variety of goods and services. A typical restaurant may not harm its reputation if it occasionally runs out of a menu item or two, but the typical hotel/casino does not have this luxury. It is especially vulnerable if it serves many high rollers who like to drop in on a moment's notice.

There must also be a sophisticated transfer accounting system in place in the typical hotel/casino. This is necessary because most properties will charge back comps to the appropriate casino department. For instance, if a guest receives a buffet comp from the slot host, the slot department will be charged internally for the menu price of that meal. In this case, money does not change hands; the record keeping is done in order to control comp privileges as well as to track their effectiveness. However, if a guest receives a food comp at a restaurant leasing space inside the hotel/casino, a method of transferring funds must be included in the system.

Along with a good transfer accounting system, management must devise a method of keeping track of comps in order to pay the government any consumption taxes that should have been collected from guests.

Since hotel/casinos usually deal in high volumes and offer several varieties of food and beverage service, it must have more labor to handle these needs than what is typically found in the normal restaurant operation. Hotel/casinos need more labor hours, and they typically need a greater level of employee skill; consequently, their labor costs are usually much higher than those experienced by most restaurants. This is especially true if a property is willing to serve high rollers anything they want, anytime they want it.

Finally, the service strategies employed by hotel/casinos must always consider the possibility that a high roller will drop in at any moment and demand service. For instance, the typical property will always leave a few tables empty in the restaurants and showrooms in order to accommodate this possibility, even though servers and guests waiting on line do not always appreciate these efforts.

OUTLOOK FOR FOOD AND BEVERAGE OPERATIONS IN A CASINO ENVIRONMENT

It appears that hotel/casinos will increase the number of tenant restaurants inside their properties. Nationally branded restaurants are especially attractive, primarily because they are familiar to guests. Properties will continue to go out of their way to solicit those that have a reputation for high value.

Food and beverage service will continue to be the key distinction offered by hotel/casinos. A case in point: When the MGM Grand Hotel and Theme Park in Las Vegas opened, there were seven rides and nine food outlets. More food outlets than rides? Enough said.

Chapter 6

Casino Marketing

The purpose of this chapter is to provide an overview of casino marketing. It begins with a discussion of the principles of marketing, offering reasons for the increase in the importance of marketing in the gaming industry. It continues with a discussion of the marketing mix and closes with an explanation of the importance of controlling the marketing function.

WHAT IS MARKETING?

Satisfying the customer should be a priority for casino managers but managers must realize that they cannot satisfy all customers. They have to choose their customers carefully, selecting players who will enable the company to meet its objectives. To compete effectively for their chosen customers, casino marketers must create a marketing mix that gives their target markets more value than their competitor's marketing mix.

Today's marketing is not simply a business function. It is a philosophy—a way of thinking about and structuring the business. Marketing is not a new ad campaign or this month's promotion. It is part of everyone's job, from the receptionist to the board of directors.[1] The task of marketing is never to fool the customer or endanger the company's image, but to design a product/service combination that provides real value to targeted customers, motivates purchase, and fulfills genuine consumer needs.

The purpose of a business is to create and maintain profitable customers.[2] Customers are attracted and retained when their needs are met. Customer satisfaction leading to profit is the central goal of casino marketing.

"What About Profits?"

Casino managers sometimes act as if today's profits are primary and customer satisfaction secondary. This attitude eventually sinks a firm as it finds fewer repeat customers and faces increasingly negative word of mouth. Successful managers see profits as the result of running a business well rather than as its sole purpose.

It is wise to assess the customer's long-term value and to take appropriate actions to ensure a customer's long-term support. Two recent studies document this. The Forum Company found that the cost of retaining a loyal customer is just 20% of the cost of attracting a new one.[3] Another study found that an increase of five percentage points in customer retention rates yielded a profit increase of 25% to 125%. Accordingly, a casino that can increase its repeat customers from 35% to 40% should gain at least an additional 25% in profits.[4]

Jan Carlzon, president of Scandinavian Airlines, summed up the importance of a satisfied customer:

> Look at our balance sheet. On the asset side, you can still see so-and-so many aircraft worth so-and-so many billions. But it's wrong; we are fooling ourselves. What we should put on the asset side is, last year SAS carried so-and-so many happy passengers. Because that's the only asset we've got—people who are happy with our service and willing to come back and pay for it once again.[5]

Nothing validates Carlzon's point more than driving down Las Vegas Boulevard past McCarran International Airport. One can see rows of "mothballed" commercial aircraft brought to the desert because lack of moisture helps preserve them. These aircraft were once worth hundreds of millions of dollars and listed on balance sheets for their full value less depreciation. Today they are worth a fraction of their balance sheet value. Why? Because the airlines whose planes are sitting on the desert are either bankrupt or were forced to cut back on their schedules because of an insufficient customer base. This is precisely the point that Carlzon was making. Without customers, our assets have little value.

Without customers, a new multi-million-dollar casino will close or go into receivership, with the receivers selling it at a fraction of its book value. Marketing will enable an organization to create and maintain customers who will increase the value of the business.

The mentality of some Las Vegas casino employees is, *we have 25 million people coming to Las Vegas, so we don't have to worry about customer satisfaction. There are thousands of guests out at the airport right now, so we'll always have a replacement for the departing guest.* The fallacy in this thinking is twofold. First, guest satisfaction is a means of creating value; casinos that treat their customers well have more demand and do not need to count on price promotions to draw in customers. Second, as competition increases, some casinos will be desperately seeking additional customers; those that are not successful will be forced to cut back on operations and lay off employees. This has already occurred in Las Vegas, Mississippi, and Atlantic City.

Successful marketers design differentiated products—ones offering new consumer benefits. Marketing means "hitting the mark." Peter Drucker, a leading management thinker, put it this way:

> The aim of marketing is to make selling superfluous. The aim is to know and understand customers so well that the product or service fits them and sells itself.[6]

This does not mean that selling and promotion are unimportant but rather that these are components of a larger "marketing mix," a set of marketing tools that work together to produce satisfied customers. The only way selling and promoting will be effective is if we first define customer targets and needs, and then prepare an easily accessible and available value package.

Robert Keith wrote about marketing's future more than thirty years ago in his classic article, "The Marketing Revolution."

> Soon it will be true that every activity of the corporation—from finance to sales production—is aimed at satisfying the needs and desires of the consumer. When that stage of development is reached, the marketing revolution will be complete.[7]

Today, for many successful gaming firms the marketing revolution is moving to completion. All departments are becoming involved in satisfying the customer. For example, accounting has to develop bills that the hotel guest can understand; maintenance people should be able to answer a guest's basic questions such as where the casino's restaurants are located; and all employees should have a genuine concern for the customer's well-being.

Peter Drucker wrote that marketing "encompasses the entire business. It is the whole business seen from the point of view of the final result, which is from the customer's point of view."[8]

A study done by the Technical Assistance Research Program found that when people have a good experience, they tell five other people. If they have a bad experience, they tell ten.[9] Spreading positive word of mouth is difficult. A few negative stories can offset many good ones. The goal is to have every guest's expectations met or exceeded.

The front desk clerk, dining-room server, changeperson, slot technician, and dealers all influence whether the guest departs satisfied. Their attitude, appearance, and willingness to handle the guest's requests help form an impression of the casino. Employees deliver the products of casinos, and through their delivery they become part of the product. It is often hard to differentiate the tangible part of the product of competing companies. Many casinos look very similar on the inside: They all purchase their equipment from the same set of manufacturers, and they all offer the same type of games (within the same jurisdiction). Product differentiation often derives from the people who deliver the service. In the gaming industry, much of the marketing activity is carried out by employees outside the marketing department, not the marketing staff. The casino's marketing program brings players to the casino, but the casino's staff must turn the first-time guest into a repeat customer. There is a positive relationship between the number of repeat guests and profit.[10]

IMPORTANCE OF CASINO MARKETING

Casino marketing director, is the hottest job in gaming, according to Dennis C. Gomes, president and COO of the Trump Taj Mahal in Atlantic City.

Every facet of gaming is undergoing tremendous growth. On the international scene, Australia has expanded its casinos to include Brisbane, Melbourne, and Sydney. Taiwan, one of the largest premium-player markets for the United States, is considering passing legislation to allow its own gaming. Gaming continues to expand throughout Asia, Europe, Central America, and South America. The premium player has a greater choice of gaming venues today, and the choices will continue to increase. Today the premium-player market has become so intense that some casinos in Las Vegas have used credit as an incentive to draw these high rollers. Credit, once a financial decision, is now being used to attract players.

Casinos compete for players by offering a larger line of credit than the competition, or by offering credit to a player who has used his line of credit at a competitive casino. The line of credit for such players can run into several millions of dollars, creating the potential of significant losses if the player defaults. Thus, the casino can lose several million dollars if the player wins or gain a note for several million dollars if the player loses. And that note may be uncollectible.[11] Nevertheless, the competitive pressure to gain these players has lead to marketing decisions that favor the player rather than the casino.

Competitive pressures are evident across the gaming industry. In Las Vegas, some older properties targeting the local customer have had to cut back on staff as new properties have cut into their market. In Mississippi, two boats have departed and the win per slot machine has dropped from $209 to $107.[12] One gaming industry expert has stated, "People who think a protected riverboat market means an area without competition should perhaps think twice."[13] Once a gaming license meant certain profits. Today that is no longer the case. The gaming industry is maturing, and competition is a feature of a mature market. In a competitive market, the casino that can profitably provide a marketing mix that provides more value for its chosen markets than the competition will be the winner. This is what marketing is about and why marketing is so important.

UNIQUE CHARACTERISTICS OF CASINO MARKETING

Casino marketers must be concerned with four characteristics of casinos: intangibility, inseparability, variability, and perishability.

Intangibility

Producers of tangible products such as automobile companies offer a physical product—a car, for example. Casinos offer an intangible product—an experience—one that cannot be seen, tasted, felt, heard, or smelled before it is purchased. When we buy a car, we can try it out first. When we purchase a holiday at a casino from a travel agent, we do not know the quality of that product until after we have bought and consumed it. When guests leave a casino resort, they have nothing to show for the purchase but a receipt—unless, of course, they have been lucky and are going home with some extra cash. Robert Lewis has observed that people who purchase a service may go away empty-handed, but they do not go away empty-headed.[14] They have memories that can be shared with others.

To reduce uncertainty caused by intangibility, buyers look for tangible evidence that will provide information and confidence about the service. The exterior of a casino is the first thing that an arriving guest sees. The condition of the grounds and the general cleanliness provide clues as to how well the casino is run. Various "tangibles" provide signals about the quality of the intangible service.

Inseparability

In a casino, customer-contact employees are part of the product. If the dealer is rude, the customer will go somewhere else. The food in a restaurant may be outstanding, but if the server has a poor attitude or provides inattentive service, customers will down-rate the overall experience. When an experience like this occurs, the customer will not be satisfied; he or she will not return and will tell others about the experience.

Inseparability also means that customers are part of the product. Some novice players do not like to play Twenty-One because if they make a mistake, by taking a card when they should pass, they will affect the results of the other players' hands. Sometimes when this occurs the other players will glare or even make comments. Training new players at novice tables not only gives them more confidence, but also eliminates some mistakes they may make when they move out to the regular tables. Managers must manage their customers so they do not create dissatisfaction for other customers.

Variability

Casino products are highly variable. Their quality depends on who provides them and when and where they are provided. There are several causes of variability. Casino products are produced and consumed simultaneously, which limits quality control. Fluctuating demand makes it difficult for casinos to deliver consistent products during periods of peak demand. The high degree of contact between the service provider and the guest means that product consistency depends on the service provider's skills and performance at the time of the exchange. A player can be having a great time, and then the dealer changes and suddenly that player is no longer having such a good time. The new dealer may be having personal problems and bring these problems to work. Once, for example, I experienced a dealer at a Crap table who acted as if he couldn't have cared less if anyone was playing or not. In listening to his conversation with the box man, I learned that he was on overtime and really wanted to be somewhere else. What he did not realize is that he did nothing to enhance the experience that the players were having.

Every casino employee should try to enhance the player's experience in a positive way. Variability or lack of consistency in service is a major cause of customer disappointment in the gaming industry.

Perishability

Casinos cannot store their products. If three Twenty-One tables are closed on a Monday, that capacity cannot be stored until Friday when there are people waiting to get on the tables. Revenue lost from not having those tables open is gone forever. If managers are to maximize revenue, they must manage capacity and demand, since they cannot carry forward unsold inventory.

THE MARKETING MIX

For tangible products, the marketing mix is composed of the "4 Ps": product, price, promotion, and place (distribution). It is called the marketing mix because these elements are blended to make a marketing offer to the customer. For example, Caesars Palace targets an upscale market. Its product includes luxurious suites, a large, well-maintained casino, excellent restaurants, and well-trained employees. It charges more for its hotel rooms than most casinos, and its table minimums are higher than some. However, Caesars knows its customers will be willing to pay these higher prices, because they value the product. Therefore, the casino advertises in magazines targeted toward the upscale traveler and also targets the international customer. The distribution effort of this organization includes hosts and branch offices. It has put together a marketing mix that is effective for its market. Conversely, The Eldorado in Henderson, Nevada, does not have rooms. It offers breakfast specials for 99¢, $2-minimum-bet tables, and plenty of 5-cent slot machines. The promotional efforts are directed at the Henderson market. It, too, has put together a marketing mix that is effective for its market.

Besides the 4Ps, casinos also have two additional Ps: the physical environment and participants.[15] The following section discusses all elements of the marketing mix.

Price

Pricing is a complex issue in casinos. Simply defined, price is the amount of money charged for a good or service, but more broadly it is the sum of the values consumers exchange for the benefits of having or using the product or service.[16] Thus, price is what someone gives up to be entertained in the casino. It is what the casino charges for its rooms and food and beverage. Some casinos charge low prices for these products to lure the player in; typically these casinos are trying to attract price-sensitive local and regional markets. Casinos provide complimentary food and beverage to premium players. These players will "pay" for these comps out of the casino's theoretical win from their play.

Another form of price is the payout rate of the slot machines. The lower the payout rate, the higher the price. Frequent players get a feel for the payout rate and avoid casinos with low payouts. The number of times a player can multiply his or her original bet in Craps when placing an odds bet is another form of pricing. Some casinos limit this to three times the initial bet, while others advertise ten times odds. The odds bet is not a money maker for the casino, but casinos offering ten times odds hope to draw players in and make their money on their other bets.

The minimum bet is another pricing technique. The table minimum is the price a player has to pay. Some casinos use low table limits to attract customers. When developing pricing strategies, the casino must be concerned with its target market. How price-sensitive that market is and what creates value for it are additional considerations. Pricing is more effective when management understands the target market. For example, some people will avoid playing $1 video poker, but will play the quarter machines, putting five quarters in each time to get the maximum payout.

Another consideration with pricing is the casino's image. Some players relate price to the quality of the product. Thus, if they see a casino resort advertising rooms for $19, they may feel that the quality of the rooms is low. Pricing in the casino industry is a complex issue, one that must be carefully thought out with the target markets in mind.

Distribution

In industries that produce tangible goods, distribution channels move the product from the factory to the customer. In the gaming industry, distribution channels move the customer to the casino. The distribution channels can be either internal or external. Casino hosts and branch offices are examples of internal channels—those controlled by the casino. Both types are aimed at the upper end of the market. External channels include junket and tour operators, travel agents, and alliances with airlines. Junket operators are aimed at the upper end of the market, while travel agents cover a broad spectrum of customers, and tour operators and airlines are aimed at a mass market.

Three key factors with distribution channels are cost, control, and communication. First, distribution channels must be cost effective. Atlantic City casinos compensate reps between 8% and 30% of the casino's theoretical win; the average is between 16% and 20%.[17]

Some casinos have gone out of business because the compensation they paid their junket operators was too high—above their theoretical win. Junket operators give the casino little control over the players: The players usually remain loyal to the junket operator. Occasionally the junket operator will not give the names of the players to the casino. Unfortunately this is also the case with some casino hosts—hosts have the players' loyalty. Casinos should get management involved in greeting and entertaining players to build up player loyalty, and they must communicate with their distribution systems. For example, casinos may set up a package and promote it to travel agents. These packages will often include a meal, show tickets, breakfast, and lodging. When the package changes, the changes have to be communicated effectively to hundreds of travel agents. Some agents will lose or misfile the message, and as a result still sell the old package, which may include a show instead of a dinner. Thus, the guest arrives expecting a show and is disappointed when he or she receives a dinner. The guest has been dealing with the travel agent for years, so he or she blames the error on the casino. This is not a good way to start with a guest. To prevent it from occurring, casinos should reduce product changes and send several notices of product changes.

Product

A product is everything the guest receives in the transaction. It includes the level of service provided by the employees, the food and beverage outlets, the type and variety of slot machines, the gaming facilities, and the casino atmosphere. When developing the casino product, managers must understand the market segment that the casino wishes to attract.

Each market segment will place a different value on the casino's product attributes. To some segments, entertainment will be important; to others it will not be important. Some segments may prefer singers, while others will prefer a show. Thus, when developing the product, the casino must understand customers and know what creates value for them.

Earlier in this chapter it was stated that the casino's product is intangible. Casinos must make their products seem more tangible,[18] via promotional material, employees' appearance, and the casino's physical environment. A casino's promotional material may provide the potential players with their first views of the casino. This material should highlight the attributes that are important to the player.

Physical Environment

Physical attributes that are not managed properly can hurt a business by sending negative messages. Examples include: signs that continue to advertise a holiday special two weeks after the holiday has passed; signs with missing letters or burned out lights; parking lots and grounds that are unkempt and full of trash; and employees in dirty uniforms at messy work stations.

The atmosphere of the casino is also an important product feature. The atmosphere of the Mirage is upscale and well done. The white tiger cage, the tropical rainforests, the large aquarium behind the front desk, and other product features all contribute to create a "WOW" effect. The Mirage targets the upper end of the market, and the atmosphere fits that market segment. The Gold Coast is another successful casino in Las Vegas. Its atmosphere does not have the WOW effect, and its customers are not seeking that. Two of the target markets for this establishment are casino employees and senior citizens, both of which would rather have inexpensive food and beverage, good slot payouts, and a good slot club.[19]

People

Richard Normann of The Service Management Group believes a key ingredient in almost all service companies to be some innovative arrangement or formula for mobilizing and focusing human energy.[20]

Normann developed the term "moments of truth," which Jan Carlzon of SAS later popularized. A moment of truth occurs when employee and customer have contact. He states that when this occurs, what happens is no longer directly influenced by the company. It is the skill, motivation, and tools employed by the firm's representative and the expectations and behavior of the client that together create the service delivery process.[21] Normann borrowed the idea from bullfighters, who used it to describe the moment when the bullfighter faces the bull in the ring. In spite of all his training and preparation, a wrong move by the bullfighter or an unanticipated move by the bull can result in disaster. Similarly, when employees and customers interact, a careless mistake by the employee or an unanticipated request by the guest can result in a dissatisfied customer.

The gaming industry is unique in that employees are part of the product—the casino must have a staff that will perform well during moments of truth. When people think of marketing, they usually think of efforts directed externally toward the marketplace, but a casino's first marketing efforts should be directed internally toward employees. Managers must make sure that employees know their products and believe that they offer good value. The employees must be excited about the company they work for and the products they sell. Otherwise, it is impossible for the guests to become excited. External marketing brings customers into the casino, but it does little good if the employees do not perform to the guest's expectations.

Marketers must develop techniques and procedures to ensure that employees are able and willing to deliver quality service. The internal marketing concept evolved as marketers formalized procedures for marketing to employees. Internal marketing ensures that employees at all levels of the organization experience the business and understand its various activities and campaigns, in an environment that supports customer consciousness.[22] The objective is to enable employees to deliver satisfying products to the guest. As Christian Gronroos notes, "The internal marketing concept states that the internal market of employees is best motivated for service-mindedness and customer-oriented performance by an active, marketing-like approach, where a variety of activities are used internally in an active, marketing-like and coordinated way."[23] A marketing perspective is used to manage the firm's employees.[24]

Internal marketing involves the following steps:

1. Establishment of a service culture.
2. Development of a marketing approach to human resources management.
3. Dissemination of marketing information to employees.
4. Implementation of a reward and recognition system.

Service Culture. Internal marketing programs flow out of a service culture. A service marketing program is doomed to fail if its organizational culture does not support serving the customer. Management must develop a service culture, that is, a culture that supports customer service through policies, procedures, reward systems, and actions.

Promotion

Promotion includes personal selling, advertising, public relations, and sales promotion. When many people talk about marketing, they mean promotion. Marketing is much more than promotion, although promotion is an important part of it.

The key to effective promotion is synergy. Casinos should try to use all the promotional elements when developing a promotional campaign. A casino may develop a sales promotion, such as a giving cars as a prize for slot players. The promotion should be advertised to the key target markets, and promotional material placed throughout the casino. Finally, a press release should be developed to announce the promotion, followed by press releases when the cars are given away.

Advertising. Advertising should support the image of the casino and communicate a clear message to the target market. The best advertisements have one main item they are trying to sell; they do not try to sell all of the casino's products. An advertisement promoting the Sports Book, placed in the sports section of the paper, can be effective. But an advertisement promoting the casino's Sunday brunch, slot club, and Sports Book placed in the entertainment section will probably create little Sports Book business. The message of the advertisement should communicate some benefit to the target audience—it should give a reason for purchasing the product. Moreover, the selection of media should match the target audience; many well-designed advertisements become ineffective when they are placed in media their intended audience does not see, hear, or read.

Public Relations. Publicity has more impact than an advertisement. Because of the intangibility of a casino's product, people seek personal sources of information. Thus, a person going to Atlantic City for the first time will seek advice on where to go and stay from friends who have already been there. Publicity is considered to be a personal source of information and so is more credible than advertising. People know that a casino can say just about anything in its advertisements; a good publicity piece can therefore be invaluable. John Romero, a casino marketing expert, gives this advice about gaining publicity.[25]

1. Create an interesting story; do not try to sell propaganda.
2. Write in the same format as that of the targeted media. For example, words or phrases are not underlined in newspapers, so do not underline them in publicity releases aimed at newspapers.
3. If a reporter follows up on your story with questions you cannot answer, do not give inaccurate responses. Tell the reporter you do not know but will find out and call him or her back.

4. Prepare for all possible questions you may receive at a press conference. There are many special-interest groups, and an unanticipated question from such a group can create an embarrassing situation.
5. Prepare the release as a story that will be interesting to the media's target audience.
6. Fill your release with meaty quotes that relate to the story.

Publicity is effective but not free. It must be managed, either externally or internally. Casinos that do not have the time or experience to manage their public relations should hire an outside firm.

Personal Selling. Casinos use casino hosts, employees, and a sales staff to sell the product. Casino hosts sell to the premium market. Employees are used to cross-sell products. The casino's slot club or casino club employees should be able to sell the features of the club. Casinos with rooms or meeting space will also have a sales staff to sell their space.

It is important that there be good communication between the sales staff and the casino's marketing department. The sales staff should seek to bring in business that will help the casino, since higher room rates often do not make up for lack of play. Some casinos provide their groups with complimentary club cards and encourage members to use them. Thus, they can track the group's play. This information determines whether the group will be invited back and what room rate it will receive if it returns. Outside sales can also be used to negotiate rates with tour and travel agents. When negotiating these rates the salesperson must know the expected win from the group.

Sales Promotion. "Sales promotion" is the name given to a collection of promotional techniques aimed at creating immediate sales. These can be restaurant promotions, car giveaways, tournaments, and reduced room prices. Slot and casino clubs are a unique type of sales promotion aimed both at immediate sales and at building a long-term relationship with the customer.

Slot clubs can be an effective marketing tool. For example, the Gold Coast increased its drop by 40% with the implementation of The Club; the Mirage experienced a 20–30% increase with Club Mirage, and the Sands experienced a 30–40% increase from the Sandsational Club.[26] One reason for the success of slot clubs is that members return more often than nonmembers.

Casinos give the players about 5% to 10% of the theoretical win back in slot club points. If a player puts $1,000 of coin into a quarter machine with a 95% payout, the theoretical win is $50, and the player will receive $2.50–$5.00 in point value. The first slot clubs traded merchandise for points. This allowed them to give the merchandise at a retail price and purchase it at a wholesale price. They were reluctant to give cash, since there was no markup. Smart managers soon found that players preferred cash, and most of them placed their cash earnings back in the casino's slot machines.

The best clubs combine slot and table games in order to track the player's total play. The better-managed club will also give more points per dollar played on machines that they want the player to use. For example, reel slots pay more points than video slots, and dollar slots pay more on a relative basis than quarter slots. Clubs also provide a good database for direct marketing.

Direct Marketing

The purpose of direct marketing is to provide interactive communication with the casino's best customers. The objective of this communication is to maintain customers over the long term. Large casinos have hundreds of thousands of customers in their club's database. This information tells which of these are the best players and what benefits the casino can provide for them. For example, do they like to golf? If they do and are top players, the casino can invite them to a golf tournament. Ideally, the database will allow the casino to get away from mass marketing and target customers who will be receptive to specific marketing offers. Sending a promotion to all 300,000 of the club's members is mass marketing and should only be used for newsletters and general promotions. Other offers should be more specific. For example, if the showroom will have empty seats in the coming weeks, local club members can be offered a reduced price on the show. This fills the showroom, gets people into the casino, and provides the members with a benefit. Likewise, members who are known to travel to the casino on weekends can be offered a room special during periods of low occupancy. This provides them with a benefit and allows the casino to sell these rooms without advertising low rates to the public. Direct marketing should be a part of every casino's marketing plan.

A MARKETING APPROACH TO HUMAN RESOURCE MANAGEMENT

Creating Jobs That Attract Good People

Managers must use the principles of marketing to attract and retain employees. They must research and develop an understanding of their employees' needs, just as they examine the needs of customers. Not all employees are the same: Some seek money to supplement their incomes;

others look for work that will be their sole income source. Marketers can use marketing research techniques to segment the employee market, choosing the best segments for the firm and developing a marketing mix to attract them.

For employees, the marketing mix is the job, pay, benefits, location, transportation, parking, hours, and intangible rewards such as prestige and perceived advancement opportunities. Just as customers look for different attributes when they purchase a product, employees look for different benefits. Some may be attracted by flexible working hours, others by good health insurance benefits, and still others by child care facilities. Flexible working hours for office or housekeeping positions, cafeteria-style benefit programs in which employees design their own benefit package, and child care can all be used to attract a certain type of employee.

Advertising should be developed with prospective employees in mind, building a positive image of the firm for present and future employees and customers. Employees choose employers and leave them in the same way that players select certain casinos and then decide to switch. It is expensive to lose both guests and employees.[27] Using a marketing approach to develop positions and company benefits helps to attract and maintain good employees.

The cost of employee turnover was estimated in the late 1980s to average $2,100 for an hourly position. This means that turnover cost over $200,000 for a casino with a 50% turnover and two hundred employees, and this cost is undoubtedly higher today.[28] A reduction in turnover can result in hundreds of thousands of dollars saved.

The Hiring Process

Employee turnover rates of 50% or more are common in the casino industry. Organizations with high turnover rates cannot develop a service culture. In such companies, managers put very little effort into hiring, basing their decisions on whether the job candidate will work for a small wage and can fill schedule vacancies. Boomtown Casino in Las Vegas has developed a game show as part of their interviewing process. The job candidates take part in this show to give management an insight into their personality. Boomtown wants to hire employees who will create a good time for their guests.

If you want friendly, courteous service, you must hire friendly, courteous people. Casinos that deliver good service seem to follow this advice. They understand that it is possible to provide employees with the technical skills needed for the job, but it is difficult to train them to be friendly and caring.

The Importance of Initial Training

If employees are not enthusiastic about the company they work for and the products they sell, it will be difficult to create enthusiastic customers. To be effective, employees must receive information regularly about their company. The company's history and current businesses, as well as its mission statement and vision are important for employees to know. Employees must be encouraged to feel proud of their employer, and managers must instill in them a desire to contribute to the company's success.

Providing Employees with Marketing Information

Often the most effective way of communicating with customers is through customer-contact employees. The Hilton provides its casino employees with passes to the dress rehearsal of a new show, allowing them to promote the show from personal experience. One casino employee who did not have this experience said she felt embarrassed when people started asking her about the show. Her manager had asked her to promote it, but sometimes when she mentioned it the guest would start asking detailed questions she could not answer. She said this made her feel like a fool after saying the show was great. Now she does not mention the show unless the guest asks about it.

Employees often have opportunities to solve guest problems before these problems become irritants. To do this they need information. Unfortunately, many companies leave customer-contact employees out of the communication cycle. The director of marketing may tell managers and supervisors about upcoming events, ad campaigns, and new promotions, but some managers may feel employees do not need this information. They *do* need information.

Reward and Recognition

Employees must know how they are doing to perform effectively. Communication must be designed to give them feedback on their performance. An internal marketing program includes service standards and methods of measuring how well the organization is meeting them. The results of any measurement should be communicated to employees. One researcher found that simply communicating information collected from customers changed employee attitudes and performance.[29] Customer service measurements have a positive effect on employee attitudes, if results are communicated and recognition is given to those who serve the customer well. If you want customer-oriented employees, seek out ways to catch them serving the customer and reward and recognize them for making the effort.[30,31]

MANAGING THE MARKETING FUNCTION

The marketing function needs to be managed. This should start with the general manager to make sure marketing is integrated throughout the organization. The casino marketing manager must be able to justify the expenses of promotional campaigns. Campaigns should be tracked by the business they bring in and their costs. Casinos going after premium players should track each player individually. Most casinos do not like to pay more than 50% of their theoretical win toward marketing costs. One important consideration with premium players is that the theoretical win varies by player. The skill of the table game player determines the theoretical win; thus, the casino marketing manager must understand each player's ability and adjust the theoretical win and the marketing offer accordingly. Each marketing tactic should be designed to provide a return on the casino's investment.

Finally, marketers should keep up with what is happening in their business environment. They should be aware of competition; travel trends; and fluctuations in local, regional, and international economies, and they should be proactive and adjust their plans to take advantage of these trends. Effective marketing does not just happen, it has to be managed.

SUMMARY

Marketing is one of the most important and dynamic areas of casino management. Casinos can no longer sit back and assume that because they have a gaming license, customers will come to them. They must create value for their customers—more value than the competition—and still operate profitably. Good marketing provides casinos with the ability to achieve this.

REFERENCES

1. Regis McKenna. *Relationship Marketing.* Reading, Mass.: Addison-Wesley Publishing Co., 1991.
2. Theodore Levitt. *Marketing Imagination* New York: The Free Press, 1986.
3. Patricia Sellers. "Getting Customers to Love You," *Fortune*, March 13, 1989, pp. 38–49.
4. James L. Heskett, Jr., W. Earle, Sasser, and W. L. Hart Christopher, *Service Breakthroughs.* New York: Free Press, 1990.
5. Karl Albrecht. *At America's Service.* Homewood, IL: Dow-Jones-Irwin, 1988, p. 23.
6. Peter F. Drucker. *Management: Tasks, Responsibility, Practices.* New York: Harper and Row, 1973, pp. 64–65.

7. Robert J. Keith. "The Marketing Revolution," *Journal of Marketing*, Vol. 20 (January 1960), pp. 35–38.

8. *Business Week,* June 24, 1950, pp. 30–36.

9. John Tschohl. *Achieving Excellence Through Customer Service.* Englewood Cliffs, N.J.: Prentice-Hall, 1991, p. 3.

10. This section draws on Chapter 1 of *Marketing for Hospitality and Tourism,* by Philip Kotler, John Bowen, and James Makens. Upper Saddle River, N.J.: Prentice-Hall, 1996.

11. John Bowen and James Makens. "Promoting to the Premium Player." Paper presented at The 9th International Conference on Gaming and Risk Taking, Las Vegas, NV, 1994.

12. J. Papkin and K. Hetter, "America's Gambling Craze." *U.S. News and World Report,* March 14, 1994, p. 42.

13. P. Doocey. "Trendline Riverboats." *International Gaming and Wagering Business,* Vol. 14 (no. 10), pp. 60–62.

14. Robert C. Lewis and Richard E. Chambers. *Marketing Leadership in Hospitality.* New York: Van Nostrand Reinhold, 1989.

15. Bernard H. Booms and Mary I. Bitner. "Marketing Services by Managing the Environment," *Cornell Hotel and Restaurant Administration Quarterly,* Vol. 23 (May 1982), pp. 35–39.

16. Philip Kotler and Gary Armstrong. *Principles of Marketing,* Englewood Cliffs, N.J.: Prentice-Hall, 1994.

17. James Makens and John Bowen. "Junket Reps and Casino Marketing," *The Cornell Hotel and Restaurant Quarterly,* Vol. 35 (October 1993), pp. 63–69.

18. G. Lynn Shostack. "Breaking Free from Product Marketing," *Journal of Marketing,* April 1977, pp. 73–80.

19. This section draws on Chapter 4 of *Marketing for Hospitality and Tourism,* by Kotler, Bowen, and Makens.

20. Richard Normann. *Service Management: Strategy and Leadership in Service Businesses.* New York: John Wiley & Sons, 1984, p. 33.

21. Normann, p. 9.

22. William R. George and Christian Gronroos. "Developing Customer-Conscious Employees at Every Level; Internal Marketing," in *The Handbook of Marketing for the Service Industries,* edited by Carole A. Congram. New York: American Management Association, p. 85.

23. Christian Gronroos. *Service Management and Marketing.* Lexington, Mass.: Lexington Books, 1990.

24. George and Gronroos, pp. 85–100.

25. John Romero. *Casino Marketing.* New York: International Gaming and Wagering Business, 1994, pp. 64–65.

26. Blair Young. "The Effectiveness of Slot Club Marketing." Unpublished paper, 1994.

27. Leonard L. Berry. "The Employee as Customer," *Journal of Retail Banking*, Vol. 3 (no. 1), pp. 33–40.
28. John J. Hogan. "Turnover and What to Do About It," *The Cornell Hotel and Restaurant Quarterly*, Vol. 33, (February 1992), p. 40.
29. Karl Albrecht and Ron Zemke. *Service America!*. Homewood, Ill.: Dow Jones–Irwin, 1985, p. 142.
30. Chip R. Bell and Ron Zemke. *Managing Knock Your Socks off Service*. New York: American Management Adds, 1992, p. 169.
31. This section draws on Chapter 11 of *Marketing for Hospitality and Tourism*, by Kotler, Bowen, and Makens.

Chapter 7

Casino Cage Operations

INTRODUCTION

The casino/cashier's cage is the operational nerve center of casino operations. As a hub of activity, it performs many vital functions on a shift-by-shift, day-by-day basis.

First, the cage, together with the vault, is responsible for the custodianship of and accountability for the casino's bankroll. This involves the daily care, control, and accounting for thousands, hundreds of thousands, and even millions of dollars. Transactions involving currency, coin, casino checks (chips), customer markers (IOUs), safekeeping funds, and customer front money flow to and from the cage and its related vault in a continuous cycle. Accurate recording procedures and adherence to sound internal controls are required to ensure bankroll safety and accountability.

Second, the cage provides a vital communication link to the casino pit or pit areas. Services include providing check fills and credits to table games, as requested; supplying information regarding customer credit status; providing financing tabulations of table game activities documented by the master game report form; and keeping casino supervisors advised of relevant information required for a smooth operation.

Third, the cage deals with countless customer transactions. Front-line window cashiers handle casino chip exchanges for currency; cash personal, payroll, and travelers checks; handle customer safekeeping and "front money" transactions; receive customer marker payment; deal with casino promotional coupons; and, provide information to customers.

Fourth, the cage interfaces with virtually every casino department—for example, transmittal of key forms to the accounting department; involvement with the hard and soft count audit teams; receiving and issuing cashiers banks to casino revenue departments (bar banks, showroom banks, Race and Sports Book banks, hotel front-desk banks, etc.); and

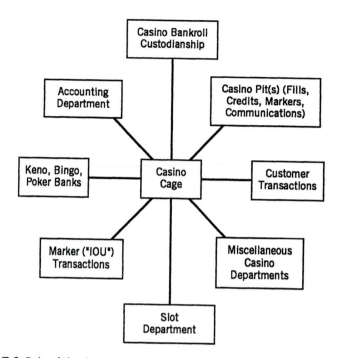

Figure 7.1 Role of the Casino Cage as a Nerve Center

working with the security department during the table game fill and credit process. In some casinos, the cage supports the slot department by providing slot fills, supplying changepersons with requested coin, and providing large jackpot payoffs.

Fifth, the cage is charged with the responsibility of preparing and maintaining countless forms required for sound internal control procedures and safeguarding the casino's assets. Additionally, compliance with requirements and procedures of the Bank Secrecy Act is a critical responsibility of casino cage personnel.

Figure 7.1 depicts the role of the casino cage as the nerve center, the hub, the heart of casino operations.

PHYSICAL STRUCTURE

Many casinos locate the cage toward the rear of the casino property and away from customer exits. One reason for this is to minimize the chances of a successful cage robbery. An occupied security booth is sometimes located within visual proximity of the cage to further deter robberies. A second reason for locating the cage in the rear is the psychological factor.

A customer cashing out at the window must walk the length of the casino toward the exit. The temptation of "one last slot pull" or "one final play at the table" can decrease the amount of money the customer takes out the front door. A third consideration is the location of the pit or live gaming areas. Live gaming is not normally conducted in the front of the casino, and because a major function of the cage is to service the needs of the pit, proximity to this area is important.

There are a number of structural possibilities for the cage facade. Some cages are protected by metal bars, others by plexiglass or shatter-proof windows. Still others are "open" cages with no protective barriers. It all depends on the environment and management's perceived need for physical security.

A small cage operation will typically offer two customer service windows and an additional window to service casino, slot, or employee requests. The larger the operation, the more service windows required, but keep in mind that customers do not like to stand in long lines to cash their chips. It is better to have too many operational windows than too few.

The cage entrance should afford maximum security with access limited only to authorized personnel. A controlled entry system providing cage occupants with a clear look at anyone requesting access is important. Many cage doors are released electronically by either a cage cashier or a security guard sitting in an adjacent booth. A good rule is to require a security officer to escort any unauthorized persons in and out of the cage. Another control is to maintain a log book for recording the name, date, and time of anyone entering and leaving. If the entrant is not an authorized person, identification is required.

Cage Layout and Equipment

Cage personnel are entrusted with a wide variety of responsibilities, which must be performed in a professional and competent manner. An overview of a typical cage layout and equipment will provide the reader with an insight to many standard items located within the cage.

Cashier's Window. Staffed by front-line cashiers whose primary duties are to conduct customer transactions. Each cashier is provided a shift-opening cash bank containing various denominations of currency and coin. This bank, normally provided by the main vault, is operated on an imprest system. Since all transactions are either at par (that is, exchanging chips for cash; encashment of personal, payroll, or travelers checks) or, in the case of payouts to casino departments, supported with cash disbursement slips, the cashier's bank must balance at the end of a shift. The cashier can be held responsible for shift shortages.

Service Windows. Depending upon the size of the casino and complexity of transactions, a variety of possibilities are available. For example, a specific window may be designated for the purpose of providing table chip fills and credits to the casino pit. Another window may be designated specifically for employee services, such as issuing and receiving bar banks, food banks, and beverage banks, as well as banks for various casino revenue departments (for example, Race and Sports Book, Keno, Bingo, lounge, showroom, hotel front desk). Still other windows may be responsible for handling customer marker transactions. Conversely, small casinos may find it practical to operate with two or three customer windows and simply designate a separate window to handle all other required transactions.

Work Counters. One or several work counters may be located at the rear or sides of the cage but away from the cashiers or service windows. They are provided to allow cashiers a suitable work area for preparing numerous forms and reports required during a shift.

Storage Cabinets. Above and below work counters or on other wall areas will be found cabinets used for storing reserve chips, casino forms, and a variety of supplies. Smaller casinos may entrust responsibility to the cage for storage and security of key or sensitive documents. Items may include current customer markers (IOUs), markers written off as uncollectible, paid customer markers, customer checks returned as uncollectible, and a myriad of forms required for daily cage operations.

Surveillance Cameras. Located in strategic areas of the cage interior are ceiling or wall-mounted surveillance cameras that are monitored on a 24-hour basis by the surveillance department. The system records all chip fill and credit transactions as well as all customer–cashier transactions.

Alarm System. A wide array of alarm systems is available for use within the cage. Most are silent systems, and all cage personnel must be familiar with procedures to be followed in the event of an attempted robbery.

Safe Deposit Boxes. Safety deposit boxes are available to customers wishing to entrust cash or valuables to the casino's cage. Customers wishing to obtain a safety deposit box must complete a data record form that is maintained by the cage. Access to the box is by the customer signing and dating the data card and providing the box key. Two keys are required to remove the box: one in the possession of the customer and the second kept by the cage. Both keys are needed to open the locks. The customer is normally charged a key deposit, which is refunded upon surrendering the key. Should a customer lose a key, the box must be drilled since the cage key alone will not open it.

Key Board or Key Panel. The cage may be entrusted with the possession, control, and issuance of a large assortment of keys. Typically, these keys allow access to gaming table drop boxes, the soft count audit room, the hard count audit room, the coin storage room, the drop box storage room, cash register audit tapes, and slot machines. Keys identified as "sensitive" must be controlled and issued via strict internal control procedures.

Phone System. Depending upon the casino's requirements, three to four counter or wall-mounted phones are available. Many casinos utilize phones that are activated by lifting the receiver and pushing a designated button or number that will instantly ring to the casino pit, casino manager's office, controller's office, cage manager's office, or other frequently called area of the casino.

Lock Box for Fills/Credits. Casinos utilizing a hand written process for table fills and credits must comply with strict controls. For example, Nevada gaming regulations stipulate

> All fill and credit slips shall be serially numbered in forms prescribed by the Board [Nevada Gaming Control Board], and shall be purchased in triplicate in a continuous series utilizing the alphabet, so that no gaming establishment may ever utilize the same numbers and series ... which series must be inserted in a consecutive order in a machine that permit the original and duplicate to be utilized by the establishment in accordance with the detailed rules for each type of slip set forth hereafter, and will only permit the third copy to be retained intact in a continuous unbroken form.

Time and Date Stamp Machines. Insertion of forms, slips, documents, customer checks into the machine's slot will automatically imprint date and time of the transaction. A cage axiom states, "If in doubt ... time and date stamp it."

Coin and Currency Processors. Vacuum counters, coin jet sorters, currency counters, and counterfeit currency detectors are now commonly used in all sizes of casino cages. They were adopted to provide faster service and more efficient and accurate work, and cage personnel are expected to become proficient in their usage.

Computer Terminals. The age of modern technology has affected large and small casino cages. Cage computer terminals are now linked to the casino pits, the credit manager, the central credit office, the controller's office, and any casino department justifying this type of interface. Request for table fills and credits; customer credit status; marker controls; and customer, data, and master-game-report form entries are just a few of the transactions that may be completed through cage computer terminals.

Miscellaneous. Check encoders, ATMs (automated teller machines), and word processors are all realities in the daily operations of today's casino cage.

Other Cage Areas

The casino cage is responsible for many cashiering functions, including customer transactions conducted by front-line cashiers; processing gaming table chip fills and credits; and processing customer credit transactions as authorized by the credit department. However, many of the daily revenue activities occurring throughout the casino require a broader overview of areas that may be considered as an integral part of the cage structure:

The Main Vault (Central Vault or Main Bank). Supervised by a vault manager or main bank cashier and employing vault cashiers, this entity serves a major banking function. It is charged primarily with the custody of the casino bankroll and acts as a conduit of cash to and from the casino cage proper.

The Soft Count Room. Access to this room is highly restricted, and strict adherence to the casino's internal control procedures must be followed. The room is designated as the location for conducting the count of the casino table drop boxes. Additionally, many casinos now include currency taken from slot machines via bill acceptors in their soft count. A soft count team, consisting of a minimum of three individuals, performs the opening of the gaming table drop boxes and sorting, counting, and recording drop box contents to the master game report form, or stiff sheet. In small casinos, all monies counted by the soft count team are verified by a designated cage supervisor, who then accepts the funds into the casino bankroll. In larger casinos, proceeds from the count are made the responsibility of the vault manager or main bank cashier supervisor.

The Hard Count Room. All coin removed from slot machines during the process of the "hard drop" is transported to a designated room. As with the soft count room, access is limited and strict control and surveillance procedures are followed. It is here that coins are weighed, sorted, counted, wrapped, and canned. Upon completion of this process, the inventoried coin is transported to a secured coin room and resulting accounting procedures accept the coin into bankroll accountability.

Table Drop Box Storage Area. The soft count previously discussed is conducted at designated times within the revenue cycle. Table drop boxes, after removal from the gaming tables, must be moved to a designated area under strict control procedures and stored until the soft count is conducted. This area, under 24-hour surveillance, may be within the soft count room or in a completely separate area.

CAGE ORGANIZATION

Nevada gaming regulations, seeking to establish minimum procedures for gaming licensees, emphasize the importance of organizational strategies in stating:

> The characteristics of a satisfactory system of internal control to be adopted by each nonrestricted licensee should include a plan of organization which provides appropriate segregation of functional responsibilities; a system of authorization and record procedures adequate to provide reasonable accounting control over assets, liabilities, revenues and expenses; sound practices to be followed in performance of duties and functions of each of the organizational departments; personnel of quality commensurate with responsibilities.

The Gaming Industry Committee of the Board of Directors of the Nevada Society of Certified Public Accountants, concerned with the problem of internal control for casinos, completed a study resulting in the following recommendations:

> With regard to the segregation of functions and duties, the committee recommends that organization of the accounting and cashiering functions should be aimed at preventing the fraudulent conversion or substitution of casino assets. As a general rule, responsibility for assets should be vested in the accounting department, while the responsibility for the custodianship of these assets should remain with the cashier's office. Furthermore, the assets controlled by one group should be physically separated from those controlled by another, and appropriate accounting records should be maintained to show each group's accountability.

The committee went on to suggest a "model" organization for a cashier's cage, consisting of four groups reporting to a shift supervisor, who, along with the credit and collection groups, reports to a chief cashier (Figure 7.2).

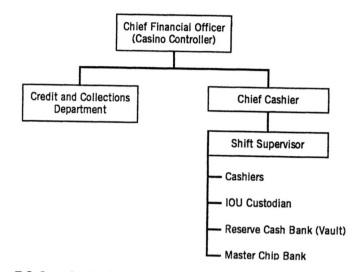

Figure 7.2 Organization for a Casino Cage

The duties and responsibilities of each area represented are as follows:

- The chief cashier and shift supervisor are responsible for overall control of assets located in the casino cage. Only these persons would be permitted to substitute in the IOU and master chip areas during the temporary absence of assigned individuals.
- Cashiers operate with imprest funds and are generally responsible for handling and recording all transactions with players and others using the cage. Transactions include, but are not limited to, receiving payments on IOUs, redeeming chips from players, cashing personal and travelers' checks, and receiving or refunding deposits. All transactions relating to IOUs and the receipt and application of monies left on deposit are recorded by the cashier and countersigned by the IOU custodian using a preprinted/prenumbered form.
- The IOU custodian receives and controls unpaid IOUs transferred to the cage. He or she is notified of payments received by cashiers, but does not have access to these funds except on a temporary basis and under strict control. The IOU custodian does not have access to blank IOUs, cash, or chips. Postdated and returned checks are processed in the same manner as IOUs.
- A senior cashier or vault cashier, specifically delegated by management, is responsible for maintaining the cash reserve bank or vault. The bank is used to replenish individual imprest funds and to buy back chips from cashiers for transfer to the master chip bank. When

chips are temporarily held in the reserve cash bank, they are not available for fills to pits.

- Pit fills come from the master chip bank. The bank also receives excess chips from pits. It receives and is charged with chips transferred from cashiers via the reserve cash bank.
- Credit and collections personnel are responsible for all matters pertaining to the approval of new credit and collection of delinquent IOUs.

Organizational strategy of the casino cage will ultimately depend on the size of the operation, management's perception of separation of duties, and the adequacy of asset protection. Regardless of the structure utilized, management's main objective is to construct an organizational plan indicating clear lines of responsibility, authority, and accountability.

BANKROLL AND REVENUE ACCOUNTABILITY

Casino gaming is a cash-intensive business requiring stringent controls and procedures to permit proper recording of gaming revenue and asset accountability. The licensee's system of internal controls must be designed to ensure that the following objectives are met: safeguarding of assets; reliability of financial records; transactions executed and recorded in accordance with casino policies and procedures; access to assets permitted only in accordance with casino policy; records complete and sufficiently accurate to permit periodic comparisons of on-hand versus book values.

The system of internal controls established by the casino must necessarily establish levels of individual accountability as well as create forms and documents to provide an audit trail of all transactions. By designating performance requirements and responsibility for completing forms and documents, management effectively creates levels of accountability. When the audit chain is broken, it is relatively easy to identify individuals responsible for violations of procedure.

The Casino Bankroll

The casino bankroll is the minimum amount of funds required to operate the casino on a daily basis. Regulatory agencies in the states of Nevada and New Jersey utilize an elaborate formula in determining the minimum bankroll requirement for each licensee. Once the bankroll has been determined, the licensee is subjected to audit by these regulatory agencies to ensure that the bankroll requirement does not fall below the established minimum. The casino bankroll is entrusted to the custodianship of the main vault or main bank for safekeeping and disbursement to the various casino revenue centers. The stipulated amount of the opening bankroll is operated as an imprest fund allowing for a shift-by-shift accountability process. The cycle of bankroll accountability is based on casino shifts, where each shift is responsible for summarizing financial transactions affecting the bankroll. This simply means that the opening bankroll amount must be the same at the beginning of each 24-hour revenue cycle, the revenue cycle consisting of the graveyard, day, and swing shifts. During the cycle, transactions will occur causing increases or decreases to funds. However, at the conclusion of the cycle, the fund or bankroll must be restored to its original amount by withdrawing excess funds (bank deposit) or restoring funds to achieve the opening bankroll amount.

Within this procedure, the following forms merit discussion: the main bank inventory form; the casino revenue summary form; and the master game report form.

The Main Bank Inventory Form

The main bank inventory form serves the following functions: It indicates the actual amount of bankroll inventory carried by the vault on a shift-by-shift basis; it serves to transfer inventory responsibility from one shift to the next; and it provides a detailed analysis of every inventory category carried. Each casino designs this form in whatever detail or format is required to serve the need of its system. However, whatever the design, the accurate recording of all bankroll items is essential. Basically, the procedure is as follows.

Assume the casino starts its first day of business with its opening at the graveyard shift. At the start of this very first shift, the vault cashiers will physically count and record every bankroll item to the main bank inventory form. This is the verified, actual bankroll. At the conclusion of the graveyard shift, the inventory is once again counted by the graveyard cashier and recorded on an inventory form. The oncoming cashiers for the day shift will verify the count and accept custodianship. Thus, the main bank inventory form serves to transfer inventory responsibility on a shift-by-shift basis since this process is repeated for each shift.

The Casino Revenue Summary Form

All revenue and expense transactions handled by the cage and vault during the three shifts of the business cycle are summarized on the casino revenue summary form. This document, which may be supported with received and disbursement summary reports, is designed to accomplish several important reporting functions:

1. As a report document, it capsulizes or summarizes all revenue and expense transactions conducted during the business cycle.

2. As a support document, it proves the accuracy of the cage inventory reported on the main bank inventory sheet.
3. As a transmittal document, it is used by the accounting department for recording daily revenues and expenses to the casino journals.
4. As a control document, it monitors transactions affecting bankroll increases and decreases and provides for the daily balancing of the imprest fund.

The Master Game Report Form

Gaming table accountability, on a shift-by-shift basis, is a critical management concern. To ensure the integrity of the revenue-reporting process, the casino cage and the casino pit must jointly unite in activities. Management seeks an accurate reporting profile regarding each table's revenue activity for each daily shift. The casino cage interfaces in table game accountability through the master game report form, which serves the following functions:

1. The cage records table opening and closing chip inventories as well as table fills and credits on it. A separate form is used for each shift.
2. It is used by the soft count audit team to record table drop and the computation of table and shift gaming results (win or less).
3. The accounting department utilizes information generated by this form to prepare the daily management report form.
4. It will be relied upon by internal and external auditors in determining proper recording and documentation of table revenue.

The master game report is prepared by two independent sources—the casino cage and the soft count audit team. The importance of two independent sources is essential in ensuring accuracy and adherence to sound procedures. As with all forms, each casino designs and utilizes a format to suit its recording needs. Regardless of the design adopted, the following data is recorded by the cage using the calculations:

- Table opener inventory
- Table chip fills
- Table chip returns (credits)
- Table name credits (markers/IOUs)
- Table closer inventory
- Table need (accountability)

With this information the Soft Count Audit Team completes the process by recording each table's drop and calculating game results (table drop minus table need equals win or loss).

Following is a brief explanation of the procedures utilized.

Each casino table game is listed by type and game number on the master game report. The designated pit supervisor prepares to open each of the tables with an opening table bank of gaming chips or tokens. This procedure requires the pit supervisor to complete a table opener/closer form, sometimes referred to as a "brownie." Assuming a three-part form is used (some casinos use a two-part form), the form is completed indicating the quantity and denomination of chips requested. This procedure is followed for each of the games to be opened. The casino cage provides requested chips, receiving one copy of the table opener/closer form, which serves as documentation for the transaction. The table opener is inserted into the proper table drop box, and play is ready to commence. The cage records each of the table opener amounts to the master game report, retaining its copy of the opener form.

During the shift, the pit executive may need to replenish table gaming chips or return excessive chips to the cage. To accomplish either task, the process is initiated with the pits' completion of a two-part request for fill or request for credit form. These forms provide the cage with documentation to complete a table chip fill or chip credit. To fulfill the requests, the cage completes either a three-part fill form or credit form. Whatever the document, all personnel involved in the process must follow established casino policy and procedure. The cage will retain one copy of these forms which, again, serves as the source document for recording to the master game report. Similarly, customer marker forms (IOUs) may be processed by the pit to the cage, which necessitates that the pit and cage complete proper credit procedures.

At the close of the gaming pit(s) shift, the chip inventory for each gaming table must be counted and recorded. Inventories are counted by a pit supervisor from that ending shift together with a pit supervisor responsible for the next shift. They are recorded by amount and denomination to a multi-part table closer/opener form. Many casinos use a combination carbonless closer-opener form for this process. The recording of the closer inventory is thus transposed to the opener form. In this way, the recorded closing inventory of one shift becomes the opening table inventory for the next shift. The table closer card is dropped into the appropriate table drop box for the ending shift, while the second part of the form, the opener, is dropped into the table drop box for the new starting shift. Whatever the process used, the cage must be provided with all supporting transactional documents containing required signatures of the individuals participating in the process for recording to the master game report.

With the conclusion of the recording process, the designated cage cashier attaches all support documents to the master game report form for that shift. These important source documents include

- Request for fill
- Fill slip
- Request for credit (chip or name credit)
- Credit slip (chip or name)
- Customer marker (IOU) transmittal form
- Table opener cards
- Table closer cards

This process is repeated for each of the three daily shifts, after which the master game reports and all support documents are picked up by the soft count audit team, which will perform the soft count recording and audit process.

The control procedures described above result in achieving cage accountability for table game revenues through proper separation of duties, adequate documentary and signatory controls as the following summary indicates:

1. *Casino pit*—initiates requests for gaming table chip openers, fills, credits, and closers while inserting documentary copies in table drop boxes and providing supporting copies of transactional forms to the casino cage.
2. *Casino cage*—releases and receives its chip inventory to and from the casino pit(s) only with written documented evidence. Each form utilized in the process is used for recording to the master game report form and retained by the cage as evidence of the recording.
3. *Soft count team*—an entity separate from the cage and gaming pits responsible for concluding this revenue process. The team opens all table game drop boxes, recovers copies of all documents contained in the boxes, verifies all entries recorded to the master game report form, counts and verifies all monies contained in the boxes, records the "soft drop," and computes and records each table and shift result to the master game report form.
4. *Main vault*—receives and verifies the soft drop from the soft count team and accepts and records these funds to the casino bankroll.
5. *Accounting department*—receives all copies of the master game report form along with all support documents, verifies all recorded entries, prepares daily management report forms, and safeguards all documents.

CONCLUSION

In the introduction to this chapter, the casino cage was described as the financial hub and nerve center for gaming transactions in a casino operation. Clearly, the cage plays a vital role in the day-to-day operations of a casino, and internal controls are rigorously applied by this important component of the organization. Additionally, it should be evident that good cage procedures require a systematic approach based upon forms utilization, signatory controls and authorizations, separation of functions, and duties. All of these lead to an easily tracked audit trail and solid internal controls. The cage is an extension of the financial controller's office and shares the fiduciary responsibility for maintaining the financial well-being of the operation. Therefore, a systematic approach to cage operations is not only important but imperative if the business is to be successful.

8

Casino Revenue Recognition

This is a review of the terminology and procedures associated with casino accounting and, more specifically, the methods by which gross gaming revenue is calculated. The two primary revenue areas in a casino are table games and slots. The most common table games are Blackjack (also known as Twenty-One), Craps, Pai Gow poker, Baccarat, Roulette, and Big-6. The slots are devices into which the player deposits coins to win a jackpot or payoffs. These devices can simulate games such as Poker or Blackjack.

The following are some key definitions that will assist the reader in understanding the procedures and methods in calculating gross gaming revenue for table games.

TABLE GAMES

Definitions

Closer card. A two-part document used to record the table inventory at the end of each 8 hour shift.

Credit slip. A three-part, serialized document that is completed and used in the table credit process to identify the specific table sending the credit, and the breakdown, by denomination, of the chips, tokens, coin and/or markers included in the credit.

Drop Box. A secured metal box attached to a game table that is used to hold currency and foreign gaming chips exchanged for house gaming chips or tokens. Also included in the drop box are orders for fills and credits, fill and credit slips, marker stubs, marker payment slips, and closer cards.

Fill slip. A three-part, serialized document that is completed and used in the table fill process to identify the specific table receiving the fill and the breakdown, by denomination, of the chips, tokens, and/or coin included in the fill.

Foreign chips. These are chips and tokens from another casino that are used in the gaming process.

Marker. A legal counter check for the purpose of granting a player credit at a gaming table or the casino cashier's cage. This is a three-part document that includes the original count check, an issue slip, and a payment slip. Original markers can be deposited in the bank for collection purposes.

Order for credit. A two-part document used by a pit floor supervisor to send a specific amount of chips, tokens, coin, and/or markers to the casino cashier's cage and to request the casino cashier's cage to prepare a fill and fill slip for a specific table game.

Order for fill. A two-part document used by a pit floor supervisor to request that the casino cashier's cage prepare a fill and fill slip for a specific table game.

Soft count. The process of counting and recording the contents of each table game's drop box. This process is on a table-by-table basis for each of the three gaming shifts.

Soft count room. The location where the contents of the drop boxes are counted and recorded by table game and shift.

Stiff sheet. The form used to record the opening inventory, closing inventory, drop, fills, credits, markers, and gross revenue or win for each table game. This is completed in total by game type and for the entire shift.

Table credits. The transfer of chips, tokens, and/or coin from a specific table game to the casino cashier's cage. Table credits are also used to transfer a gaming marker from a pit to the casino cashier's cage when the marker has not been repaid by the player within a specified period of time.

Table fills. The transfer of chips, tokens, and/or coin from the casino cashier's cage to a specific table game.

Table game drop. The process of removing the drop box from each of the table games for the shift that is just ending and replacing it with a new drop box for the shift that is about to begin. This process also includes the transportation and securing of the drop boxes onto the drop box cart in the soft count room.

Table inventory. The supply of chips, tokens, and coin used by the dealer to pay off winning bets, to exchange with a player for currency, and to store losing bets from players.

Table Game Transactions

The calculation of table-game gross gaming revenue begins with the player. The player at a table game plays with house chips for which he or she exchanged cash or credit (a marker). Cash or markers exchanged for chips are placed in the table's drop box, which is physically attached to the table game.

During play, if a table game is running low or in need of a particular denomination of chip(s) or tokens, an order for fill is prepared that requests the casino cashier's cage to make up a table fill. The casino cashier's cage then prepares the fill, as specified by the order, as well as a fill slip. In cases where too much of one denomination of chips is on a table, a table credit will be initiated. As described for a table fill, an order for credit is prepared by a pit floor supervisor. The chips and/or tokens are then sent to the casino cashier's cage along with the original part of the order for fill. The casino cage cashier prepares a credit slip, which is transported back to the specific table game. The original fill or credit slips are deposited into the table's drop box by the dealer after it has been properly verified and signed. These processes occur each and every time that chips and/or tokens need to be transferred to or from a table game.

Table Game Drop

The revenue accounting process begins with a procedure called the table game drop, which consists of several regimented procedures that have been established by state gaming authorities. The table game drop occurs, at predetermined times, every eight hours during the day. Each drop is separately designated in order to provide for strict accountability by shift: day, swing, and graveyard.

The table-game drop process begins with the counting and recording of the table inventory. Obviously, the ending table inventory for the just-completed shift is the opening table inventory for the shift about to start. The table inventory is conducted by two casino supervisors. Usually, one supervisor represents the just-completed shift and one represents the new shift. This provides for a "check and balance" between shifts in order to ensure statistical fairness and consistency.

The table inventory is counted, recorded, and verified by both casino supervisors. It is then recorded on the "hard" or closer card by denomination of chips, coin, and tokens. Both casino supervisors sign the closer card designating its accuracy, and once signed the card is placed in the table drop box for the just-ended shift. The closer card is dropped into the box by someone other than a casino supervisor—for example, the table's dealer or a member of the drop team, which is made up of several security officers and laborers. Once the closer card has been dropped into the drop box, nothing else may be deposited.

Usually, the drop team follows closely behind the casino supervisors conducting the table inventory count. When the closer card has been dropped, the drop box for the just-ended shift is removed from the table and replaced by a new drop box, for the shift that is about to begin. When the drop box is removed from the table, its locking mechanism automatically locks the drop slot. The just-removed box is placed on the drop cart by one of the drop team members. The cart is closely watched by one of the security officers assigned to the team.

When all of the drop boxes for the just completed shift have been removed and are on the drop cart, at least two members of the drop team (usually security officers) and the two casino pit supervisors who took the table inventory transport the drop cart to the soft count room. The doors of the drop cart are locked with padlocks, and the cart(s) is stored in the locked soft count room, which is under closed-circuit surveillance 24 hours a day. Only the soft count team is permitted to handle the drop boxes once they are secured in the soft count room.

Soft Count

At a time designated and reported to gaming regulatory authorities by the casino, the soft count team counts the contents of the table drop boxes and calculates the gross gaming revenue for the just completed shifts. The team consists of a minimum of three people, either from independent departments—for example, cage, accounting, and casino—or assigned as a part of a permanent count team. Prior to beginning the count, the count team must obtain the table drop box keys from the casino cashier's cage. All count team members must be present when the keys are taken from the cage.

Each table drop box requires two keys. The first key opens the contents door of the drop box, permitting the emptying of all currency, chips, tokens, and paper work from the box. The second key resets the drop slot door into the open position so that the box can be used on its designated shift.

Each member of the count team is assigned a particular position. The positions are box opener, counter, and recorder. The box opener opens the drop boxes, empties the contents of the drop box onto the count table, shows that the box is empty, resets the drop slot, and returns the locked box to the drop cart. The box opener also assists the counter in the sorting of the currency, chips, tokens, and paper work. It is the responsibility of the box opener to ensure that uncounted funds from one drop box are not commingled with the uncounted funds of another drop box or funds that have already been counted. The counter is responsible for sorting the currency, chips, and tokens by denomination and then physically counting these items. A total, by denomination, is verbally communicated to the recorder. (In larger casinos, the count team may be expanded to four people, the fourth member serving as a verifier of the results of the counter's work).

The recorder receives all of the paper work from the drop box. This person is responsible for matching and stapling all orders for fills and credits with their respective fill and credit slips. A total of the fills and credits as well as the markers issued and payments received is verified, by drop box, with the totals recorded on to the stiff sheet by the casino cashier's cage. The recorder also records the verbally communicated totals, by denomination, of the currency, chips, and tokens on the closer card.

The stiff sheet, which is also known as the master games report, is the first document to bring each of the revenue calculation components together. The stiff sheet is prepared by table game number for each shift. Prior to the start of the soft count process, the casino cashier's cage enters the following data on the sheet: table opener (beginning table inventory), table closer (ending table inventory), total fills, credits, marker issues, and marker payments. All that remains is for the soft count team to record the table drop and calculate the win or loss by table and in total for that shift. Once the total table drop is determined and recorded on the stiff sheet, the recorder calculates the table's win or loss. Table 8.1 illustrates the calculation for table-games gross gaming revenue.

Table 8.1   Calculation of Table-Game Gross Gaming Revenue

Given the following transactions for a table game:	
Beginning table inventory	$ 15,000
Ending table inventory	$ 11,000
Table fills	$ 5,000
Table credits	$ 2,000
Cash and chips (from drop)	$ 7,000
Markers issued and outstanding (from drop)	$ 1,000
Gross gaming revenue is calculated as follows:	
Cash and chips (from drop)	$ 7,000
plus markers issued and outstanding (from drop)	1,000
	$ 8,000
less beginning table inventory	$ 15,000
plus table fills	$ 5,000
minus table credits	$ (2,000)
minus ending table inventory	$(11,000)
	$ (7,000)
Gross gaming revenue of win	$ 1,000

It should be noted that any corrections to the stiff sheet or any related gaming document must be made in the following manner: The amount in error is crossed out with a single line, the correct figure is written above the crossed out figure, and two members of the count team initial the correction.

Upon completion of the count for each of the tables, the entire drop of cash, chips, and tokens is verified against the totals for the shift listed on the stiff sheet. Everything must be in balance before the drop funds can be transferred to the casino cashier's cage. When the drop has been balanced, all members of the soft count team are required to sign the stiff sheet attesting to its accuracy.

A cage cashier, independent from the soft count and usually the main bank cashier, receives the funds and the stiff sheet from the count team. He or she counts and verifies the total funds with the total drop listed on the stiff sheet. If everything is in balance, the cage cashier signs the sheet and accepts the funds into the cage's accountability. All of the count documentation, including the stiff sheet, must be transported to the accounting offices by a member of the soft count team, since it is strictly prohibited that soft count documentation be left in the control of the casino cage. It is permissible to place the soft count documentation in a locked or sealed bag that is delivered to accounting at a later time, as long as only accounting can gain access to the actual documents.

The following are some key definitions that will assist the reader in understanding the procedures and methods in calculating gross gaming revenue for slot and video games.

SLOT AND VIDEO GAMES

Definitions

Coin-in. The amount of coins inserted into the coin slot, measured by one of several electronic meters installed on a slot or video game.

Drop. Coin-ins that were diverted from the hopper into the drop bucket held in the slot cabinet below the machine. The total amount of coins in the drop bucket constitutes the drop. (Note that when a machine is permanently removed from the casino floor, the coins held in the hopper are also dropped into the drop bucket to be counted. Not all of these coins are included in the drop figures. The coin in the hopper less the initial fill for that machine equals drop win or loss.

Drop bucket. A bucket or pail used to catch and hold coins/tokens that were diverted from the hopper.

Hard count. The process of weighing the contents of the drop buckets, by slot or video game. The weight of the coins/tokens is converted, by the computerized scale, into a dollar value based on the denomination being weighed.

Hard count room. The location used to weigh, wrap, and verify the contents of the slot drop buckets.

Hold. The percentage of actual win divided by the total amount of coin-in for each game.

Hopper. An internal holding area within each slot game. The contents of the hopper are used to pay small jackpots to players. Included in the hopper are coins from the slot game's initial fill as well as coin-in played.

Initial fill. A predetermined amount of coin placed in the hopper when a slot game is placed in service on the casino floor. Initial fills are not deductible expenses for gaming tax purposes and are held as an inventory on the balance sheet.

Machine fill. The transfer of coins or tokens from a slot booth or cage to a slot game when the hopper has been emptied.

Jackpot (handpays). Winning results on a slot or video game exceeding a predetermined amount, which are required to be handpaid by slot supervisory personnel.

Weigh/wrap verification. The process of comparing, by denomination, the total value of the weigh to the total value of the wrapped or racked coins/tokens. The difference is used to determine if an additional investigation is warranted for the variance.

Wrap. The process of wrapping the coin and/or racking the tokens after the weigh has been completed.

Slot and Video Game Transactions

The calculation of gross gaming revenue for slot and video games is much like that for table games. The process begins with the player. Coins or tokens are inserted into the coin slot and fall into the hopper. As the coin or token falls it triggers an electronic sensor that validates it as genuine and registers one coin-in. (Modern-day slot devices also include currency acceptors that place credits on a slot device for play. Although the currency inserted in these acceptors does not fall into the hopper, it does register an appropriate amount of coin-in for statistical purposes).

When a low-level jackpot is won by the player, it is paid by the slot device itself. The coins held in the hopper are used to make these small payouts. If the hopper does not have enough coins or tokens to complete the payout, a machine fill becomes necessary. At least one slot supervisor and another slot employee complete a jackpot/fill slip and obtain a fill bag or bucket from a slot change booth. The amount of coins/tokens used to make a machine fill are predetermined by management and are counted and prepared by slot booth personnel. Upon replenishment of the hopper, the slot device is permitted to complete the payout. For jackpots that exceed specified amounts, the slot device will "lock up" and require that a handpaid jackpot be made. According to Internal Revenue Service code, all slot device jackpots that exceed $1,200 require that a form W2-G be completed and filed. Because a special IRS document is required, it is logical to assume that all jackpots that exceed $1,200 require the completion of a jackpot/fill slip.

In an attempt to gain more control over slot operations, most casinos place the jackpot/fill slip requirement at a level well below the $1,200 amount—Many will place it at a $1,000 level. It is important for management to institute a balance between customer service and internal controls. The faster that a casino can get the cash into the hands of the player, the greater the opportunity for the player to resume gaming activities and hopefully return the just-won jackpot.

Coins or tokens that fall into a hopper that has reached its predetermined level are automatically diverted into the drop bucket located in the slot cabinet below the slot device.

Slot and Video Game Drop

At a time designated by management, the revenue accounting process for slot devices begins with the slot drop. The drop process begins with a security officer and the slot drop team leader obtaining the slot cabinet keys from the casino cashier's cage. The slot drop team consists of employees from the hard count/coin room, security, and accounting.

The hard count employees are responsible for pulling the slot drop, security officers watch the drop buckets as they are loaded on to a hydraulic cart, and the accounting employee is an observer. As drop buckets are pulled from the slot cabinets, a tag with each respective slot machine number is placed on top of the coins/tokens. This will be used to identify where that bucket came from when the weigh process begins. Once the hydraulic cart is filled with the buckets, the entire drop team transports the buckets to the hard count room. If the drop is not yet completed, the buckets are securely locked in the hard count room. Upon completion of the drop, the slot cabinet keys are returned to the casino cashier's cage.

Hard Count

At a time designated and reported to gaming regulatory authorities by the casino, the hard count team weighs the contents of the slot drop buckets. This is the where the calculation of gross gaming revenue for slot devices begins. Prior to beginning the weigh process, the hard count supervisor or team leader must perform a weigh test on the weigh scale. Using set weights of 10 and 25 pounds, the scale determines the dollar value, by denomination, for each of those weights.

These results are compared to the calibration results, calculated when the scale was last serviced, in order to determine if a significant variance exists. If one does exist, the hard count supervisor must contact both the manufacturing contractor responsible for maintaining the scale and the controller's office about these problems. If no significant variance is found, the weigh process can continue.

Each drop bucket is emptied, individually, into the weigh-scale holding hopper. The identification tag is used to enter the specific slot device number from which that bucket originated into the weigh scale computer. The weigh scale computer has been programmed to convert the weight of coins, by denomination, into specific dollar values, which are recorded on to a weigh journal that also includes the slot device number. Once the scale has weighed the contents of the drop bucket, the coins/tokens automatically drop onto a conveyor belt, which transports them to wrapping machines. As the coins/tokens are wrapped, the rolls of coin drop on to another conveyor belt, which takes them to a canning station.

At the canning station, the rolls of coin are placed in metal or plastic cans that hold a specific dollar amount based on the denomination of coin. These cans are stacked in a manner that facilitates the overall counting of the wrapped coins/tokens. When the weigh process is completed, the weigh scale computer runs a summary report totaling the weigh by denomination. These totals are recorded on the weigh/wrap verification report.

When the wrap portion of the count is completed and all of the rolled coins have been canned and stacked, they are counted by denomination. These totals are also recorded on the weigh/wrap verification report. The variance in both dollar amounts and percentages, for each denomination, is calculated. Variances that exceed plus or minus 2% or are $1,000 or greater (whichever is less) must be investigated by the hard count supervisor, who writes an explanatory report. If no significant variances exist, all members of the hard count team sign the weigh/wrap verification report. The casino cashier's cage is then notified that the slot drop is ready to be transferred into cage accountability.

A cage cashier, usually the main bank cashier, performs an independent count and verification, by denomination, of the wrap. If everything is in balance, the main bank cashier signs the weigh/wrap verification report accepting the slot drop into cage accountability. It is at this point that the actual calculation of slot gross gaming revenue can be determined. Table 8.2 illustrates the calculation of slots gross gaming revenue.

If we assume that the coin-in totals for this period are $7,500, the hold percentage for this particular machine is 2.6% ($200/$7,500).

Table 8.2 Calculation of Slot Gross Gaming Revenue

Given the following transactions for a slot device:	
Slot drop	$ 1,900
Machine fills	$ 800
Hand-paid jackpots	$ 900

Gross gaming revenue is calculated as follows:	
Drop (from weigh tape)	$ 1,900
minus Machine Fills	$ (800)
minus hand paid jackpots	$ (900)
Gross Gaming Revenue or Win	$ 200

CONCLUSION

The process by which gross gaming revenue is calculated for either table games or slot devices is directed by the internal control standards required by gaming regulatory authorities. Calculating gross gaming revenue is much more than adding and subtracting a group of numbers and recording a win total. It begins with a set of operational internal control procedures that dictate how things must be done and who must be present when they are done.

Chapter
9

Reporting of Cash Transactions

HISTORY

Concerned that casinos provided a means for drug traffickers to launder their illicit profits, the Secretary of the Treasury determined in 1985 that casinos would fall within the definition of a financial institution. As financial institutions, casinos would then be required to report all transactions involving more than $10,000 in cash during any 24-hour period. In addition to stopping money laundering, it was hoped that the required reporting would help the Internal Revenue Service identify tax evaders.

For years, general businesses like automobile dealerships, jewelry stores, hotels, and even restaurants have been required to report to the Internal Revenue Service all cash transactions in excess of $10,000 received in a trade or business. But until 1985, casinos were exempt from this requirement.

Before the inclusion of casinos, financial institutions were limited to the following:

1. Banks
2. Brokers or dealers in securities
3. Currency dealers or exchangers
4. Issuer's, sellers, or redeemers of traveler's checks or money orders
5. Licensed transmitters of funds
6. Telegraph companies

As a financial institution, every casino within the jurisdiction of the federal government is now subject to reporting under Title 31 of The Bank Secrecy Act.

Friday, January 22, 1993/**Las Vegas Review-Journal**

10 Atlantic City casinos fined

♥**Treasury Department officials accuse the resorts of failing to comply with money-laundering laws.**

Associated Press

WASHINGTON - The Treasury Department fined 10 Atlantic City, N.J., casinos $2.48 million Thursday for alleged civil violations of the law designed to prevent money laundering.

The department accused the casinos of "willfully failing to report" currency transactions over $10,000 to the Internal Revenue Service as required by the Bank Secrecy Act.

The law has applied to banks since 1974 and to casinos and other large cash-based businesses since 1985. The requirement is designed to help the government track and combat money laundering.

"Reporting failures, whatever their cause, ... potentially deprive Treasury of financial information which is a vital weapon in the battle against organized crime, drug trafficking and tax evasion," said John P. Simpson, acting assistant Treasury secretary.

The alleged violations that led to the fines were found in audits covering the years 1985 through 1988. Since 1988, "the casinos have invested substantial time and resources to improve compliance and cooperate with the government," the department said.

It said the penalties were based on the casinos' failure to comply with reporting requirements and that it had no evidence of criminal violations.

Six of the 10 casinos have agreed to settle the charges by paying fines. They are Bally's Grand Hotel and Casino, $126,000; Bally's Park Place Casino, $9,000; Showboat Hotel and Casino, $58,500; Tropworld Hotel and Casino, $414,000; Trump Castle Hotel and Casino, $175,500, and Trump Plaza Hotel and Casino $292,500.

The four other casinos were assessed the maximum civil money penalties authorized by law. They are Caesars, Atlantic City Hotel Casino $145,000; Claridge Casino Hotel $402,000; Harrah's Atlantic City Casino Hotel, $730,000, and Sands Hotel and Casino, $130,000.

In May of 1985, the following paragraph was added to Title 31:

Each casino shall file a report of each deposit, withdrawal, exchange of currency, gambling tokens or chips, or other payment or transfer, by, through, or to such casino which involves a transaction in currency of more than $10,000. Multiple currency transactions shall be treated as a single transaction if the casino has knowledge that they are by or on behalf of any person and result in either cash in or cashout totaling more than $10,000 during any twenty-four hour period.

Classifying casinos as financial institutions was, to say the least, an unwelcome change in the industry. Operators felt that this would discourage or severely curtail an extremely profitable segment of casino customers, the high roller. At first, the industry argued against the change altogether. However, after weeks and months of dialogue, it became evident that nothing could be done about the impending reclassification. Casinos would soon report under Title 31 (see Table 9.1, which outlines the type of reporting required).

Nevada's regulators felt that individual reporting to the Treasury was an intrusion by the federal government that should be avoided if possible. They felt that direct involvement by the federal government could, in the long term, threaten the industry and they were successful in persuading the Secretary of Treasury to allow each jurisdiction, if it so desired, to develop its own method of implementing the necessary controls and reporting procedures. The final decision by the Treasury gave each jurisdiction two options.

1. Obtain an exemption from direct reporting to the Department of Treasury by developing its own system of implementing and monitoring for compliance with the reporting requirements.
2. Report directly to the Department of Treasury subject to Title 31 of the Bank Secrecy Act with the Department of Treasury responsible for monitoring compliance.

Nevada's regulators, with the support of Nevada's gaming industry, decided on the first option, and so Regulation 6A was written. Before implementation, Regulation 6A had to be accepted by officials from the Treasury, which after months of negotiations, accepted Nevada's self-regulation model. Even though the system is administered by Nevada's gaming regulators, copies of all reports are sent to the Internal Revenue Service.

At the time, the only U.S. jurisdictions, other than Nevada, with casinos were located in Atlantic City and Puerto Rico.

Both Atlantic City and Puerto Rico opted for the second option. Consequently, each casino in both jurisdictions reports to and communicates directly with the Department of Treasury.

Table 9.1 Department Affected, Incidence and Type of Report Required under Regulation 6A

Cage

1. Sale of more than $10,000 in chips for cash in a single transaction. .030
2. Redeeming more than $10,000 in chips for cash, in a single transaction, that were not won or wagered. .030
3. Accepting more than $10,000 in cash as front money or safekeeping deposit. .040
4. Accepting more than $10,000 in cash as payment for markers. .040
5. Any receipt or disbursement of more than $10,000 in cash not specifically covered. .040
6. Redemption of more than $1,000 worth of another casino's chips for cash. .040
7. If the $10,000 was exceeded by aggregating the transactions, a .040 report is always used.
8. Redeeming more than $10,000 in chips for cash, that were won or wagered. .050
9. Player wins on a wager of more than $10,000 (in chips or cash) and payoff is in cash. .050

Card Games

1. Sale of more than $10,000 in chips for cash in a single transaction. .030
2. Redeeming more than $10,000 in chips for cash, in a single transaction, that were not won or wagered. .030
3. Sale of more than $10,000 in chips for cash in multiple transactions. .040
4. Redeeming more than $10,000 in chips for cash, in multiple transactions, that were not won or wagered. .040
5. Redeeming more than $10,000 in chips for cash, that were won or wagered. .050

Table Games

1. Sales of more than $10,000 in chips for cash in a single transaction. .030
2. Accepting more than $10,000 in cash as payment for markers. .040
3. Any receipt or disbursement of more than $10,000 in cash not specifically covered. .040

Table 9.1 *(continued)*

4. Sale of more than $10,000 in chips for cash in multiple transactions.   .040
5. Player loses more than $10,000 in cash in single or multiple transactions.   .040

Bingo & Keno

1. Sale of more than $10,000 in chips for cash in a single transaction.   .030
2. Redeeming more than $10,000 in chips for cash, in a single transaction, that were not won or wagered.   .030
3. Accepting more than $10,000 in cash as payment for markers.   .040
4. Any receipt or disbursement of more than $10,000 in cash not specifically covered.   .040
5. Redemption of more than $1,000 worth of another casino's chips for cash.   .040
6. If the $10,000 was exceeded by aggregating the transactions, a .040 report is always used.
7. Player wins on a wager of more than $10,000 (in chips or cash) and payoff is in cash.   .050
8. Redeeming more than $10,000 in chips for cash, that were won or wagered.   .050

Race and Sports

1. Sale of more than $10,000 in chips for cash in a single transaction.   .030
2. Redeeming more than $10,000 in chips for cash, in a single transaction, that were not won or wagered.   .030
3. Placing a single wager of more than $10,000 in cash.   .030
4. Accepting more than $10,000 in cash as front money or safekeeping deposit.   .040
5. Accepting more than $10,000 in cash as payment for markers.   .040
6. Any receipt or disbursement of more than $10,000 in cash not specifically covered.   .040
7. Redemption of more than $1,000 worth of another casino's chips for cash.   .040
8. Player wins on a wager of more than $10,000 (in chips or cash) and payoff is in cash.   .050

Nevada's Regulation 6A Model

PROHIBITED TRANSACTIONS

Three types of transactions are strictly prohibited:

1. Since Nevada's system is designed to prevent even subtle money laundering, cash-for-cash transactions in excess of $2,500 are prohibited. This does not include tokens for cash, **but does include U.S. coins for cash.**
2. No check for cash in excess of $2,500. The one exception is a check for winnings. For example, if the patron wins a large slot jackpot, he or she can accept the winnings by check.
3. Issuing a check or wire transfer for winnings to a third party (it must be in the name of the winning patron).

TYPES OF REPORTS

There are two types of reports required under Regulation 6A: The currency transaction report (CTR) (Figure 9.1), and the currency transaction incidence report (CTIR) (Figure 9.2).

The CTR is the only report where the patron must provide positive identification. The CTIR merely lists the type of transaction and the amount involved. Identification of the patron or inclusion of his or her name in the CTR is not necessary.

Since both Title 31 and Nevada's Regulation 6A require reporting any patron whose total transactions, during a 24-hour period, exceed $10,000, some method was necessary to keep track of multiple transactions. The multiple transaction log (MTL) (Figure 9.3) was designed to do just that and is used in all gaming areas affected by the regulation.

Currency Transaction Report (CTR)

Although the same form is used, CTRs are further classified as type .030 or .040. The type of transaction involved determines whether it requires an .030 or .040.

On both .030 and .040, the report must contain

1. Date and time of the transaction.
2. Amount of the transaction.
3. Patron's name.
4. Patron's permanent address.
5. Method used to verify the patron's identity and residence, and description of credential, including number (e.g., drivers license, military I.D., passport).

Form **8362**		**Currency Transaction Report by Casinos**					
(Rev. May 1992)		File a separate Form 8362 for each transaction. Please type or print.				OMB No. 1545-0906	
Department of the Treasury Internal Revenue Service		*(Complete all applicable parts—see instructions)*					

Part I — **Individual or Organization for Whom This Transaction Was Completed**

Individual's last name		First name	Middle initial	Social security number
Organization's name		Employer identification number (EIN)	Passport number	Country
Address (number, street, and apt. or suite no.)		Occupation, profession, or business	Alien registration number	Country
City	State	ZIP code	Country (if not U.S.)	Driver's license (number and state)

Part II — **Identity of Individual Conducting the Transaction** (Complete only if an agent conducts a transaction for the person in Part I)

Last name		First name	Middle initial	Social security number
Address (number, street, and apt. or suite no.)		Passport number	Country	Alien registration number	Country
City	State	ZIP code	Country (if not U.S.)	Driver's license (number and state)

Part III — **Patron's Account or Receipt Number ▶**

Part IV — **Description of Transaction**
If more space is needed, attach a separate schedule and check this box . . . . ▶ ☐

1 Type of transaction. Check the applicable boxes to describe transaction.

a ☐ Currency exchange (currency for currency)

b CASH IN:
- (1) ☐ Deposit (front and safekeeping)
- (2) ☐ Chips purchased
- (3) ☐ Check purchased (see item 6 below)
- (4) ☐ Wire transfer of funds
- (5) ☐ Collection on account
- (6) ☐ Other cash in .... (specify)

c CASH OUT:
- (1) ☐ Withdrawal of deposit (front and safekeeping)
- (2) ☐ Check cashed (see item 6 below)
- (3) ☐ Chips redeemed
- (4) ☐ Credit advance
- (5) ☐ Other cash out .... (specify)

| **2** Total amount of currency transaction (in U.S. dollars) $ .00 | **3** Amount in item 2 in $100 bills or higher $ .00 | **4** Date of transaction (month, day, and year) |

5 If other than U.S. currency is involved, please furnish the following information:

| Currency name | Country | Total amount of each foreign currency (in U.S. dollars) $ .00 |

6 If a check was involved in this transaction, please furnish the following information (see instructions):

| Date of check | Amount of check (in U.S. dollars) $ .00 | Payee of check |
| Maker of check | | Drawee bank and city |

Part V — **Casino Reporting the Financial Transaction**

Name	Employer identification number (EIN)
Address (number, street, and apt. or suite no.) where transaction occurred	
City	State	ZIP code

Sign Here ▶

| (Casino employee who handled the transaction) | (Title) | (Date) |
| (Casino official reviewing and approving the Form 8362) | (Title) | (Date) |

For Paperwork Reduction Act Notice, see back of form.   Cat. No. 62291Z   Form **8362** (Rev. 5-92)

Figure 9.1 Currency Transaction Report by Casinos

CURRENCY TRANSACTION INCIDENCE REPORT

File up to 5 separate transactions on this report. Please type or print.
(Complete all applicable parts — see instructions)

INCIDENCE #1:

Trans. date	Trans. time	Trans. amount	Trans. type	Name of employee handling transaction

Name of person adeasing to gaming

Evidence of gaming

Confirmation with _____ pit personnel

INCIDENCE #2:

Trans. date	Trans. time	Trans. amount	Trans. type	Name of employee handling transaction

Name of person adeasing to gaming

Evidence of gaming

Confirmation with _____ pit personnel

INCIDENCE #3:

Trans. date	Trans. time	Trans. amount	Trans. type	Name of employee handling transaction

Name of person adeasing to gaming

Evidence of gaming

Confirmation with _____ pit personnel

INCIDENCE #4:

Trans. date	Trans. time	Trans. amount	Trans. type	Name of employee handling transaction

Name of person adeasing to gaming

Evidence of gaming

Confirmation with _____ pit personnel

INCIDENCE #5:

Trans. date	Trans. time	Trans. amount	Trans. type	Name of employee handling transaction

Name of person adeasing to gaming

Evidence of gaming

Confirmation with _____ pit personnel

CASINO REPORTING THE FINANCIAL TRANSACTIONS

Name
TROPICANA HOTEL — LAS VEGAS   88-0158259

Number and Street
3801 Las Vegas Boulevard So.

City	State	Zip Code
Las Vegas	Nevada	89109

Sign Here _____

(Casino employee reviewing this form) (Title) (Date)

Figure 9.2 Currency Transaction Incidence Report

6. Signature of person handling the transaction and recording the information.
9. Signature of person reviewing the report (frequently the internal audit department).

Distinctions between the .030 and .040 reports are

10. If it is an .030 report, an *attempt must be made to obtain the patron's social security number.*
11. If it is an .040 report, *it is not necessary to ask the patron for a social security number;* however, the regulation states that the number must be included in the report if known by the casino

MULTIPLE TRANSACTION LOG

Casino name: _____

Date: _____

Area: _____

Date	Time	Description of patron	Name of patron (if known)	Table/ station number	Trans amount	Cumulative amount	Trans type	Remarks/evidence of gaming & pit supervisor's name	Employee signature

Note: This form should be used in all areas of the Casino. Cage personnel need not fill in the "Table/station number" column.

Transaction types:
1. Chip redemption (with evidence of gaming)
2. Chip redemption (no evidence of gaming)
3. Chip purchase
4. Front money or safekeeping deposit
5. Marker payment
6. Redemption of foreign chips ($1,000)
7. Payoff of winning wager in cash
8. Other cash transaction (specify in remarks)

Figure 9.3 Multiple Transaction Log

There are only three types of transactions that require an .030 report and therefore require asking for the patron's social security number:

1. Redemption by the casino of more than $10,000 in chips for cash that the patron did not win from gambling. This applies to all departments where chips are redeemed for cash, (that is, the casino cashier and the Race and Sports Book).
2. The accepting of a cash wager of more than $10,000 in any game where chips are not customarily used for betting. Departments where this type of betting occurs are the Race and Sports Book, Keno, and Bingo.
3. The sale of more than $10,000 in chips for cash. Certainly this can occur in the pit and cage, but it can also occur in the card room or in any other department where chips can be purchased.

All transactions requiring an .030 report are single transactions. If the patron redeems more than $10,000 in chips in two or more transactions, it does not require an .030 report.

There are five types of transactions that require reporting under .040. Here the significant difference in the report preparation is that *the patron's social security number is not required.*

1. Receipt from a patron of more than $10,000 in cash as a front money deposit or for safekeeping. The only departments where cash is accepted in this manner are the cage and Race and Sports Book.
2. Repayment of any marker or markers totaling more than $10,000 in cash. The cage, the pit, and the Race and Sports Book can accept cash as payment for a marker.
3. Regulation 6A.040 includes the following catch-all that requires an .040 report: receipt from or disbursement of more than $10,000 in cash to a patron not specifically covered elsewhere. This sentence prevents any large transaction from slipping through on a technicality. It also allows the casino to classify chip purchases in a different category from money play loses.
4. The redemption of more than $1,000 worth of another casino's chips for cash. This affects any department where chips can be redeemed for cash.
5. The loss of more than $10,000 in cash in a game where chips are normally used for wagering. Transactions of this type are limited to the table game area.

All multiple transactions where the aggregate exceeds $10,000 require reporting under .040.

Currency Transaction Incidence Report (CTIR)

The CTIR is referred to as an .050 report. An .050 report differs materially from the .030 or .040 report in that it does not require identification of the patron or even inclusion of his or her name if known by the casino. The .050 reports only that the transaction has occurred and the amount of money involved.

The .050 report contains:

1. Date and time of the transaction.
2. Amount of the transaction.
3. Name or initial of persons handling transaction and recording information.
4. Name or initial of persons who provided information that chips were won or wagered by patron.
5. A brief description of the evidence used to verify that the cash being paid out resulted from wagers, or the chips being exchanged resulted from winnings or wagering at the gaming tables (i.e., sports pool payout ticket number, poker tournament winnings, twenty-one winnings from x hours of play in y pit, etc.).
6. Signature of person reviewing the report (usually internal audit).

Two transactions require entry into an .050 report:

1. If a patron wagers more than $10,000, wins the bet, and the payoff is in cash. The total amount of the payoff (including the wager) is entered in the report. The wager can be accepted in either chips or cash. If in cash, it is necessary to prepare an .030 report prior to accepting the wager. The only departments that pay off in cash are Keno, Race and Sports Book, Bingo, and handpaid jackpots in slots.
2. The redemption of more than $10,000 in chips from a patron for cash where it can be reasonably assured that the patron won, substantially won, or wagered in gaming the entire amount. The "substantially won" and "wagered in gaming" statements leave much to interpretation. Therefore, the Gaming Control Board has provided this explanation:

> For this purpose the amount "wagered in gaming" by a patron is the sum of the largest single amount wagered by the patron with his money (rather than house money) plus amounts lost by the customer in wagering with his money.

Although attempting to clarify its meaning, this does little. I don't believe the patron can ever wager the house's money. If the wager is won by the patron, it becomes *the patron's* money.

Multiple Transaction Log (MTL)

Finally, to keep track of individual transactions that, in total, may exceed $10,000 during a 24-hour period, it is necessary to keep a multiple transaction log (MTL). MTL is required in all departments responsible for the preparation of either .030 or .040 reports. Any type of transaction exceeding $2,500 requires entry in the MTL, which contains

1. A description and, if known, the name of the patron.
2. If occurring in the pit, the table number.
3. Time, date, type, and amount if greater than $2,500.
4. Signature of pit or cage personnel recording the entry.

These logs are maintained for 24 hours, after which they are turned in to the accounting department for storage. Every 24 hours, each department receives a new MTL.

Front Money and Safekeeping Deposits

The regulation provides unique ways of handling player deposits of front money or for safekeeping. Each casino has two options:

1. Physically segregate the cash deposited in a designated location and return the same cash to the patron.
2. Record the number of bills in each denomination of the cash deposit. When the deposit is taken down, it is returned in the same denominations and number of bills of each denomination as in the original deposit.

What If the Patron Refuses to Comply?

Since the casinos are forced by regulation to obtain the necessary information, the casino has no choice but to bar the patron from gaming until he or she complies. Each pit is required to maintain a "barred patron log," which lists the patron's name, if known, and description. All pit personnel are expected to routinely review this log.

Benefit of Choosing 24-Hour Window

The regulation allows each casino to determine when its 24-hour day begins and ends. This has proven extremely beneficial in minimizing the effect on individual players. For instance, if the casino's 24-hour period begins at midnight, one night to the player could be two nights for the purpose of reporting. If the player loses, or if he or she buys in for $10,000 or less before midnight and then buys in for another $10,000 after midnight, reporting is not necessary. When the regulation was first enacted, many casinos chose early morning as the 24-hour cutoff. It did not take long for them to change to a time that more closely cut the player's play time in half.

Benefit of Segregating Like Transactions

Another huge benefit of Regulation 6A is the categorizing of "like" transactions. Chip purchases, money play loses, and marker payments are all separate. Regulation 6A states that a transaction of a given type has to exceed $10,000 in order to be reportable. This allows a player to purchase chips in the amount of $10,000, have money play loses up to $10,000, buy back $10,000 worth of markers, make Race and Sport wagers of $10,000, and deposit $10,000 in cash as front money during the casino's 24-hour day—*ALL* without having to prepare an .030 or .040 report.

Regulation 6A and Title 31 were reluctantly accepted by both management and players. It is extremely difficult to approach a player just after he has lost a bet that brought him over the $10,000 threshold and request his driver's license. At this point, the player is in no mood to comply.

Since 1985, players have grown accustomed to Regulation 6A. In the process, many have developed their own ways to avoid reporting. It is not uncommon for today's players to ask the casino personnel what their total is so they can stop their play just before the reporting is necessary or change from one type of transaction to another. Once the player reaches $10,000 in chip purchases, he or she may start betting cash.

It is also important that if the casino has the necessary information on file, the player need not be bothered. Many casinos photocopy a player's driver's license when an application for credit or check cashing is made. If this information is on file, there is no need to ask the patron for identification. Also, once a positive player identification is made for a report, subsequent reports can be made based upon the prior identification.

It is not necessary to inform the player the report is being prepared. It is only necessary if the casino does not know the player and, consequently, must see his or her identification. When first implemented, many casinos felt obligated to notify the player that a report was being prepared. By and large, most casinos now simply prepare the report if the information is available.

Nevada's Regulation 6A provides a uniform method of complying with the regulations of the Treasury. Every casino knows what is expected of it and how to handle every situation.

Title 31 Reporting

Unlike Nevada, where cash for cash over $2,500 is strictly prohibited, other U.S. casinos do not have the same restrictions. However, if the total of the exchange or exchanges exceeds $10,000, a CTR must be prepared. In these jurisdictions, all cash-in is aggregated for the purpose of reporting.

Examples of cash-in are front money or safekeeping deposits, as well as chip purchases in the pit. If a player deposits $5,000 in front money with the cage and then purchases another $5,001 in chips—with cash—in the pit, a report is required under Title 31. Atlantic City's casinos are required to use their casino computer systems for aggregating pit buy-ins and cage transactions.

Title 31 itself does not provide for CTIR. Therefore, *ALL cash-in* and *ALL cash-out* is aggregated separately and, if the cash-in or cash-out exceeds $10,000, preparation of a CTR is mandatory. *ALL cash-out includes winnings,* whereas Nevada's Regulation 6A exempts verifiable winnings.

Nevada's permitting of cash wagers, pit marker redemptions, and aggregating by transaction type has done much to alleviate the negative effects of Regulation 6A. This, along with verifiable winnings required only on the CTIR, has made Nevada's the most easy-to-manage and player-friendly system in the United States.

 *Part Three*

Gaming

Chapter 10

The Mathematics of Casino Games

INTRODUCTION

The purpose of this chapter is to provide a brief look into probability theory and mathematics as they apply to gaming analysis. The chapter looks at probability theory and odds—odds are required to determine specific bet payoffs. Expected value theory is developed for selected table games. Also, selected table games are analyzed to the point that the reader can develop a complete analysis for each one. Five Card Poker is also partially analyzed. The final section of the chapter develops a relationship between "hold, drop, win, and the game PC."

PROBABILITY THEORY AND ODDS

Odds and game payoffs frequently denote the same thing to the player. If the bet payoff is equal to the true odds against the event, the terms have the same meaning. However, the casino manager seldom sets game payoffs equal to true odds. If he or she did, the game value would be zero.

Odds are another format for presenting probability. They are shown as follows, with P being the probability for the game.

$$\text{ODDS} = \left[\frac{1}{P} - 1\right] : 1$$

Odds are always expressed in whole numbers. For example, rather than expressed as 1.4 to 1, they are expressed as 7 to 5. The above relationship is used to express odds against the event. Thus, 7 to 5 against the event means that if a game is played 12 times, the player loses 7 times and wins 5 times. Likewise, if the game payoff for a win is 7 to 5, the player breaks even when playing with the payoff set equal to true odds.

Two additional examples of odds follow. The probability of tossing a 7 with dice is 1/6. The odds are

$$Odds = \left[\frac{1}{\frac{1}{6}} - 1\right] : 1$$
$$= [6 - 1] : 1$$
$$= 5 : 1 \text{ against the event}$$

Confusion develops between odds and payoffs if the odds are incorrectly stated as "6 for 1" for the above example. Incorrectly stated, their meaning is that if the player makes a bet on rolling a 7 on the next toss of the dice, and places a 1-unit bet on the table, this bet belongs to the casino because it has accepted the player's bet. If the player rolls a 7 on the next toss, the casino pays the player a total of 6 units; it is returning the player's original bet plus 5 additional units. The player has gained 5 units with the 1-unit bet. Hence, a payoff of *5 to 1* is equal to a payoff of *6 for 1*. The casino uses the *6 for 1* notation because it appears as a larger win for the player.

In a second example, the probability of rolling a 6 with dice on the next toss is 5/36. Thus, the true odds are shown as *31 to 5* or as *36 for 5*.

$$Odds = \left[\frac{1}{\frac{5}{36}} - 1\right] : 1$$
$$= [36 - 5] : 5$$
$$= 31 : 5 \text{ against the event}$$

Another fact concerning probability theory is that the sum of the probabilities for a game must equal 1. This is shown as

$$\sum P = P_1 + P_2 + P_3 + \ldots = 1$$

The following is also true:

$$EV_{\text{Player}} = -EV_{\text{House}}$$
$$-EV_{\text{Player}} = EV_{\text{House}}$$

where *EV* is the "game expected value." The above simply states that if the player wins, the house loses, and if the player loses, the house wins. This is a "zero sum" game. Casino poker is not a zero sum game when the house takes a percentage or "rake" from the player's pot.

Here is the "game expected value" relationship:

$$EV = P_1 \times O_1 + P_2 \times O_2 + P_3 \times O_3 + \ldots$$

The application of the above equation to the previous example of rolling a 7 on the next toss of the dice follows. Assume that the house pays the player at the *5 to 1* rate.

$$EV = \frac{1}{6} \times 5 + \frac{5}{6} \times (-1)$$

$$EV = \frac{5}{6} - \frac{5}{6} = 0$$

As the casino is paying off at true odds, the expected value is 0. In the next example the payoff is *4 to 1*.

$$EV = \frac{1}{6} \times 4 + \frac{5}{6} \times (-1)$$

$$EV = \frac{4}{6} - \frac{5}{6} = -\frac{1}{6}$$

The expected value is written for the player in the above examples; hence, the player loses 1/6 of each wager each time it is made.

The expected value is used to determine the "house PC" (or P. . . . C . . . .) for the wager. It is shown below for the previous example (*4 to 1* payoff).

$$\text{House PC} = \frac{EV}{\text{Bet}} \times 100$$

Example:

$$\text{House PC} = \frac{+\frac{1}{6}}{1} \times 100 = +16.67\%$$

The above house PC can be expanded to determine the PC for any game and combination of player wagers. Assume that the player bets

Table 10.1 Sample Player Bets in Craps

Bet Type	Bet Amount	Wager PC
Pass	$1500	1.414%
Don't pass	$2000	1.402%
Come-out 7	$500	16.7%
Field	$800	2.7%

shown in Table 10.1 are made; also shown is the amount of each bet and the PC for each bet.

The general relationship for the house PC for the bet types, amounts, and wager PCs in Table 10.1 are

$$\text{House PC} = \frac{PC_1 \times W_1 + PC_2 \times W_2 + PC_3 \times W_3 + PC_4 \times W_4}{W_1 + W_2 + W_3 + W_4} \cdot$$

$$\text{House PC} = \frac{1500 \times 1.414 + 2000 \times 1.402 + 500 \times 16.7 + 800 \times 2.7}{1500 + 2000 + 500 + 800}$$

$$\text{House PC} = 3.2156\%$$

The *house PC* for a specific game or for all casino games should not be confused with other terms in the casino industry. The common terms *hold, drop,* and *win,* are discussed later in this chapter. The house PC expressed in dollars is equal to the house win. The win is the accumulation of all bets, and the theoretical house win is considered for each bet type. House PC should be used as a player evaluator: how players are making bets and what types of bets they are making.

CRAPS, THE GAME

Craps is probably played by more people who do not understand the basic game than any other game in the casino. Blackjack is played by a greater number of people, but most of them understand how to add points and know when they have busted. Many Craps players understand some bets, but not all. Some know how game probabilities are obtained. Fewer players know how to determine the game PC for selected bets, and very few can determine all of the game PCs for all possible Craps bets. Selected game PCs are shown in this section.

"Pass" or "Come" is one of the best bets a player can make in a casino. The house advantage for this bet is only 1.414%.

Pass and Come Wagers

The probabilities of dice outcomes are shown in Table 10.2.

The initial toss of the dice results in one of the following:

1. 7 or 11: Player win.
2. 2, 3, or 12: Player loses.
3. 4, 5, 6, 8, 9, or 10: Player establishes a point.
4. The point must be repeated before a 7 is rolled for the player to win.
5. If the Player rolls a 7 before he or she repeats the point, the player loses.

The point analysis is

1. 4 or 10: 3 chances to win (to make a 4 or 10).
           6 chances to lose (to make a 7).
           9 chances to affect the point outcome.

$$P_4(\text{Win}) = \frac{3}{9} = \frac{1}{3} : \text{Payoff}(+1)$$

$$P_7(\text{Loss}) = \frac{6}{9} = \frac{2}{3} : \text{Payoff}(-1)$$

2. 5 or 9: 4 chances to win (to make a 5 or 9).
          6 chances to lose (to make a 7).
          10 chances affect the point outcome.

$$P_5(\text{Win}) = \frac{4}{10} = \frac{2}{5} : \text{Payoff}(+1)$$

$$P_7(\text{Loss}) = \frac{6}{10} = \frac{3}{5} : \text{Payoff}(-1)$$

Table 10.2   Probability of Dice Outcomes

Number	Probability	Number	Probability
2	1/36	8	5/36
3	2/36	9	4/36
4	3/36	10	3/36
5	4/36	11	2/36
6	5/36	12	1/36
7	6/36	Total*	36/36

*The game payoff is 2 for 1, or 1 to 1.

3. 6 or 8: 5 chances to win (to make a 6 or 8).
6 chances to lose (to make a 7).
11 chances affect the point outcome.

$$P_6(\text{Win}) = \frac{5}{11} : \text{Payoff}(+1)$$

$$P_7(\text{Loss}) = \frac{6}{11} : \text{Payoff}(-1)$$

The expected value of the game for the player is

$$EV_P = \frac{1}{36} \times (-1) \ [2 : \ 1\text{st Roll}]$$

$$+ \frac{2}{36} \times (-1) \ [3 : \ 1\text{st Roll}]$$

$$+ \frac{3}{36} \times \left\{ \frac{1}{3} \times (+1) + \frac{2}{3} \times (-1) \right\} \ [4 : \ \text{Repeat 4 before 7}]$$

$$+ \frac{4}{36} \times \left\{ \frac{2}{5} \times (+1) + \frac{3}{5} \times (-1) \right\} \ [5 : \ \text{Repeat 5 before 7}]$$

$$+ \frac{5}{36} \times \left\{ \frac{5}{11} \times (+1) + \frac{6}{11} \times (-1) \right\} \ [6 : \ \text{Repeat 6 before 7}]$$

$$+ \frac{6}{36} \times (+1) \ [7 : \ 1\text{st Roll}]$$

$$+ \frac{5}{36} \times \left\{ \frac{5}{11} \times (+1) + \frac{6}{11} \times (-1) \right\} \ [8 : \ \text{Repeat 8 before 7}]$$

$$+ \frac{4}{36} \times \left\{ \frac{2}{5} \times (+1) + \frac{3}{5} \times (-1) \right\} \ [9 : \ \text{Repeat 9 before 7}]$$

$$+ \frac{3}{36} \times \left\{ \frac{1}{3} \times (+1) + \frac{2}{3} \times (-1) \right\} \ [10 : \ \text{Repeat 10 before 7}]$$

$$+ \frac{2}{36} \times (+1) \ [11 : \ 1\text{st Roll}]$$

$$+ \frac{1}{36} \times (-1) \ [12 : \ 1\text{st Roll}]$$

$$EV_P = \$ - 0.01414$$

The Come bet is identical to the Pass bet. If the crap table is clear of all previous Pass, Come, or other point-related bets, the next toss of the dice is a Pass bet. If a crap game is in progress—that is, a point has been established and is still on the table—and if the player wishes to make a pass bet on the next toss of the dice, that is called a Come bet. Thus, there can be a total of six point-type bets on the table at one time, as there are six possible points that can be made. There will be one original Pass bet that establishes the first point and five Come bets that establishes the next five points. If this situation exists on the table, and if a 7 is the next roll of the dice, all the point bets will be decided as losses.

Craps: Don't Pass/Don't Come

"Don't pass" is favored by more Craps players than is Pass. Basically, it is the opposite of the Pass bet, with one minor house change. It is this minor change that gives the house its advantage. The game analysis follows:
The game payoff is: *2 for 1*, or *1 to 1*.
    The initial toss of the dice is

1. 2 or 3: Player wins.
2. 7 or 11: Player loses.
3. 4, 5, 6, 8, 9, or 10: Player establishes a point.
4. The Player must roll a seven before the point is repeated to win. If the point is repeated before a 7 is made, the player loses.
5. The 12 is barred with this wager, meaning it does not count.
6. Hence, there are only 35 outcomes with Don't Pass.

Note that it is item 5 that represents the minor change made by the house to change a disadvantage to an advantage. Barring a number is equivalent to a "push," or a no bet. Its effect is shown next.
    The point analysis:

1. 4 or 10: 3 chances to lose (3 ways to make a 4 or 10).
            6 chances to win (6 ways to make a 7).
            9 chances affect the point outcome.

$$P_4(\text{Loss}) = \frac{3}{9} = \frac{1}{3} : \text{Payoff}(-1)$$

$$P_7(\text{Win}) = \frac{6}{9} = \frac{2}{3} : \text{Payoff}(+1)$$

2. 5 or 9: 4 chances to lose (4 ways to make a 5 or 9).
            6 chances to win (6 ways to make a 7).
            10 chances affect the point outcome.

$$P_5(\text{Loss}) = \frac{4}{10} = \frac{2}{5} : \text{Payoff}(-1)$$

$$P_7(\text{Win}) = \frac{6}{10} = \frac{3}{5} : \text{Payoff}(+1)$$

3. 6 or 8: 5 chances to lose (5 ways to make a 6 or 8).
   6 chances to win (6 ways to make a 7).
   11 chances affect the point outcome.

$$P_6(\text{Loss}) = \frac{5}{11} : \text{Payoff}(-1)$$

$$P_7(\text{Win}) = \frac{6}{11} : \text{Payoff}(+1)$$

The expected value of the game for the player is

$$EV_P = \frac{1}{35} \times (+1) \text{ [2 : 1st Roll]}$$

$$+ \frac{2}{35} \times (+1) \text{ [3 : 1st Roll]}$$

$$+ \frac{3}{35} \times \left\{ \frac{1}{3} \times (-1) + \frac{2}{3} \times (+1) \right\} \text{ [4 : 7 before Repeat 4]}$$

$$+ \frac{4}{35} \times \left\{ \frac{2}{5} \times (-1) + \frac{3}{5} \times (+1) \right\} \text{ [5 : 7 before Repeat 5]}$$

$$+ \frac{5}{35} \times \left\{ \frac{5}{11} \times (-1) + \frac{6}{11} \times (+1) \right\} \text{ [6 : 7 before Repeat 6]}$$

$$+ \frac{6}{35} \times (-1) \text{ [7 : 1st Roll]}$$

$$+ \frac{5}{35} \times \left\{ \frac{5}{11} \times (-1) + \frac{6}{11} \times (+1) \right\} \text{ [8 : 7 before Repeat 8]}$$

$$+ \frac{4}{35} \times \left\{ \frac{2}{5} \times (-1) + \frac{3}{5} \times (+1) \right\} \text{ [9 : 7 before Repeat 9]}$$

$$+ \frac{3}{35} \times \left\{ \frac{1}{3} \times (-1) + \frac{2}{3} \times (+1) \right\} \text{ [10 : before Repeat 10]}$$

$$+ \frac{2}{35} \times (-1) \text{ [11 : 1st Roll]}$$

$$EV_P = \$ - 0.014026$$

$$EV_P = -1.4026\%$$

The differences between Pass and Don't Pass is

EV(Pass: player)	–0.014141
EV(Don't pass: player)	–0.014026
Difference	0.000115 in favor of Don't Pass, or 115 out of 1,000,000 games

The meaning of expected value and the percentage of the time the house wins for Don't Pass follows:

$$\%(\text{House}) - \%(\text{Player}) = +1.4026\%$$

$$\%(\text{House}) + \%(\text{Player}) = 100\%$$

$$\%(\text{House}) = 100\% - \%(\text{Player})$$

$$\%(\text{House}) = +1.4026\% + \%(\text{Player})$$

$$+1.4026\% + \%(\text{Player}) = 100\% - \%(\text{Player})$$

$$2 \times \%(\text{Player}) = 100\% - 1.4026\%$$

$$\%(\text{Player}) = \frac{98.4974\%}{2} = 49.2487\%$$

$$\%(\text{House}) = 50.7513\%$$

$$1000 \text{ Games :}$$

$$\text{House wins :} \quad (50.7\% \times 1000) = 507 \text{ Games}$$

$$\text{Player wins :} \quad (49.3\% \times 1000) = 493 \text{ Games}$$

$$\text{House advantage} = 14 \text{ Games}$$

In the previous section, it was determined that with the Pass bet the house would win 50.7% of the time and the player would win 49.3% of the time. This implies that in 1,000 games there is no advantage to the player when betting either Pass or Don't Pass. If one were to make 1,000 consecutive bets, it would require a continuous playing time of approximately seven to eight hours and the dice would be tossed around 3,350 times. To get the advantage, which is the difference between 1.4141% and 1.4026% (0.014141 − 0.014026 = 0.000115), or 0.0115%, one would have to make 10,000 consecutive bets of Don't Pass versus 10,000 consecutive bets of Pass to have an advantage of one more win. Or, from a realistic point of view, if a player played an average of 40 hours per week for 2 weeks, the net effect of Don't Pass and Pass would be $1, if all $1 bets were made. To the casino this has a meaning; but does it have any real meaning to the casual player who may visit a casino two or three times a year?

Pass/Come with Free Odds

"Free odds" means that the house offers a player a bet with which it has no advantage. Mathematically, this means the house expected value is 0. Likewise, if the house expected value is 0, the player's expected value when accepting the bet is also 0. An example of free odds follows.

Pass with Free Single Odds

General Conditions. If the player has established a point with the Pass or Come wager, and if the house offers free Single odds, the house will allow a second wager, normally equal to the first wager, and will pay "full true odds" on it. If the player makes his or her point, the player wins the second bet and is paid off at full true odds and also wins the first bet and is paid off at *1 to 1*. If the player rolls a seven before making the point, he or she loses the second and first bets.

First one must determine the *second bet payoffs*. Full true odds must be determined for each possible point. They are correct true odds for various points are as follows:

4 or 10: True odds are *2 to 1* against the player. Recall that there are three ways to make a 4 or 10 and six ways to make a 7; hence, there are nine outcomes that affect these points, $P_4 = 1/3$. Inserting this probability into the odds relationship, the following results:

$$\text{Odds} = \left[\frac{1}{\frac{1}{3}} - 1 \right] : 1$$

$$= [3 - 1] : 1 = 2 : 1$$

5 or 9: True odds are *3 to 2* against the player. Recall that there are four ways to make a 5 or 9 and six ways to make a 7, so there are 10 outcomes that affect these points, $P_5 = 2/5$. Inserting this probability into the odds relationship, the following results:

$$\text{Odds} = \left[\frac{1}{\frac{2}{5}} - 1 \right] : 1$$

$$= [5 - 2] : 2 = 3 : 2$$

Table 10.3 Payoffs Involving Points

| | Payoff | | | |
Point	1st Wager	2nd Wager	Total	Loss
4 or 10	1	2	3	2
5 or 9	1	1.5	2.5	2
6 or 8	1	1.2	2.2	2

6 or 8: True odds are *6 to 5* against the player. There are five ways to make a 6 or 8 and six ways to make a 7. Therefore, 11 outcomes affect these points, $P_6 = 5/11$. Inserting this probability into the odds relationship, the following results:

$$\text{Odds} = \left[\frac{1}{\frac{5}{11}} - 1 \right] : 1$$

$$= [11 - 5] : 5 = 6 : 5$$

If fractional payoffs are made by the casino, the following payoffs result when points are involved with the Pass bet. Payoffs when points are involved are shown in Table 10.3.

The table shows decimal payoffs. If the player were betting in 10 or 5 units, these payoffs would be multiplied by 10 or 5. "Total" means that the player has won or repeated his or her point before tossing a 7 with the dice. The player's expected value can be determined for a pass bet or free single odds as follows.

$$EV_P = \frac{1}{36} \times (-1) \, [2 : \text{ 1st Roll}]$$

$$+ \frac{2}{36} \times (-1) \, [3 : \text{ 1st Roll}]$$

$$+ \frac{3}{36} \times \left\{ \frac{1}{3} \times (+3) + \frac{2}{3} \times (-2) \right\} \, [4 : \text{ Repeat 4 before 7}]$$

$$+ \frac{4}{36} \times \left\{ \frac{2}{5} \times (+2.5) + \frac{3}{5} \times (-2) \right\} \, [5 : \text{ Repeat 5 before 7}]$$

$$+ \frac{5}{36} \times \left\{ \frac{5}{11} \times (+2.2) + \frac{6}{11} \times (-2) \right\} \, [6 : \text{ Repeat 6 before 7}]$$

$$+ \frac{6}{36} \times (+1) \ [7 : \text{1st Roll}]$$

$$+ \frac{5}{36} \times \left\{ \frac{5}{11} \times (+2.2) + \frac{6}{11} \times (-2) \right\} \ [8 : \text{Repeat 8 before 7}]$$

$$+ \frac{4}{36} \times \left\{ \frac{2}{5} \times (+2.5) + \frac{3}{5} \times (-2) \right\} \ [9 : \text{Repeat 9 before 7}]$$

$$+ \frac{3}{36} \times \left\{ \frac{1}{3} \times (+3) + \frac{2}{3} \times (-2) \right\} \ [10 : \text{Repeat 10 before 7}]$$

$$+ \frac{2}{36} \times (+1) \ [11 : \text{1st Roll}]$$

$$+ \frac{1}{36} \times (-1) \ [12 : \text{1st Roll}]$$

$$EV_P = \$ - 0.01414$$

The effect of free single odds is 0 for the second wager because the house is paying full true odds on the second wager.

While the expected value for the game did not change, the "house percentage" for the game does change. The average bet is determined as follows: one-third of the time the game is completed with the initial toss of the dice—that is, if a 2, 3, 7, 11, or 12 is rolled; and two-thirds of the time the game involves a point and a second wager is made—that is, if a 4, 5, 6, 8, 9, or 10 is initially rolled. Therefore the average bet is

$$\text{Average Bet} = \frac{1}{3} \times \$1 + \frac{2}{3} \times \$2 = \$1.6667$$

$$\%\text{Player} = \frac{-0.01414 \times 100}{1.6667} = -0.84848\%$$

The player reduces the percentage loss by betting larger sums of money, but the expected value for the game does not change. Technically there is no limit to the number of free odds a casino may offer.

Some of the other common craps bets are "Place Bets, To Win and To Lose," the "Big-6," and the "Big 8;" and proposition bets, such as the "Come Out" bets, field bets, and hardway bets.

Combination Betting

There are *two important facts* regarding combination betting: First, the player's PC generally decreases when a proper combination bet is made;

second, the player's expected value for the combination bet is the sum of the expected values for each of the single bets. Both of these facts are shown in the following example of a combination bet.

Assume the player bets Pass and Don't Pass at the same time. The *net effect* of this combination bet is to lose only when a 12 is tossed with the Pass bet. All other dice rolls cancel each other, so the expected value is

$$EV_P = \frac{35}{36} \times (0) + \frac{1}{36} \times (-1) = \$ - 0.02778$$

$$\text{Average bet} = 1 + \frac{35}{36} \times 1 = \$1.9722$$

$$\%\text{Player} = \frac{-0.02778 \times 100}{1.9722} = -1.40858$$

Or, if the expected values for each bet are taken into account, and if the Don't Pass Expected Value is adjusted by the barred 12, the result is as follows:

$$EV(\text{Pass} + \text{Don't Pass}) = -0.01414 + \frac{35}{36} \times (-0.014026) = \$ - 0.02778$$

KENO

The game of Keno has a board of 80 numbers (1 through 80), 20 of which are picked randomly. The player can select from 1 through 15 numbers, and if enough of those match the 20 randomly picked, the player wins. The win payoff depends upon the number of matched numbers.

The examples shown below should further an understanding of game payoffs. The payoffs are examples from one casino, which has the option to change the payoffs in an effort to increase the game play frequency. For this reason many casinos have specials or progressive keno jackpots, which are unique to the individual operation.

Example Keno Bets and Payoffs

One-Number Spot. The player selects one number, which must match one of the 20 drawn numbers. The player has complete freedom in selecting any one of the 80 numbers in the universe. The probability of a win is 20/80.

The Payoff is *3 for 1* or *2 to 1*.

$$P(\text{Win}) = \frac{20}{80}$$

$$P(\text{Loss}) = \frac{60}{80}$$

$$EV_P = \frac{20}{80} \times (+2) + \frac{60}{80} \times (-1) = \$ - 0.25$$

$$\%\text{Player} = -25\%$$

Two-Number Spot. The player selects 2 numbers, and these must match two of the 20 drawn numbers to win. The combination equation is used to determine the potential combinations for both the universe and player wins.

The Payoff: 12 for 1, or 11 to 1. The universe of potential two-spot bets is

$$\frac{80!}{2! \times 78!} = \frac{80 \times 79}{1 \times 2} = 3160$$

And the potential wins are

$$\frac{20!}{2! \times 18!} = \frac{20 \times 19}{1 \times 2} = 190$$

$$P(\text{Win}) = \frac{190}{3160}$$

$$P(\text{Loss}) = \frac{2970}{3160}$$

$$EV_P = \frac{190}{3160} \times (+11) + \frac{2970}{3160} \times (-1) = \$ - 0.27848$$

$$\%\text{Player} = -27.848\%$$

Three-Number Spot. The player selects 3 numbers. If 2 of them match 2 of the 20 drawn numbers, the player wins, and if all 3 numbers match any of the drawn numbers, the player wins an additional amount. The analysis follows:

Payoffs: *Three Numbers:* 42.5 for 1, or 41.5 to 1.

Two Numbers: 1 for 1, or 0 to 1.

The universe of potential three-number bets is

$$\frac{80!}{3! \times 77!} = \frac{80 \times 79 \times 78}{1 \times 2 \times 3} = 82,160$$

The potential three-number wins are

$$\frac{20!}{3! \times 17!} = \frac{20 \times 19 \times 18}{1 \times 2 \times 3} = 1140$$

The potential 2-number wins are

$$\frac{20!}{2! \times 18!} \times \frac{60!}{1!} = \frac{20 \times 19 \times 60}{1 \times 2 \times 1} = 11,400$$

With a 2-number win, two of the numbers must match 2 of the 20 drawn numbers, and the 3rd number can be 1 of the 60 remaining numbers that were not drawn. There are 60 combinations of the 60 remaining numbers not drawn.

The previous percentages are minimum house percentages and assume all players are fully paid at the exact winning payoffs. However, if $50,00 is the maximum total payoff for the house, and if a typical six-spot number is used, the house percentage rises from 28.75% to:

$$\frac{300,450,200}{300,500,200} = +99.93336\%$$

Most casinos offer "Way" tickets, on which a player can bet various combinations. Each Way becomes a separate bet. The total loss is the sum of the expected values for all the individual bets, but the player's percentage loss may decrease. Keno is a game where a player can strike it rich in a couple of minutes, assuming that he or she has a rather large bankroll to start with.

Some casinos offer progressive jackpots, and more than the aggregate $50,000 (some casinos have a $500,000 aggregate payout) can be won by the players. A percentage of each player's bet is added to a progressive jackpot. The house may also elect to reduce its normal payoffs with a progressive game. The probability of hitting the correct combination of numbers is very small for progressive games.

BLACKJACK

Number of Decks and Significance

A casino manager may question the significance of computations with a varying number of card decks for the game of Blackjack. Consider the following examples.

First, a single deck of 52 cards and the probability of drawing a single card from a decreasing deck:

$$\text{First card}: \ P = \frac{1}{52} = 0.0192307$$

$$\text{Second card}: \ P = \frac{1}{51} = 0.0196078$$

$$\text{Third card}: \ P = \frac{1}{50} = 0.020000$$

$$\text{Fourth card}: \ P = \frac{1}{49} = 0.020481$$

$$\text{26th card}: \ P = \frac{1}{26} = 0.0384615$$

Next, two decks, with a total of 104 cards and the probability of drawing a single card from a decreasing deck:

$$\text{First card}: \ P - \frac{1}{104} = 0.0096153$$

$$\text{Second card}: \ P = \frac{1}{103} = 0.0097087$$

$$\text{Third card}: \ P = \frac{1}{102} = 0.0098039$$

$$\text{Fourth card}: \ P = \frac{1}{101} = 0.0099009$$

$$\text{Fifth card}: \ P = \frac{1}{100} = 0.0100000$$

$$\text{52nd card}: \ P = \frac{1}{52} = 0.0192307$$

Next, four decks, with a total of 208 cards and the probability of drawing a single card from a decreasing deck:

$$\text{First card}: \ P = \frac{1}{208} = 0.0048076$$

$$\text{Second card}: \ P - \frac{1}{207} = 0.0048309$$

$$\text{Third card}: \ P - \frac{1}{206} = 0.0048543$$

$$\text{Fourth card}: \ P = \frac{1}{205} = 0.0048780$$

$$\text{Fifth card}: \ P = \frac{1}{204} = 0.0049019$$

$$\text{104th card}: \ P = \frac{1}{104} = 0.0096153$$

Finally, six decks, with a total of 312 cards and the probability of drawing a single card from a decreasing deck:

$$\text{First card}: \ P - \frac{1}{312} = 0.0032051$$

$$\text{Second card}: \ P = \frac{1}{311} = 0.0032154$$

$$\text{Third card}: \ P = \frac{1}{310} = 0.0032258$$

$$\text{Fourth card}: \ P = \frac{1}{309} = 0.0032362$$

$$\text{Fifth card}: \ P = \frac{1}{308} = 0.0032467$$

$$\text{152nd card}: \ P = \frac{1}{156} = 0.0064102$$

While the above shows an apparent, large difference between specific probabilities—for example, one deck (0.0192307) versus six decks (0.0032051)—a common question is, what effect does this have on management control of the game? Most casinos keep records that reflect a 0.0001 level of statistical significance, so in general anything smaller than 0.0001 has a rounding effect. hence, 0.00005 is rounded to 0.0001 and 0.00002 is rounded to 0.0000. Therefore, the fifth or sixth decimal places apparently do not affect the casino hold PC.

Moreover, the casino is probably not too concerned if its hold percentage is 0.2000, 0.2020, or 0.1980, because its statistical standard deviation is approximately 5%, which is 0.0500. If a computer program uses a statistical 95% confidence level, which uses *two standard deviations* for determining a significant mean difference, which is (2 × 0.05) 0.1000, or 10%. In practice, then, the theoretical differences between single-, two-, four-, or six-card decks should have minimal impact on the overall hold percentage, unless the casino has players who are very skillful. Note from the above probabilities that very little difference exists between probabilities when drawing to a full deck versus a decreasing deck. The exception to this is when the wagers are *very large* in respect to the casino total hold or drop.

Example computations in this chapter are rounded to four decimal places, which agrees with most current casino reporting techniques. Some players are concerned about the overall effect of 100 games, which would require a significance level of 0.01, and 0.001 or less has little or no meaning. A significance level of 0.0001 is equivalent to one game out of 10,000 or about 250 hours of casino playing time, which at eight hours per day is about one month of continuous play.

Blackjack, Game Value Analysis

The probability of being dealt a natural blackjack with a single deck is shown below. The "combinations" of natural blackjacks are

$$P_{21} = \frac{64}{1326} = 0.0482654 = 0.0483$$

Hence, about 48 hands out of every 1,000 will have a natural blackjack dealt. If the player is dealt a blackjack, the probability that the dealer will be dealt a blackjack in the same game is (with a decreasing deck):

$$P_{21} = \frac{45}{1225} = 0.0367346 = 0.03647$$

The probability of both the dealer and the player having a blackjack in the same game is

$$0.0483 \times 0.0367 = 0.0017726 = 0.0018$$

or about 2 games in 1,000 that will have a blackjack tie. The above is repeated for two, four, and six decks and is summarized in Table 10.4.

In all of the above cases, the effects of considering a decreasing or full deck are minimized, or 0 per 1,000 games.

Table 10.5 shows the probability of making various point totals and busts when the dealer stands on a Soft 17 for various initial two-card hands. (The totals are weighted averages.) Table 10.6 is a dealer up-card analysis.

Table 10.4 Probability of a Tie with One or More Decks

Number of Card Decks	Player BJ	Dealer BJ	Decreasing Both BJ	Full Both BJ
1	0.0483	0.0367	0.0018	0.0018
2	0.0478	0.0421	0.0020	0.0023
4	0.0476	0.0448	0.0021	0.0023
6	0.0475	0.0456	0.0022	0.0023

Table 10.5 Dealer Must Stand on Soft 17—Point Totals and Busts

Points Two Cards	Hands	Probability of Making					
		21	20	19	18	17	Bust
21	0.0483	1	0	0	0	0	0
20	0.1026	0	1	0	0	0	0
19	0.0603	0	0	1	0	0	0
18	0.0649	0	0	0	1	0	0
17	0.0724	0	0	0	0	1	0
16	0.0649	0.0769	0.0769	0.0769	0.0769	0.0769	0.6155
15	0.0724	0.0828	0.0828	0.0828	0.0828	0.0828	0.5860
14	0.0769	0.0892	0.0892	0.0892	0.0892	0.0892	0.5540
13	0.0845	0.0960	0.0960	0.0960	0.0960	0.0960	0.5200
12	0.0890	0.1034	0.1034	0.1034	0.1034	0.1034	0.4830
11	0.0483	0.3422	0.1114	0.1114	0.1114	0.1114	0.2122
10	0.0407	0.1114	0.3422	0.1114	0.1114	0.1114	0.2122
9	0.0362	0.0608	0.1200	0.1200	0.1200	0.1200	0.2284
8	0.0287	0.0694	0.1286	0.1286	0.3594	0.1286	0.2446
7	0.0241	0.0749	0.0749	0.0618	0.1564	0.3695	0.2625
6	0.0165	0.0972	0.1017	0.1064	0.1063	0.1655	0.4229
5	0.0121	0.1095	0.1140	0.1175	0.1246	0.1234	0.4110
4	0.0044	0.1113	0.1161	0.1202	0.1274	0.1306	0.3944
Soft 16	0.0121	0.1292	0.1292	0.1292	0.1292	0.1292	0.3540
Soft 15	0.0121	0.1346	0.1346	0.1346	0.1346	0.1346	0.3270
Soft 14	0.0121	0.1400	0.1400	0.1400	0.1400	0.1400	0.3000
Soft 13	0.0121	0.1455	0.1455	0.1455	0.1455	0.1455	0.2725
Soft 12	0.0044	0.1510	0.1510	0.1510	0.1510	0.1510	0.2450
Total*	1.0000	0.1213	0.1761	0.1343	0.1395	0.1465	0.2823

Table 10.6 Dealer Up-Card and Dealer Must Stand with Soft 17

Up Card	Probability	Probability of Making					
		21	20	19	18	17	Bust
Ace	0.0769	0.3612	0.1304	0.1304	0.1304	0.1304	0.1172
10	0.3077	0.1114	0.3422	0.1114	0.1114	0.1114	0.2122
9	0.0769	0.0608	0.1200	0.3508	0.1200	0.1200	0.2284
8	0.0769	0.0694	0.0694	0.1286	0.3594	0.1286	0.2446
7	0.0769	0.0741	0.0786	0.0787	0.1378	0.3686	0.2622
6	0.0769	0.0971	0.1017	0.1062	0.1062	0.1939	0.3949
5	0.0769	0.1083	0.1128	0.1164	0.1236	0.1223	0.4166
4	0.0769	0.1113	0.1142	0.1201	0.1273	0.1305	0.3966
3	0.0769	0.1148	0.1201	0.1242	0.1320	0.1351	0.3738
2	0.0769	0.1181	0.1237	0.1282	0.1366	0.1399	0.3535
Total	1.0000	0.1201	0.1800	0.1330	0.1399	0.1473	0.2797

Game Value: Player versus Dealer

Certain assumptions are made about how the player will play the game prior to determining the game value. If one knows how the player is going to play each hand against the dealer, certain assumptions do not have to be made. The basic assumption is that the player follows house rules, that is, he or she attempts to make 17 through 21 points or "bust" on each hand. If this is true a game value can be determined. The General game expected value is shown below.

$$EV_P = P(\text{Player bust}) \times (-1)$$

$$+ P(\text{Player makes } 17-21) \times P(\text{Dealer bust}) \times (+1)$$

$$+ P(\text{Player makes } 17-21) \times P(\text{Dealer makes } 17-21)$$

$$\times \{P(\text{Player win}) \times (+1) + P(\text{Dealer win}) \times (-1) + P(\text{tie}) \times (0)\}$$

$$+ \{P(\text{Player Blackjack}) - P(\text{Player + Dealer Blackjack})\} \times (+0.5)$$

EV_P is the expected value for the player. The first term in the above equation refers to the fact that the player plays first; hence, if the player busts, the game is over.

The second term assumes that if the player does not bust, he or she makes 17 through 21 points and forces the dealer to play. The second part of the second term is the probability of a dealer bust. (Note that in the joint probability relationship, first the player must make 17 through 21 points before the dealer can bust.)

The third term (shown in two lines in the equation) assumes that neither the player nor the dealer busts, so both have 17 through 21 points. If the player has a higher point total than the dealer, the player wins. If the dealer has the higher point total, the player loses. If both have the same point total, there is a tie and the game is a "push."

The fourth term (the last line of the equation) is an adjustment term for a blackjack. The house plays the player *3 to 2 (1.5 to 1)* if the dealer does not have a blackjack. All 21-point hands were included in terms 2 and 3 of the equation with a payoff of +1. The last term corrects the +1 payoff to +1.5 by considering those blackjack hands dealt to the player, less the probability of the dealer having a blackjack at the same time. The additional payoff is +0.5 for these hands.

A series of computations is required to determine the various probabilities needed for several of the above terms.

First Term. The probability of a player bust, taken from Table 10.6, is 0.2823.

Second Term. The probability of a player making 17 through 21 points is also taken from Table 10.6. It is $(1 - P(\text{bust})) = 0.7177$. The probability of a dealer bust is the same as that of the player bust, and it is 0.2823.

Third Term. The probabilities of either the player or the dealer making 17 through 21 points is identical: both 0.7177. If the player has 21 points, he cannot lose but either wins or ties. If the player has 20 points, he loses when the dealer has 21 points, ties when the dealer has 20 points, and wins whenever the dealer has 19, 18, or 17 points. This process continues for player's hands of 19, 18, and 17 points.

Player wins are the probability of the player having various point totals times the probability of winning against all dealer point distributions, calculated as

$$\text{Win Total} = 0.1690 \times 0.8310 + 0.2454 \times 0.5856 + 0.1871 \times 0.3985$$

$$+ 0.1944 \times 0.2041 + 0.2041 \times 0 = 0.3984$$

Player ties, shown below, are the probability of the player having various point totals times the probability of tieing against all dealer point distributions.

$$\text{Tie Total} = 0.1690 \times 0.1690 + 0.2454 \times 0.2454 + 0.1871 \times 0.1871$$

$$+ 0.1944 \times 0.1944 + 0.2041 \times 0.2041 = 0.2032$$

Player losses are the probability of the player having various point totals times the probability of losing against all dealer point distributions:

$$\text{Loss Total} = 1 - \text{Win} - \text{Tie}$$

$$= 1 - 0.3984 - 0.2032 = 0.3984$$

Fourth Term. This is the adjustment term for the higher payoff when the player has a blackjack.

$$P(\text{Blackjack}) = 0.0483$$

$$P(\text{Player Blackjack}) \times P(\text{Dealer Blackjack})$$

$$= 0.0483 \times 0.0483 = 0.0023$$

The results are inserted back into the general equation for the game value. They follow.

$$EV_P = 0.2823 \times (-1) + 0.7177 \times 0.2823 \times (+1)$$

$$0.7177 \times 0.7177 \times \{0.3984 \times (+1) + 0.2032 \times (0) + 0.3984 \times (-1)\}$$

$$+ \{0.0483 - 0.0023\} \times (+0.5)$$

$$= -0.0567, \text{ or about } -5.67\%$$

Many casino managers feel that a good Blackjack player significantly reduces the casino's advantage from 5.67% to about 1% to 2% by applying various strategies and by card counting. In some cases, the card counter may also have an advantage if the deck becomes favorable to the player. A common technique used by many casino managers who allow card counters to play is to restrict all of the player's bets to their first bet.

ROULETTE

Introduction

Some casino managers agree with the myth that certain roulette dealers (*croupiers*) can control the spin and movement of the ball to place it in some wheel number slots. If specified numbers are involved, this is a myth. But what if the dealer, through ball spin, wheel revolutions per minute, and ball release, controls the quadrant the ball will come to rest in? Is this possible? Many dealers claim it is. It may have occurred in Las

Vegas in a roulette game in 1988. An unnamed player was betting $1,000 chips, one at a time, but placing a series of bets all in one quadrant, and was over $500,000 ahead in less than 10 hours of play. According to probability theory, this "win" was possible but unlikely. Many casino supervisors were not too concerned with the win as long as the player continued to play. Others were very concerned, concerned enough to do things that would discourage the player from continuing play. Naturally, if the player quit, the casino would be the loser. During the next 6-hour period, the player lost back to the casino about $150,000, but was still ahead by over $1/3 million. The concerned supervisors were not content with the losses they recaptured, so they made the fatal mistake of replacing the wheel, claiming that it must be out of balance. The player cashed in his chips and walked out with over $1/3 million in cash after 16 hours of continuous play.

Did the casino do the right thing? There was nothing wrong with the wheel that was replaced. Flaws could not be found with the dealers. Was it chance? Was it a controlled spin? Was it an experienced dealer? Was it a new type of wheel spin combined with ball release? Was it mathematically possible? Yes, it was. Would it repeat? Yes, it would.

The following analysis is based on a wheel with both the 0 and 00. Example bets are indicated and their expected values are developed.

Roulette Bets

The Straight-Up or Single-Number Bet. The player is betting on a single number. If any other number appears, he loses. The normal payoff for the bet is *35 to 1*. The usual maximum bet allowed in Nevada for this bet is $1,000.

There are 38 outcomes for the game, and so the following is true:

$$P(\text{Win}) = \frac{1}{38}$$

$$P(\text{Loss}) = \frac{37}{38}$$

$$EV_P = \frac{1}{38} \times (+35) + \frac{37}{38} \times (-1) = \$ -0.0526$$

$$\%\text{Player} = -5.25\%$$

The Split Bet or Two-Number Bet. The player is betting that one of two adjacent numbers will appear. The payoff for this bet is *17 to 1*.

$$P(\text{Win}) = \frac{2}{38}$$

$$P(\text{Loss}) = \frac{36}{38}$$

$$EV_P = \frac{2}{38} \times (+17) + \frac{36}{38} \times (-1) = \$ - 0.0526$$

$$\%\text{Player} = -5.26\%$$

The Street Bet or Three-Number Bet. The player is betting that one of three numbers in a line and adjacent to the middle number will appear. The payoff for this bet is *11 to 1*.

$$P(\text{Win}) = \frac{3}{38}$$

$$P(\text{Loss}) = \frac{35}{38}$$

$$EV_P = \frac{2}{38} \times (+11) + \frac{35}{38} \times (-1) = \$ - 0.0526$$

$$\%\text{Player} = -5.26\%$$

The Column Bet or Twelve-Number Bet. The player is betting that one of 12 numbers in the same column will appear. The payoff for this bet is *2 to 1*.

$$P(\text{Win}) = \frac{12}{38}$$

$$P(\text{Loss}) = \frac{26}{38}$$

$$EV_P = \frac{12}{38} \times (+2) + \frac{26}{38} \times (-1) = \$ - 0.0526$$

$$\%\text{Player} = -5.26\%$$

The Red- or Black-Number Bet. The player is betting that either a red number will appear *or* a black number will appear. The numerals 0 and 00 are not considered to be numbers in Roulette and have a green background. The payoff for this bet is *1 to 1*.

$$P(\text{Win}) = \frac{18}{36}$$

$$P(\text{Loss}) = \frac{20}{36}$$

$$EV_P = \frac{18}{38} \times (+2) + \frac{20}{38} \times (-1) = \$-0.0526$$

$$\%\text{Player} = -5.26\%$$

All of the above game percentages are reduced by one-half if 00 is eliminated.

BACCARAT, THE GAME

Baccarat is an interesting game of rules—one set of rules for the player and another set for the bank. Unlike blackjack, one may bet as the player or as the bank prior to any cards being dealt. In a normal Baccarat game, the minimum bet is usually $20, and all the betters around the table can bet on the "player's hand" or on the "bank's hand." With a bet on the bank's hand, if the hand wins, there is a 5% commission against the player win, so 5% of the minimum bet of $20 is a $1 commission. There is no card counting system developed to date that can significantly affect the game's house PC.

Baccarat is a big-money game. Many Las Vegas casinos have special Baccarat areas, semi-separated from the main casino area, and some even have completely segregated areas where the game is played for $100,000 to $250,000 per hand. While it is a low-percentage house game (close to 1% house advantage), it is extremely possible for either the house or the player to have a 10-hand win margin over the other, resulting in a $1 to $2.5 million house win or loss after a 10-hour session. Many casinos report their "house hold," or PC, with and without Baccarat. Personal fortunes have been lost by Baccarat players because they think they cannot be hurt if the house only has a 1% advantage.

Baccarat can be played with one to eight decks of cards.

Card Values and Counts

The card suit, such as ♥♦♣♠, has no value. All suits are equal. Ace through 9 are counted as face value, so Ace = 1, 5 = 5, and 9 = 9. The normal 10-point cards (from Blackjack), such as 10, J, Q, and K have no value and are equal to 0. The same rule applies to 10-point hands when adding the value of the cards as shown below. Thus, a 9 and a 6 have a value of 5 points, not 15. This is because 15 = 10 + 5, and the 10 has 0 value.

$$10 + 10 = 0$$
$$10 + 1 = 1$$
$$10 + 9 = 9$$
$$7 + 7 = 10 + 4 = 4$$

The Initial 2-Card Hands

Both the player and the bank are dealt two cards. The initial distribution of possible 2-card hands is extremely important to properly analyze the game. As a single 52-card deck is used as the computational base, the potential number of 2-card hands must be determined. That number is

$$\frac{52!}{2! \times 50!} = \frac{52 \times 51}{1 \times 2} = 1326$$

The 2-card hands and corresponding probabilities are shown in Table 10.7.

Game Analysis

The expected value for the game when betting on the player is as follows (the house pays *1 to 1*):

$$EV_P = 0.4582 \times (-1) + 0.0959 \times 0 + 0.4459 \times (+1) = \$-0.0123$$
$$\%\text{Player} = -1.23\%$$

Table 10.7 Probabilities of Initial 2-Card Hands and Bank "Win, Tie, and Loss"

2-card points	Probability			
	Hands	Win	Tie	Win
9	0.0965	0.9035	0.0935	0
8	0.0935	0.8100	0.0935	0.0965
7	0.0965	0.5703	0.1443	0.2854
6	0.0935	0.4305	0.1401	0.4292
5	0.0965	0.4046	0.0850	0.5101
4	0.0935	0.3518	0.0860	0.5618
3	0.0965	0.3249	0.0805	0.5944
2	0.0935	0.3099	0.0782	0.6116
1	0.0965	0.2938	0.0785	0.6276
0	0.1433	0.2750	0.0809	0.6437
Total	1.0000	0.4582	0.0959	0.4459

However, many authors report a slightly higher house game advantage by ignoring the ties. If there is an adjustment for ties, the following expected value results:

$$EV_P = \frac{0.4582 \times (+1) + 0.4459 \times (-1)}{1 - 0.0959} = \$ - 0.0136$$

$$\%\text{Player} = -1.36\%$$

The player can also bet on the bank. If he does, there is a 5% charge (commission). The expected value, including ties, follows:

$$EV_P = 0.4582 \times (+0.95) + 0.0959 \times 0 + 0.4459 \times (-1) = \$-0.0106$$

$$\%\text{Player} = -1.06\%$$

Note that the win is not $1, but $1 less the 5% commission, that is, only $0.95 for each $1 bet.

Once again, many authors report a higher negative value because they make an adjustment for ties. Their analysis follows.

$$EV_P = \frac{0.4582 \times (+0.95) + 0.4459 \times (-1)}{1 - 0.0959} = \$ - 0.0117$$

$$\%\text{Player} = -1.17\%$$

Baccarat is a low-percentage game for the player, but it is not played that frequently in a casino, probably because of the minimum bet requirements (frequently $20). Some casinos have attempted to change the commission in an effort to improve player betting. However, usually when attempts are made to alter the basic game, the player has to give up something in exchange. Lowering the commission requires players to lose ties; they are no longer pushes. Very large casino bets are frequently allowed in Baccarat; however, the casino must be prepared to lose large amounts of money. It is entirely possible for the player to win 10 more hands than she loses after a large number of hands (700 in a 10-hour session). At $100,000 or more a hand, the potential casino win or loss could be $1 million or more, a very probable event. A small casino can not afford such a one-day loss, even though probability is on its side for a large number of sessions.

5-CARD POKER

Most Poker analysis is based on the 5-card hand and initial 5-card deal. The ranking of hands is based on the probability of being dealt various 5-card hands from a 52-card decreasing deck. Unfortunately, this same ranking is also used for all variations of Poker, including 7-card hands and wild-card versions of the game. The ranking is used even when an extra card, typically the Joker, is added to the deck, making it 53 cards. If probability theory is used to rank the hands, different rankings should be established for each of these games. However, this would add confusion to the game. A good Poker player is aware of the changing probability relationships and will play his hands with this added knowledge and usually win more hands than his or her opponents.

There are many types of Poker. Only the basic mathematical concepts relating to playing-card distributions are shown in this chapter. Poker games and rules generally vary from one geographic region to another, but the ranking of various Poker hands remains fairly constant. The ranking exceptions generally apply to games in which there are more than one wild card.

There are *13 ranks of cards*. The normal ranking starts from the highest-ranked card and proceeds to the lowest-ranked card: Ace (A), King (K), Queen (Q), Jack (J), 10, 9, 8, 7, 6, 5, 4, 3, 2, and [Ace (A)]. Note that A can be the highest-ranking card or the lowest. Suits generally are not ranked; one suit does not over-rank another as in some card games, such as bridge. The suits are Spades (♠), Hearts (♥), Clubs (♣), and Diamonds (♦). As there are 4 suits and 13 ranks for each suit, there are (4 × 13) = 52 different cards in the playing deck.

Number of 5-Card Hands

The universe of 5-card hands that can be dealt from a 52-card deck follows.

$$\frac{52!}{5! \times 47!} = \frac{52 \times 51 \times 50 \times 49 \times 48}{1 \times 2 \times 3 \times 4 \times 5}$$

$$= 2,598,960 \text{ combinations}$$

5-Card Poker Rankings

Selected examples of the initial deal of 5-card Poker hands are shown below.

Royal Flush. The best 5-card Poker hand is the royal flush. It is the highest-ranked cards from one suit, dealt in any order—for example, A♥-K♥-Q♥-J♥-10♥. The possible number of royal flush hands that can be dealt follow.

$$\frac{1!}{1! \times 0!} \times \frac{1!}{1! \times 0!} \times \frac{1!}{1! \times 0!} \times \frac{1!}{1! \times 0!} \times \frac{1!}{1! \times 0!} = 1 \times 1 \times 1 \times 1 \times 1 = 1$$

$$P = \frac{1}{2,598,960}$$

Any Royal Flush

$$P = \frac{4}{2,598,960}$$

Four of a Kind. The following is an example of four of a kind: A♣-A♥-A♦-A♠ X. The X can be any of the remaining 48 cards. The possible number of Ace four-of-a-kind hands follows.

$$\frac{4!}{4!} \times \frac{48!}{1! \times 47!} = 1 \times 48 = 48 \text{ each rank}$$

13 Ranks

$$13 \times 48 = 624$$

$$P = \frac{624}{2,598,960}$$

Full House. The hand A♥-A♦-A♣-K♠-K♥ is an example of a full house. This hand must have three of a kind plus a pair. Naturally, as there are four As, only three are necessary, and as there are four Ks, only two are required to produce the example full-house hand.

$$\frac{4!}{3! \times 1!} \times \frac{4!}{2! \times 2!} \times \frac{44!}{0! \times 44!} = 24 \text{ Combinations}$$

13 Ranks 3 Kind

12 Ranks 2 Kind

$$\text{Total} = 24 \times 13 \times 12 = 3744$$

$$P = \frac{3744}{2,598,960}$$

Three of a Kind. The hand A♥-A♦-A♣-XY is the highest-ranking three-of-a-kind hand that can be dealt. The lowest ranking three-of-a-kind hand is 2-2-2-XY. XY are any two other nonpaired cards; naturally, one of these cards cannot match the three of a kind. The computation for three of a kind will include full houses, so an adjustment is made to eliminate these hands. The computation follows.

$$\frac{4!}{3!\times1!} \times \frac{48!}{2!\times46!} = 4512$$

13 Ranks

Less Full Houses : 3744

$$Total = 4512 \times 13 - 3744 = 54,912$$

$$P = \frac{54,912}{2,598,960}$$

One pair. The hand A♥-A♠-XYZ is an example of a one-pair hand, with XYZ three different ranked cards that do not match the pair. The first computation determines the following number of hands for this specific combination: A-A-K-Q-J.

$$\frac{4!}{2!\times2!} \times \frac{4!}{1!\times3!} \times \frac{4!}{1!\times3!} = 384$$

13 Ranks of Pairs

Combinations of 12 Ranks 3 at a Time

$$\frac{12!}{3!\times9!} = 220$$

$$Total = 384 \times 13 \times 220 = 1,098,240$$

$$P = \frac{1,098,240}{2,598,960}$$

Table 10.8 is a summary of all possible 5-card hands that can be dealt from a 52-playing card deck (Bridge or Poker).

5-Card Draw Poker Analysis

The current most popular slot machine is 5-card video Draw Poker. While similar casino games have been available for years as mechanical flip card machines, they never gained the popularity of the current video versions. The casino can also have bonus payoffs; the common example is the royal flush if the player inserts a maximum number of units (coins). Another common bonus is a progressive jackpot. Payoffs other than the royal flush

Table 10.8 Summary of 5-Card Hands That Can Be Dealt from a 52-Card Deck of Bridge or Poker Cards

Hand	Number
Royal Flush	4
Straight Flush	36
4 of a Kind	624
Full House	3744
Flush	5108
Straight	10200
3 of a Kind	54912
2 Pair	123552
Pair	1098240
No Pair	
A high	502860
K high	335580
Q high	213180
J high	127500
10 high	70380
9 high	34680
8 high	14280
7 high	4080
Total	2598960

are multiple payoffs, meaning that if the payoff for two pairs is *2 for 1* for one unit of play, it will be *10 for 5* for five units of play.

One reason for the popularity of Video Poker is that the game requires some level of player skill, which is totally lacking in all other slot machine games. The player should know the best way to improve his hand after the initial 5-card deal.

HOLD, WIN, AND DROP

Hold, win, and *drop* are invented terms used to evaluate casino operations. At times there is considerable confusion regarding their meaning. Casino managers generally look for terms that can be applied to their operations and that will provide a fair evaluation of their efforts. The basic relationship between hold, win, and drop is

$$\text{Hold} = \frac{\text{Win}}{\text{Drop}}$$

The actual definitions of the above terms are established by the government agency having jurisdiction over gaming. The following definitions are used in Nevada.

$$\text{Hold} = \text{Closing Bank} + \text{Credit Slips Cage} + \text{Drop}$$
$$- \text{Opening Bank} - \text{Fills}$$
$$\text{Drop} = \text{Total(\$)} + \text{Chips} + \text{Tokens} + \text{Credit Slips}$$

Hold is a critical term. Casino holds for different games are frequently compared, and many casino managers are evaluated by their average casino hold for all games. One problem is, what is an ideal hold? The following example may assist in determining what is ideal.

$$\text{Purchase}: \$10,000 \text{ chips}$$
$$\text{Drop} = \$10,000$$
$$\text{Player loss} = \$10,000$$
$$\text{Win} = \$10,000$$
$$\text{Hold} = \frac{\$10,000}{\$10,000} = 100\%$$

Ask yourself, "Is the above good for the casino? The players?" The answer should be *NO!* A casino with a 100% hold will not have customers.

Win is a term that depends on four variables for each game. These variables are the type of bet, the bet amount, the bet frequency, and the bet percentage (PC). If a player makes large bets, the win should be high, as it should if a player makes the same bet over a long time. If the bet PC is high, the win may be high. Naturally, a large win is important to the casino manager, but it may not always generate a large hold. Table 10.9 shows typical holds for selected games in Nevada and New Jersey.

The major difference between Nevada and New Jersey holds is in the handling of credit slips purchased back by the player. In Nevada this can be done at the table where the credit slip originated; in New Jersey, credit slips can only be repurchased in the casino cage.

The relationship between hold and the house PC can only be estimated. The house PC is the game percentage advantage for the house. While there is a specific house PC for each type of bet, Table 10.10 indicates an average House PC for normal player bets in New Jersey.

The house PC is important when one considers how many bets must be made to generate a specific win for the house. Two examples each generate the same win, but each has a different average bet. Figures 10.1 and 10.2 show the number of bets that must be made to generate the specified win.

Table 10.9   Typical Holds

Game	Hold	
	Nevada	*New Jersey*
Blackjack	18.9%	15.8%
Craps	18.4%	15.8%
Roulette	27.9%	24.7%
Big-Six	53.2%	47.5%
Baccarat	21.3%	14.8%
House average	19.7%	16.5%

Table 10.10   Average House PC in New Jersey

Game	Hold	House PC
Blackjack	15.8%	1.33%
Craps	15.8%	1.33%
Roulette	24.7%	2.63%
Big-Six	47.5%	15.0%
Baccarat	14.8%	1.25%

Goal: WIN = $1000

BET = $500

Game	Number
Baccarat	160
Blackjack	150
Craps	150
Roulette	76
Big-Six	13

Figure 10.1   Casino Win and Bet Frequency on a $500 Bet

Goal: WIN = $1000

BET = $100

Game	Number
Baccarat	800
Blackjack	750
Craps	750
Roulette	380
Big-Six	67

Figure 10.2 Casino Win and Bet Frequency on a $100 Bet

Both figures clearly show that the amount and bet frequency are important and must be considered for specific house wins. Gaming analysis is very difficult if one must keep track of each bet type and amount. If the casino manager did this, however, he or she could accurately compute the actual win and hold for each game. As this information is not recorded, an alternative approach must be taken. One technique is to graph the house PC and the hold, as shown in Figure 10.3.

It is apparent from the figure that games with a high house PC should be offered by the casino to generate a large hold. However, experience has shown that players do not make large bets or frequently play games with a high house PC. This can be verified by looking at the house win for each

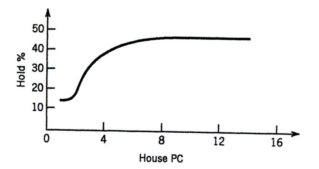

Figure 10.3 Game PC versus Hold Percentage

of the previous games. Generally, games with lower house PCs generate higher wins.

Figure 10.4 shows the development of a game "factor." Figure 10.5 shows average factors for New Jersey that are dependent on the house PCs shown above. Note that factors are probably different for each casino because of the types of bets, average bets, and the frequency of each type of bet, all of which are dependent on the types of players in the casino.

Figure 10.6 shows that low house PCs are related to large factors. A large Factor implies either a combination or all of the following: high bet frequency and a high average bet.

The casino manager's goal should be to generate high factors. Figure 10.6 also shows that high factors are generated with games or bets that

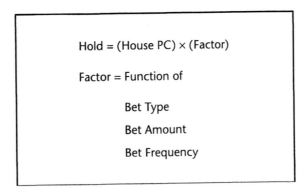

Hold = (House PC) × (Factor)

Factor = Function of

Bet Type

Bet Amount

Bet Frequency

Figure 10.4 Game Factor Development

Game	Factor	House PC
Blackjack	10.5	1.33
Craps	10.5	1.33
Roulette	9.39	2.63
Big-Six	3.17	15.0
Baccarat	11.8	1.25

Figure 10.5 Game Factors for Selected Casino Games in New Jersey

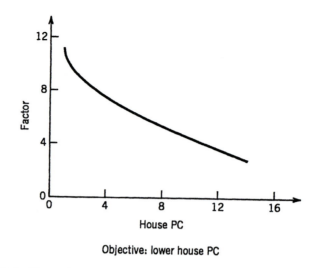

Objective: lower house PC

Figure 10.6   House (Game) PC versus "Factor"

have a low house PC. In other words, players are looking for "fair games." Players may also practice money management. Such players look for games that have low house PCs. However, some look for games that have a high payoff, such as the "Mega-Buck" slot machines. In practice casino games should offer both types of bets for the player: those that have a low house PC and those that have a high payoff regardless of the house PC.

SUMMARY

This chapter concludes with a recommendation for the casino: Make the game fair for the player. The player recognizes fair games and generally plays these games for longer periods than games with a high game PC, except for games with a very high win ratio (keno and Mega-Bucks slot machines). Players can analyze games and will readily play one if their analysis is correct and different than the casino's.

REFERENCES

There are numerous gaming and gambling books, but they may be difficult to obtain unless one is located in a legalized gaming area such as Nevada or Atlantic City, New Jersey. Many probability texts include gaming references because gaming is applied probability theory. Much of the current emphasis in gaming books is on betting systems, since people want to know how to beat the theory.

In addition, most gaming books are short-run publications. That is, a limited number of books are printed and when they are sold out, there is rarely a second production run. Thus, the book goes out of print. Finally, many excellent books were written in Europe and are in a foreign language. Only selected references are listed below.

Three Excellent References for Many Games

Frank D. Borsenik, *Mathematics of Casino Games: Hotel Administration C436* (correspondence course). Reno, NV: Division of Continuing Education, Independent Study Department.

Darwin Ortiz. *Darwin Ortiz on Casino Gambling.* New York: Dodd, Mead & Company, 1986.

Edward W. Packel. *The Mathematics of Games and Gambling.* The Mathematical Association of America, 1981.

General Casino Books

J. Edward Allen. *Beat the Odds.*

Frank Barstow. *Beat the Casino.*

John Gollehon, *Casino Games.*

Dr. Edward O. Thorp. *The Mathematics of Gambling* (a very good reference text).

John Scarne. *Scarne's New Complete Guide to Gambling* (also a very good reference text).

Alan Wykes. *Complete Illustrated Guide to Gambling* (published in England).

Baccarat

Russell T. Barnhart. *Bankers Strategy at Baccarat Chemin de Fer, Baccarat en Banque and Nevada Baccarat* (a very good reference text).

Blackjack

Edward O. Thorp. *Beat the Dealer* (very good).

Peter Griffin. *The Theory of Blackjack* (1988 ed.) (very good).

Craps

John Scarne. *Scarne on Dice* (very good).

Keno, Roulette, and Slots

See the books listed as "excellent references" for appropriate treatment of these games.

Probability

Lester E. Dubins and Leonard J. Savage. *Inequalities for Stochastic Processes* (very good).
Murray R. Spiegel. *Statistics* (very good).
Richard Epstein. *Theory of Gambling and Statistical Logic* (very good).

Poker

Doyle Brunson, *Super System: A Course in Poker Power* (very good).
Dave Sklansky. *Winning Poker* (very good).

Card Games, General

John Scarne, *Scarne on Cards*; also *Scarne's Encyclopedia of Card Games* (very good).
The United States Playing Card Company. *Official Rules of Card Games*.

This list is not intended to be complete. For example, sports and handicapping are not included. The books I have noted as very good do provide a mathematical analysis to prove percentages and "systems." Thousands of publications cover personal gaming experiences, but these are not included here. Nevertheless, the above books should provide one with an excellent reference library.

Utility Analysis of Gaming Motivation

What motivates people to gamble? One might answer that money is the motivation—it is plausible that a gambler is motivated by the expected monetary gain or the expected value of the game. However, the expected values of casino games are always to the advantage of the house. Otherwise, how can casinos pay off all kinds of expenses and still earn profits? There must be something beyond expected value that motivates the player to participate in gambling. This chapter introduces the expected utility theory that explains the motivation of gambling. The theory was first proposed by some mathematicians in the eighteenth century.

THE EXPECTED VALUE OF A GAME

The conventional analysis of gambling is based on the expected values of games. The expected value of a game is defined as the sum of the outcomes multiplied by their relevant probabilities. Mathematically, it is

$$EV(g) = \Sigma P_i O_i$$

where

$EV(g)$ is the expected value of the game.
O_i is the ith outcome.
P_i is the probability of the ith outcome.

The expected value of a game is always negative for the player and positive for the casino house. The absolute values of the two are exactly the same. Therefore, what the player loses equals what the house wins. If the expected value of a game for the player is 0, then the game is "fair." It has "true odds" against the player. But fair game would earn zero revenue for the casino, so the casino cannot afford to provide players with fair games. If casino games were all fair, the casino would be out of business.

To earn revenue for the casino, games must be "unfair," to the advantage of the house.

The "unfairness" of casino games is well known to the players. The players, however, knowingly play the "unfair" games. Evidently, the expected value of a game does not explain why people gamble. Early in the eighteenth century, the motivation of gambling puzzled many scholars who tried to use expected value to explain it but failed. A typical example is the "St. Petersburg Paradox," an experimental game first designed by mathematician Nikollaus Bernoulli of Switzerland in the eighteenth century. Unlike today's casino games, the St. Petersburg experiment has odds to the advantage of the player or a positive expected game value for the player. To play the game, the player tosses a coin with one side of heads and the other side of tails. The player continues to toss the coin until the heads side lands upward on the ground and the game is over. The player is awarded one ducat (Swiss currency in the eighteenth century) if he or she has heads at the first toss, two ducats if heads appear at the second toss, four if at the third, eight at the fourth, and so forth. Each additional toss will double the amount of the prize. To maximize the prize, the player wants to see heads appear as late as possible. The purpose of the experiment was to determine the fair price at which the player was willing to play the game.

The expected value of the game is the sum of possible outcomes multiplied by their probabilities. The prize for the game earned at the nth toss is 2^{n-1} ducats. If the coin has heads at the first toss, the prize is one ducat (2^{1-1}) and the probability of the outcome is $1/2$, since the coin has only two sides. The probability to have tails at the first toss is also $1/2$. If the player does not get heads at the first toss, he or she is allowed to toss a second time. The prize for having heads at the second toss is two ducats, or 2^{2-1}. Isolated from the first toss, the probability of heads at the second toss is still $1/2$, since the second toss is completely independent of the first one. The joint probability of tossing heads at the second toss but not at the first is $1/4$ ($1/2 \times 1/2$), or $1/2^2$. The joint probability of having heads at the third toss but not at the previous tosses is $1/8$ ($1/2 \times 1/2 \times 1/2$). Therefore, the joint probability that heads will not appear until the nth tosses should be $1/2^n$. Table 11.1 illustrates the possible outcomes and corresponding prizes of the coin-tossing game.

The expected value of the game can be shown as:

$$EV(g) = 1/2 \times 1 + 1/4 \times 2 + 1/8 \times 4 \ldots + 1/2^n \times 2^{n-1} + \ldots$$
$$= 1/2 + 1/2 + 1/2 + \ldots + 1/2 + \ldots = \infty$$

As shown in the above equation*, the expected value of the game is

_____

*From Levy, 1984, by permission of Prentice Hall.

Table 11.1   Probabilities and Prizes of the St. Petersburg Game

nth Flip at Which Heads First Appear	Outcome (H—Heads T—Tails)	Probability of the Outcome	Prize (Ducat)
1st	H	$1/2$	1
2nd	TH	$1/4$	2
3rd	TTH	$1/8$	4
4th	TTTH	$1/16$	8
5th	TTTTH	$1/32$	16
.	.	.	.
.	.	.	.
.	.	.	.
nth	$(n-1)$TH	$1/2^n$	2^{n-1}

Reprinted with permission of Prentice Hall.

infinity. It appears that, based on the criterion of expected value, any price charged for playing this game would be a fair one. It is always a fair game whatever the price is.

An experiment was conducted among a group of university students to determine the prices that people would be willing to pay for the game. The results show that most were willing to pay only two or three ducats; The maximum price was eight ducats. The contradiction between the expected value of the game and the price that people were willing to pay for the game is the "St. Petersburg Paradox."

In reality, no one can pay an infinite amount of money for playing such a game. Theoretically, the game could continue forever and the prize could grow infinite. Most people, however, will pay a small amount of money for a ticket to play the game. Obviously, what motivates people to play a gambling game is not the expected value of the game but something beyond that.

THE EXPECTED UTILITY OF A GAME

The expected value analysis does not explain why people gamble. The motivation of gambling is explained by the utility theory, which was first proposed by some famous mathematicians of the eighteenth century.

Bernoulli's Utility Function

Bernoulli's solution to the St. Petersburg Paradox is that expected utility, rather than expected value, is involved in peoples' decisions to participate in a game. The utility of a gambling game can be defined as the satisfaction derived form it. It is a function of the monetary gain or loss (w) from the game.

The basic idea of Bernoulli's utility function, a logarithmic function ($U(w) = \alpha \log w/\beta$), is that the utility derived from additional money decreases as the player's wealth increases. Therefore, while the total utility or satisfaction from the game increases as the winnings increase, the marginal utility or pleasure decreases. The expected utility of a game is the sum of the utility of each outcome multiplied by its probability.

Based upon Bernoulli's utility function, the expected utility of the St. Petersburg game, which has an infinite expected monetary value but has uncertainty associated with the outcomes, is equivalent to the expected utility of two ducats with absolute certainty. Since the individual is sure to lose the two ducats for the ticket, the probability associated with the two ducats is 100%. The individual is willing to pay no more than two ducats because the game can derive an expected utility only equivalent to the expected utility of the two ducats with certainty. The logarithmic utility function provides a satisfactory solution to the St. Petersburg Paradox. For an individual with the Bernoulli logarithmic utility function in its general form, the expected utility of the game is

$$EU\,(w) = \alpha\log 2 - \alpha\log \beta = \alpha\log 2/\beta$$

where α and β are coefficients for different individuals.

Therefore, the expected utility of the game is the same as the individual's expected utility he or she can derive from two ducats with certainty, or a probability of 100%, whatever the coefficients α and β may be. If an individual's satisfaction is featured with Bernoulli's utility function, the individual will be equally satisfied with the St. Petersburg game with uncertain outcomes or with two ducats in hand, since the two events have exactly the same expected utility. Therefore, the maximum price that the individual is willing to pay for playing the game is two ducats.

Cramer's Utility Function

Another mathematician of the 18th century, Gabriel Cramer, proposed a different utility function as a solution to the St. Petersburg paradox. Cramer's utility function describes an individual's utility as the square root of monetary value:

$$U(w) = w^{1/2}$$

Like Bernoulli's utility function, Cramer's utility function shows that incremental wealth brings in decreasing marginal utility. Thus, if a player who has Cramer's utility function is asked to pay for playing the St.

Petersburg game, he or she is only willing to pay the money that will generate utility equal to the game's expected utility, which, in this case, is between two and three ducats.

Both utility functions explain mathematically why most people are willing to pay only two or three ducats for playing the St. Petersburg game, which has an infinite expected value. The two solutions show that players are motivated to gamble by the expected utility of a game rather than its expected value. If the expected utility of the game is greater than the expected utility loss on the ticket cost, people will play. If the expected utility loss is greater than the expected utility of the game, people will not play.

UTILITY FUNCTION AND GAMBLING DECISION

Gambling is a risk-taking behavior. There are three types of individuals with different attitudes toward risk: risk-averse, risk-neutral, and risk-taking. An individual's decision to participate in games is affected by his or her attitude toward risk.

Risk Averter's Utility Function

An individual characterized by Bernoulli's or Cramer's utility function is typically a risk-averter.

For an individual with the Cramer utility function, the utility derived from different wealth or monetary gain is demonstrated in Table 11.2.

It is a utility function with diminishing marginal utility. Graphically, the function is concave with positive first derivative and negative second derivative (Figure 11.1). For a risk-averse individual with such a utility function, additional wealth will bring in increasing satisfaction but at a decreasing rate. Will a risk-averter gamble? Consider this example: If the

Table 11.2 Utility Derived from Monetary Gain Based on Cramer's Utility Function

Monetary Gain (w)	Utility $U(w) = w^{1/2}$
$1	1.00
$5	2.24
$10	3.16
$20	4.47
$30	5.48
.	.
.	.
.	.

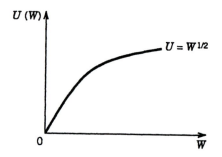

Figure 11.1 Risk-Averter's Utility Function

individual characterized by Cramer's utility function is offered a lottery ticket that costs $10 and has a 20% chance to win $50 and an 80% chance to win nothing, will he or she buy the lottery ticket? The expected value of the lottery game is equal to the price of the ticket. This is a fair game, or a game with true odds. Based upon the expected value criterion, the individual may be willing to participate in the lottery game. Based upon the expected utility theory, however, the game is less than the utility of the $10 the person has to pay for the ticket. Using Cramer's formula, $U(w) = \sqrt{w}$, the expected utility of the $10 is

$$U(w) = \sqrt{w}$$
$$= \sqrt{10}$$
$$= 3.16$$

where w is the monetary value of the ticket. The value 3.16 is the expected utility loss on the cost of the ticket.

The expected utility gain from the lottery game is $1.41(0.8 \times \sqrt{0} + 0.2 \times \sqrt{50})$, less than the expected utility loss on the ticket. Therefore, this risk-averse individual is not likely to buy the lottery ticket. In fact, he or she may not want to participate in the game even if the prize is raised. Assume the prize is now doubled at $100 and the chance of winning the prize remains 20 percent. The expected value of the lottery game is $20 $(0.2 \times \$100 + 0 \times \$10)$, twice the price of the lottery ticket. The game is now an "unfair" game to the advantage of the player. According to the expected value criterion, the individual will definitely participate in the game. Nevertheless, the expected utility gain from the game is $2(0.8 \times \sqrt{0} + 0.2 \times \sqrt{100})$, still lower than 3.16, the expected utility loss on the ticket.

Based upon the expected utility of the game, a risk averter with diminishing marginal utility may not want to gamble even when the expected value of the game is greater than its price. For this type of individual, less money with certainty may be preferable to more money with uncertainty. For this individual, $10 with certainty is more valuable than $50 or $100 with uncertainty.

The Risk-Neutral Individual's Utility Function

While the risk averter's utility function is featured by diminishing marginal utility, the utility function of a risk-neutral individual is linear with constant marginal utility. It has positive first derivative, but zero second derivative. For a risk-neutral individual, additional money will generate greater satisfaction, and the satisfaction will increase at a constant rate as wealth increases. Will a risk-neutral individual gamble? Let's answer the question by analyzing his or her utility function. A simple example of risk-neutral utility function has the form:

$$U(w) = \alpha w$$

where α is a positive constant (Figure 11.2).
The expected utility loss on the lottery ticket is

$$EU(\$10) = (1.00) \times U(\$10) = 10 \times \alpha = 10\alpha$$

The expected utility gain from the game is $10\alpha(0.8 \times 0 + 0.2 \times 50\alpha)$, exactly the same as the expected utility loss on the ticket. Therefore, the risk-neutral individual should be indifferent; he or she may or may not participate in a fair lottery game whose expected value is the same as the

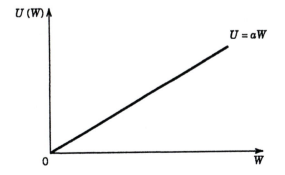

Figure 11.2   Risk-Neutral Utility Function

price of the ticket. However, he or she will not buy the lottery ticket at a price greater than the expected value of the game. If the ticket price is $11, the expected utility loss on the ticket, 11α, will be greater than the expected utility of the game, and he or she will not play.

Risk Taker's Utility Function

The utility function of a risk-taker is convex with positive first and second derivatives. It features increasing marginal utility. In other words, each additional dollar of gain brings in greater incremental satisfaction for the risk taker.

A simple example of a risk taker's utility function is $U(w) = w^2$, which has as its first derivative $U'(w) = 2w$ and as its second derivative $U''(w) = 2$. Figure 11.3 shows the graph of the utility function.

It can be seen that as the risk taker's wealth increases, his or her utility increases at an increasing rate. For the risk-loving individual, the expected utility loss on the ticket is

$$EU(\$10) = (1.00) \times U(\$10) = (1) \times 10^2 = 100$$

The expected utility gain from the game is $1,250(0.8 \times 0 + 0.2 \times 50^2)$, far greater than the expected utility loss on the ticket. Therefore, the risk taker will definitely buy the lottery ticket. He or she is even willing to participate in an "unfair" lottery game that has an expected value to his or her disadvantage. Assume that the prize of the previous game is reduced to $30 and the probability of winning remains 20%. The expected value of the game is now

$$EV = (0.8) \times \$0 + (0.2) \times \$30 = \$6$$

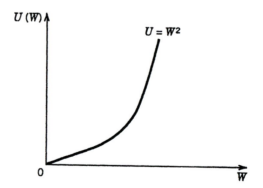

Figure 11.3   Risk-Taker's Utility Function

Table 11.3 Risk Attitudes and Game Participation

Type	U'(w)	U''(w)	EU(g)	vs.	EU($10)	Gamble
Risk-Averter	> 0	< 0	EU(g)	<	EU($10)	No
Risk-Neutral	> 0	= 0	EU(g)	=	EU($10)	Indifferent
Risk-Taker	> 0	> 0	EU(g)	>	EU($10)	Yes

which is less than the ticket price, $10. For this risk taker, the expected utility gain from the game is $180(0.8 \times 0 + 0.2 \times 30^2)$, still greater than the utility loss on the ticket even though the game becomes "unfair." Table 11.3 summarizes the risk attitudes of the three types of individuals.

WILL A RISK AVERTER GAMBLE

Millions of people participate in gambling, either by buying lottery tickets or by going to casinos. Are they all risk takers? Do they all have convex utility functions with positive first and second derivatives? If they do, their marginal utility of money must increase as their wealth increases, and this seems to contradict the reality. In reality, most people consider a dollar on a rainy day more valuable than a dollar when they are wealthy. It is appropriate to assume that most people are rational risk averters whose marginal utility decreases as their wealth increases. Their utility functions should be concave. The fact that most people are risk averters makes the presumption that all gamblers are risk takers implausible.

It is also plausible that most gamblers are covered by various kinds of insurance, and buying insurance is a typical risk-averse behavior. This again contradicts the presumption that all gamblers are risk takers. The fact that risk averters may participate in games cannot be explained by their utility function. The next section introduces three hypotheses that attempt to explain why risk averters can play gambling games.

The Subjective Utility Hypothesis

One of the hypotheses that explains risk averter's participation in gambling is the subjective utility hypothesis, which holds that the player's expected utility is not based upon the objective or true probability of the game, but on the player's subjective or biased beliefs about the probabilities of the game. Yarri (1965) hypothesized that an individual's subjective probability tends to be higher than the objective probability when the objective probability is low, and lower than the objective probability when the latter is high. The essence of the hypothesis is that the player has a tendency to believe what is contrary to the reality. Because of the subjective probability assigned by the risk averter to a game, he or she may have higher expected utility than the true expected utility of a game.

Consider a roulette game with 0 through 36 on the wheel: The player bets on a single number. If the wheel stops at the number, the player wins. The payoff ratio, which is set by the casino house, is typically *35 to 1 or 36 for 1*. Since the wheel is equally divided by 36 radii, the objective probability of winning the game is 1/37, and the objective probability of losing the game is 36/37. Also assume that the player will bet $10 if he or she decides to play the game. If the player wins, he or she will win $350. If he or she loses, the loss will be the bet, $10.

Based upon the objective probabilities of roulette, the game expected utility for the risk averter is negative. Gambling implies a loss of utility, and so the risk averter will not play.

Now assume that the risk-averse player has a *subjective* probability of winning the game of 3/37 and a subjective probability of losing of 34/37. Applying the subjective probabilities to the game, the player's subjective expected value is

$$EV = \left(\frac{3}{37}\right) \times \$350 - \left(\frac{34}{37}\right) \times \$10$$

$$= \$28.35 - \$9.19$$

$$= \$19.16$$

The expected value becomes positive when the objective probabilities are replaced by the subjective probabilities. With this subjective probability, or this misconception of the probabilities, the risk-averse individual can have positive expected utility from the roulette game, and thus he or she may play it. In reality, many players participate in gambling simply because they feel that they have "good luck." When such feelings prevail, players tend to use their subjective probabilities to replace objective probabilities. Subjective probability is often a result of casino or lottery administration's publicizing of the numbers and names of winners. Repeated advertising can mislead people in their judgment about the "true odds" of a game and encourage them to participate in gambling.

The Two-Segment Utility Function Hypothesis

The expected values of casino games are typically negative for the players. According to the expected utility theory, a risk averter will never participate in a fair game, let alone the unfair casino games that are to the advantage of the house.

To explain the same individual's two conflicting behaviors—gambling, a risk-taking behavior, and buying insurance, a risk-averse behav-

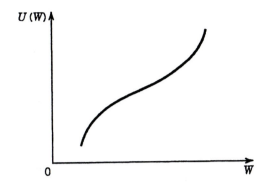

Figure 11.4   Two-Segment Utility Function

ior—Friedman and Savage (1948) proposed that the utility functions for individuals may have two segments, one concave and the other convex, as demonstrated in Figure 11.4. The shape of the utility function changes from concave to convex as the wealth of the individual increases.

Individuals in the concave segment are less wealthy—they are not likely to participate in gambling. Individuals in the convex segment are wealthier and are likely to participate. Individuals in the middle segment (or the middle class) have utility functions very close to a linear function. They may buy insurance and participate in gambling at the same time, having the features of both risk averters and risk takers.

The Pleasure-of-Gambling Hypothesis

This hypothesis assumes that the gambler derives his or her utility not only from the monetary gain or loss but also from the nonmonetary pleasure of gambling. With two variables determining the utility, the utility function is represented as shown in Figure 11.5.

The points on the same curve represent equal levels of utility. The same level of utility, such as U3, can result from small monetary gain with great pleasure, such as point A, or more monetary gain with less pleasure, such as point B. The curves that are farther from the origin, represent higher levels of utility. U1 and U2 are higher levels of utility than U3. Higher levels of utility can be achieved by increasing either pleasure or wealth, or both.

The essence of the pleasure-of-gambling hypothesis is that the gambler's utility is a multivariate model, and the utility loss on money lost can be compensated by the utility gain from the pleasure of gambling. The utility of gambling is actually a combination of the utility of the game itself and the pleasure amenities associated with it. Free drinks and meals,

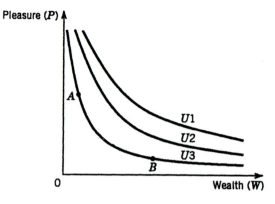

Figure 11.5 The Pleasure of Gambling *Reprinted with permission of Prentice Hall.*

free or low-rate rooms, and free circus shows (such as those in Circus Circus Casino Hotel in Las Vegas) are examples of amenities that can increase gambling pleasure.

Given a negative expected value and a negative expected utility, a risk averter will probably not play. But if the casino provides the incentive of a free amenity, such as a drink, whose probability is 100%, the risk averter may change his or her mind. While the expected value of the game and the drink combined may still be negative for the risk averter, the expected utility can become positive. Therefore, the risk-averse individual may be willing to play the game and enjoy the free drink. The player's negative expected value implies a positive expected value for the casino, or the casino's win revenue.

SUMMARY

The purpose of this chapter is to analyze the motivation of gambling using the expected utility theory. Different hypotheses with regard to the gambler's utility function are discussed and numerical examples are presented.

A typical gambler is a risk taker whose utility function is featured by increasing marginal utility of wealth. He or she may participate not only in fair games but also in unfair games, which is to the advantage of the house. The increasing marginal utility of wealth implies that the more he or she wins, the greater the satisfaction he or she enjoys. This type of gambler is not likely to quit when winning, since big wins can stimulate a strong desire for even greater winnings.

A risk-neutral individual's utility function is represented graphically by a straight line. For this individual, additional wealth brings in more satisfaction at a constant rate. He or she will be indifferent to fair games, but will not participate in unfair games that are to the advantage of the house.

Theoretically, a risk averter is a nongambler who has a concave utility function with decreasing marginal utility. He or she will never participate in an unfair game that is to the advantage of the house or in a fair game. The risk averter may not even participate in an unfair game that is to his or her advantage. In reality, not many people are irrational risk lovers whose marginal satisfaction increases as wealth increases. Most people have decreasing marginal utility of wealth, which characterizes a risk averter's utility function.

While gambling is a risk-taking behavior, the gaming market is probably composed mainly of risk averters. For the gaming industry to increase its revenues, it must encourage risk averters to participate. There are two ways to promote games among risk averters. One is to raise their subjective probability; the other is to increase gaming amenities. The more profitable way of promoting gaming among risk averters is to raise their subjective probability of winning and consequently raise their subjective expected utility. Increasing gaming amenities may cost more than the efforts aimed at increasing potential gamblers' subjective probability and reduce the profitability of the gaming operation. To avoid harming profitability, increasing gaming amenities to attract players should be kept within a reasonable range. Gaming operations should search for the optimum level of amenities at which the combined expected value is still negative for players while the expected utility is positive.

An individual's attitude toward risk is affected by his or her wealth, as indicated in the two-segment utility function hypothesis. When an individual becomes wealthier, the graph of his or her utility function tends to become convex, and his or her behavior may incline toward risk taking. International gaming promotions should focus on newly wealthy regions, such as Hong Kong and Thailand, and those experiencing fast economic growth, such as China and Brazil. Wealth is the garden soil of risk takers, and the rapidly growing wealth in those regions will cultivate increasing number of gamblers. The potential for the development of new gaming markets is tremendous, and the U.S. gaming industry should seize the new opportunities.

BIBLIOGRAPHY

Alchian, A.A. The Meaning of Utility Measurement, *American Economic Review* (March 1953).

Bernoulli, D. Exposition of a New Theory on the Measurement of Risk, *Econometrica* (January 1954).

Friedman, M., and L.J. Savage. The Utility Analysis of Choices Involving Risk, *Journal of Political Economy* (August 1948).

————. The Expected Utility Hypothesis and the Measurability of Utility, *Journal of Political Economy* (December 1952).

Levy, H. and M. Sarnat. *Portfolio and Investment Selection: Theory and Practice.* Englewood Cliffs, N.J.: Prentice-Hall, 1984.

Markowitz, H.M. The Utility of Wealth, *Journal of Political Economy* (December 1952).

Nevada State Gaming Control Board *Nevada Gaming Abstract*, 1993.

Senneti, J.J. Bernoulli, Sharp, Financial Risk and the Petersburg Paradox. *Journal of Finance* (June 1976).

Von Neumann, J., and O. Morgenstern. *Theory of Games and Economic Behavior.* Princeton, N.J.: Princeton University Press, 1947.

Yaari, M.E. Convexity in the Theory of Choice Under Risk, *Quarterly Journal of Economics* (May 1965).

Part Four

Casino Management and Gaming Education

Chapter

12

Gaming Management and the College Curriculum

Gaming education may rank among the more controversial issues faced by hospitality educators. Many schools (and their state funding agencies) currently struggle with the social, legal, economic, and moral issues that arise when exploring gaming curricula. The controversy that surrounds gaming as an industry is not unique. The oil industry, commercial fishing, and meat packing all have colorful pasts filled with rough characters, questionable business practices, and irresponsible treatment of the environment.[1] Similarly, educators and others in new and potential gaming jurisdictions have expressed concern about the social welfare and behavioral problems characterized by addictive gambling behavior and reckless spending habits that some claim surround the current growth of gaming in the United States.[2] Further, questions about the desirability of gaming as an entertainment industry are being addressed in town halls and state legislatures. In the end, it is the people of each state or jurisdiction who must decide the fate of gaming in their area. When that happens, and it is projected to continue to happen,[3] it will be the job of educators to provide leadership in legal oversight, certification, and professionalism for this new entertainment industry.

GAMING COMES TO THE PEOPLE

> People enjoy gambling and state governments like and need the revenue (G. Vallen, 1993)

Despite the controversies, the explosive growth of the gaming industry in this country and the resulting increase in gaming career opportunities makes it increasingly important to address the issue of gaming in hospitality education. Seventy years ago gambling was banned in all states. From 1931 to 1989, casino gaming was legal in only New Jersey and

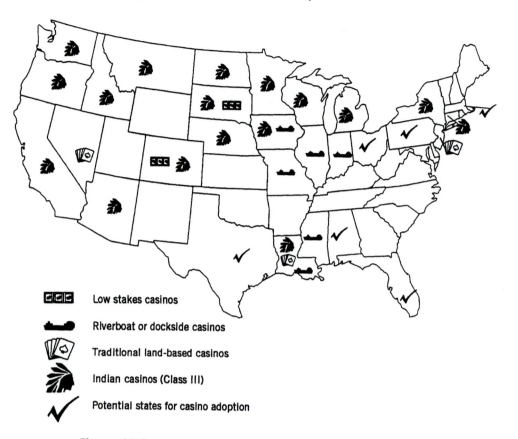

Low stakes casinos

Riverboat or dockside casinos

Traditional land-based casinos

Indian casinos (Class III)

Potential states for casino adoption

Figure 12.1 Expanding Numbers of Gaming Operations Prompt the Need for Employees with Gaming Education

Nevada. Since 1989, however, the number of states authorizing casino operations has mushroomed to nearly two dozen.[4] Six more states have a high probability of passing legislation in 1994 or 1995[5] (see Figure 12.1). By the year 2000, 95% of all Americans are expected to live within a 3- to four-hour drive of one or more casinos.[6] While they may not yet have casinos, jurisdictions in 48 states (all but Utah and Hawaii) allow gaming in some form.[7]

Legalized casino gaming began in Nevada in 1931, with the single addition of Atlantic City in 1976. Two events influenced the rapid increase in the number of gaming jurisdictions:

1. In 1988, the Federal Indian Gaming Act became effective, declaring that once a state has legalized any form of gambling, the Native Americans in that state have the right to offer the same game without governmental restrictions.

2. In 1989 the people of Deadwood, South Dakota, and the State of Iowa voted for legalized gaming. By 1991 the first riverboat was operational in Iowa.

These were the true bellwethers of the expansion of gaming. Since that time nearly two dozen states have passed casino-type gaming (including traditional, slots only, and riverboat casinos as well as Native America gaming).[8] Further, while gaming operations are growing regionally, residents in all parts of the country are boosting the popularity of such operations. A breakdown of the total visitors to casinos in 1994 shows that 24% were from the West, 28% from the North Central region, 23% from the Northeast, and 25% from the South.[9] Additional statistics support the increase in the popularity of gaming:

- The number of U.S. households that gambled in a casino was up from 17% in 1990 to 30% in 1994.[10] U.S. households made 125 million visits to casinos in 1994, nearly three times the number of visits in 1990.[11]
- Sixty-six million of the 125 million visits were to traditional gaming destinations (Las Vegas, Reno, Atlantic City). New destinations (riverboats, Native American gaming jurisdictions, and low-stakes casinos) accounted for 59 million visits.[12]
- In 1993, 74% of adults in the United States considered a visit to a casino to be a fun night out.[13] This rose to 82% in 1994.

The growing popularity of gaming ensures a bright future for this industry. A 1993 study conducted by Home Testing Institute and Yankelovich Partners, Inc., projected that Native American gaming revenues will triple from 1993 to 1997. Additionally, the study indicated that riverboat gaming revenues of 1 billion dollars in 1992 will quadruple by the year 2002, and land-based casino gaming will be legal in 13 states by the year 2002.[14]

The employment and career opportunities in the industry appear strong. Many jobs demand specialized skills and training, and a deficit in trained and experienced employees currently exists. The need to prepare individuals to work in this industry is apparent.

Implications for Hospitality Education

As casino gaming moves from the loose-cash business "that couldn't lose" in the 1950s to "the growth industry of the 1990s,"[15] professional managers will be needed to direct this growth. As regulation increases and competition heats up, professional management skills will be an important contribution to success—perhaps even the difference between the profitable and the bankrupt. In addition to expanded career opportunities for students, gaming education provides the opportunity to contribute to the professionalism of gaming as an industry.

Expansion of Gaming Education in the Hospitality Management Curriculum

Until recently, only a few programs in the country included gaming education in their curricula. It is not a surprise that those programs were located in or near one of the traditional gaming jurisdictions of Nevada and Atlantic City. The state system in Nevada has offered gaming-related courses at its two universities as well as in the community college system for more than 20 years. On the other side of the country, programs in New Jersey and a few surrounding states have included gaming courses in their curriculum for at least 17 years. Currently, programs in Texas, Colorado, Missouri, Michigan, Mississippi, Pennsylvania, New Jersey, Nevada, New York, and Indiana either offer specific gaming courses, are developing such courses, or are integrating gaming industry issues into existing courses.[16] However, important considerations should be weighed when planning and developing courses in this unique area.

EDUCATION AND CAREERS

Gaming Education and Career Success

In professional programs such as hospitality administration, business, and the like, education planners generally have an obligation to consider the entry-level employment and long-term career options for which students are to be prepared. Accordingly, the mission statement of the institution and department or program should serve as a guide to understanding the program's purpose and level of responsibility. In the case of gaming curricula, two questions should be addressed:

1. For what gaming career opportunities do we expect a graduate of this program to be qualified?
2. Does the gaming industry employment market warrant inclusion of all aspects of this program?

The answers to these questions may depend on the regulations within the local or regional gaming jurisdiction. For example, in the state of Nevada all casinos must include hotel rooms, therefore, it makes sense to address aspects of gaming in hotel courses as well as in specific gaming courses. Other programs may find themselves sandwiched between jurisdictions with differing regulations and therefore differing needs. Moreover, a program may be faced with difficult choices concerning the courses that can be offered, given limited financial, faculty, and content resources.

Education certainly is an investment. Hospitality education, including gaming education, is no exception. This education requires time, money, hard work, opportunity cost, and risk, so the program must be relevant to the career needs of its students. For that reason there are at least four critically important roles that general and gaming education play in supporting the gaming industry careers of students.

First, education fundamentals such as reading, writing, speaking, arithmetic, and problem solving, as well as knowledge about the surrounding world, are foundations in life and work. Education specific to gaming can enhance this infrastructure by further developing the knowledge, skills, and abilities (KSAs) needed for success. These could include providing familiarity with the language of gaming and an awareness of gaming issues (knowledge), developing prowess with gaming tools and conventions (skill), and identifying and refining innate aptitudes and talents (ability) such as capability in solving gaming-related problems. The gaming industry seeks KSAs in terms of competencies. Concretely, employers view competencies as an individual's ability to take his or her KSAs and apply them to accomplish a given task, such as supervising staff, preparing a report, or analyzing a statistical question.

Second, education is a potential gaming industry launch pad. Today, it is a key to advancement toward positions of higher responsibility, visibility, challenge, and compensation. For this reason, many people who entered the gaming industry with little related education are returning to classes.

A third role of gaming education is the improved vision it offers when the student returns to the job. There is a saying that a person with 20 years of experience may really have only one year of experience—repeated 20 times. By providing exposure to new ideas and procedures, and promoting evaluation and feedback for continuous improvement on the job, education can boost experience to become its own education. The combination of professional education and experience that involves working with people, things, money, or timelines, or that requires problem solving and decision making, is the quintessential education. Thus, it is not surprising that employers frequently select the student with *good* grades combined with strong, relevant, experience over the student with *excellent* grades and no experience.

Never has the fourth role of education been more important; that role is *lifelong learning.* Educational growth allows students to stay abreast of career opportunities and changes. Because of the dynamism in our society and economy, few people entering the workforce in the nineties and the twenty-first century will start and end their working careers in the same industry. Even today, many people have a series of careers and subcareers, some of which are related and others unrelated to previous positions. Those expecting to remain gainfully employed are well advised to continue this investment in the form of continuing education and self-development. Among the most useful techniques are the formal methods of classes, seminars, and workshops, as well as less formal methods such as conferences, associations, media (books, computer and video, etc.), and mentoring.

A Gaming Career

Education can mean the difference between a career and a job. While the terms *career* and *job* are often used synonymously, in the context of educational preparation they take on separate connotations. In this sense, references to a gaming industry "career" reflect the idea of a planned progression in responsibility and expertise, as in "climbing the career ladder." Often a career involves one or more college degrees in preparation for a profession such as accounting or administration. This does not contradict the fact that most hospitality graduates can expect to begin in an entry-level role. Also, from an entry position it is not unusual for a gaming career to span a wide range of diverse roles (from dealing cards to supervising security), numerous departments, and several parent companies. But each experience can provide exposure to and understanding of complementary and competing operations, and about a variety of strategies and styles to support a successful long-term career.

In contrast to career, the term *job* refers less to an occupation and more to entry-level, repetitive tasks of relatively modest status or prestige. In this interpretation, a job usually does not require a college degree, although it may involve specialized training and require a particular knowledge, skill, or ability. Typically the wage for a job is relatively low, and in patron service jobs income may derive substantially from tips. Gaming examples of jobs include serving beverages, cleaning gaming devices, cashiering, and operating games that require little skill to present.

Gaming Education for Advancement: Why Not?

For those interested in gaming management and education, it is important to consider some reasons that individuals often stay in entry-level jobs for much of their working life. First, elective education, including technical school or college, is not affordable to all. Nor does such schooling appeal to everyone. Instead, individuals are often sufficiently comfortable with the earnings, expectations, and working conditions that a repetitive, predictable job offers. Second, many individuals lack the basic language and mathematical skills, or have physical, emotional, or mental limitations such that an entry-level job best suits their needs or abilities. Third, some employees genuinely lack the time for self-development or job hunting, perhaps because they are a single parent, work multiple jobs, or have other intense time demands. Additionally, some employees remain in entry-level jobs because they believe they have "topped out" and simply have no idea of how to progress.

Unfortunately, there also is always a group that seems to lack the courage to try to move ahead, refusing to study, seek promotions and transfers, or apply for other alternatives, fearing failure or reprisal. Finally, particularly difficult are those who have poor performance records and are therefore either unsuitable for promotion or do not remain with one employer long enough to progress. Some of these individuals may not be receptive to education, training, or other support, and therefore perpetuate their entry-level existence. However, many of the traditional barriers attributed to career success can be overcome through educational interventions.

PROGRAMS AND COURSES

Formal Formats for Gaming Education

Given the variety of employment opportunities emerging for those who do choose formal gaming education, two- and four-year college programs, as well as technical and vocational schools, are introducing gaming course content to prepare students for gaming industry careers.

The knowledge, skills, and abilities needed for careers in specific industries highlight the importance of orienting a gaming program toward industry-specific subjects and skills. Table 12.1 provides a glimpse of gaming and related career opportunities. Viewing alternative program orientations in this format can provide curriculum ideas relevant to student needs. Although some gaming programs may choose to emphasize the administrative and accounting elements, others the mechanics of the games, and still others technical support areas, no single educational program has the resources to prepare for all gaming industry possibilities. Planners must allocate resources with purpose and intelligence.

Community (Two-Year) College, Technical, and Vocational Programs

Two-year or community, college programs with a gaming component typically include vocational and technical courses and also offer college preparatory courses. Though they serve community students interested in one or more classes, they also offer a range of Associate of Arts (two-year college) degrees in gaming-allied areas such as business, hotel, or food and beverage administration. As shown in Table 12.1, column A, a gaming-oriented two-year program might provide formal technical

Table 12.1 Examples of Gaming and Gaming-Related Employment Opportunities

(A) Potential Gaming Positions— Two-Year Degree	(B) Related Careers— Two- or Four-Year Degree	(C) Potential Gaming Positions— Four-Year Degree
Dealer for casino table and dice games	Hotel management	State lottery operations or pari-mutuel operations management
Cage cashier or clerk	Facilities management	Pit and/or slot operations or management
Slot technician	Lounge/cabaret entertainer	Gaming accounting, auditing, and internal control
Gaming surveillance	Food and beverage production/service	Gaming regulation and enforcement
Slot route operations	Computer technology specialist	Gaming marketing and marketing research

preparation in, for example, cage (banking) operations, specific game procedures, or security and surveillance specialties.

The duration of these programs varies widely. Programs often specialize in preparing students for very specific positions (an example of this might be a short course in dealing the card game Twenty-One). Others may require one or more years, preparing students for a skilled trade occupation like maintenance and repair of gaming devices such as slot, lottery, and video poker machines. Note that vocational-technical occupations often are hands-on: repairing the video terminal, preparing food, and so forth.

Column B of Table 12.1 lists a sampling of occupations that may be accessible for a two-year or four-year degree program, but for which one might prepare with little or no formal *gaming* education. For example, the administrative assistant could prepare in a business or clerical program.

A general college prep curriculum directed toward hospitality or business administration generally is the most appropriate avenue for two-year students interested in transferring to a four-year gaming-oriented program. If gaming electives are available at the two-year institution, taking one or two prior to transferring is recommended. A strong performance therein could test a student's interest in gaming, provide a head start on industry knowledge, and strengthen his or her college application.

Four-Year College Programs

Column C of Table 12.1 lists selected gaming industry employment possibilities for those graduating from four-year baccalaureate programs. In contrast to technical or two-year programs, baccalaureate programs focus to a greater degree upon gaming operations management or professional support careers rather than on technical or trade positions. A curriculum with a gaming management emphasis generally strives to prepare students for entrance as a gaming operations assistant supervisor, management trainee, or in a support staff position (e.g., auditing), parallel to the preparation provided by a traditional general business or hospitality administration degree.

As noted earlier, entry into the gaming industry may be in a hands-on position such as dealer or accounting clerk even with a baccalaureate degree. This is especially likely for students with only slight exposure to gaming in their college program or for those with little actual gaming industry experience. Why? First, gaming is both specialized and complex; a basic-level position should provide valuable learning time. Second, until recently relatively few gaming operations existed, few educational programs included gaming, and even fewer programs mandated gaming experience and internship work. Thus, in order to survive, the tradition in gaming operations has been that supervisory and other managerial and gaming specialist positions generally came through promotions from within or by drawing the best employees away from rival operations. Only in the last few years have gaming operations begun to look to higher education for entry-level talent. And because the gaming industry is expanding so rapidly, those in a proven gaming organization who combine a quality education with consistent performance and self-development, are likely to find themselves rewarded with a wide variety of advancement opportunities.

Gaming Courses and Subjects

Table 12.2 provides a list of major gaming subjects distilled from the suggestions of expert gaming practitioners and educators, as well as from the curricula of leading college gaming programs. As presented, the gaming subjects are conceived as potential courses in a program with numerous elective or required gaming course offerings. They also can be adopted as subjects to be combined with or integrated into other courses. This list is by no means a comprehensive inventory of possibilities, but rather gives priority educational needs.

Table 12.2 organizes gaming subjects based on their content as well as their specificity to gaming. Column A lists gaming topics that essentially

Table 12.2 Selected Gaming Subjects or Courses

(A) *Refocus the Familiar*	(B) *Games and Gaming*	(C) *Unique to Gaming* *(Nongames)*
Orientation to the gaming industry	Dealing games of chance (cards, dice)	Gaming in Indian nations
Casino *operations* (I&II)	Mathematics of games	Gaming regulation and control
Riverboat gaming *operations*	Protection of games of chance	Casino cage operations
Gaming *marketing*	Slot machine operations	Gaming technologies
Accounting in the gaming industry	Pari-mutuel and charitable games operations	Casino security and surveillance
Gaming *internship*	Race and Sports Book Management	Sociology of gaming

refocus familiar hospitality courses to gaming-specific content. Italicized words indicate subjects that may already be present in the curriculum in a general form. For example, simply substitute *Hotel, Hospitality,* or *Food & Beverage* for the nonitalicized portion of the title; then "Orientation to the Gaming Industry" refocuses to become "*Orientation* to the Hospitality Industry."

Column B of Table 12.2 suggests subjects involving games of chance, as well as expertise relating to games. "Mathematics of Games," for example, includes instruction in gaming-related statistics; students would learn such applications as how to determine the expected house win, given a particular type of poker game and rule set. Since the games are the product sold by the gaming industry, it is important for managers to understand probabilities and why the games provide the expected revenues.

Finally, column C of Table 12.2 lists subjects other than the games themselves that are more or less unique to the gaming industry. Most courses in column C probably would be provided within the main college or department, but other colleges also may contribute. Thus, a Sociology department might be most qualified to provide a course in the sociology of gaming.

Gaming Education Specialization and Proximity Considerations

As planners delve into the details of subject matter and courses, decisions must be made regarding the exact nature of the gaming curriculum. Should it prepare students for careers in specific segments of the gaming industry? Or should the preparation be more general? This may depend upon the gaming labor market to be addressed, national or local. Some programs may direct their program toward a nationwide gaming preparation, not specific to any particular environment or jurisdiction. Others may recognize and be instrumental in preparing a workforce for a specific gaming job market, typically one in local, state, or nearby gaming jurisdictions. Again, these issues can be guided by a program's mission statement in conjunction with feedback from potential gaming industry employers. The answer also must be a function of the vitality of the overall gaming and labor markets, and of the proximity of potential gaming employers to the institution.

Illustrating the above, a program within or near a jurisdiction that permits parimutuel betting and charitable gaming but disallows casino gaming, might offer course content specific to those gaming activities and operations. In contrast, the gaming curriculum for a program imbedded in and/or nearby one or more casino or riverboat gaming areas might provide courses and gaming subject relevant to these operations. Although the two educational programs should have many gaming fundamentals in common, in other ways casino and riverboat operations differ substantially from parimutuel and charitable operations. A well-planned curriculum will reflect this by, for instance, providing students different information and emphases concerning gaming regulations and controls, other gaming environment factors, types of operations and games, patrons, trends, and so forth, of the chosen gaming specialization. Likewise, when student preparation targets employment within a particular geographical area, gaming curricula must adapt to appropriate cultural and regulatory considerations, as well as to the style and scale of regional operations.

Gaming Major Caveat for a Professional College

A curriculum with a very general gaming emphasis such as "gaming and gambling in society" exemplifies a pitfall cautioned against in a professional college. We have encountered suggestions of such programs. They contain a very different commitment to gaming education from that advocated here in that they include *no* gaming management or operations components. Instead, they are built completely around such courses as "Gaming around the World" (discussing different games here and abroad as cultural phenomena), the "History of Gaming," "Social Issues in Gaming," and the "Psychology of the Gambler." The eternal debate for educators concerns the noble position a social science-oriented curriculum enjoys in higher education.[17] However, if preparing and placing students in gaming operations and/or managerial positions is an objective, totally excluding operations and administration courses is inappropriate. Such a curriculum educates students about a society inclusive of gaming while it omits the essential "how gaming works" and "effective gaming management" elements that the industry is beginning to seek, and should expect, from professional programs claiming a gaming emphasis.

Gaming Course and Curriculum Development

The next phase, planning the actual gaming topics and courses to include in a curriculum, can be a difficult process, fraught with compromises and perennially ripe for adjustment. Significantly, each year a main theme at the Conference of Hospitality, Restaurant, and Institutions Educators is curriculum re-engineering—a review and fresh look at *what* should be taught and *how* it should be interpreted and arranged in hospitality programs. Educators discuss how they have re-examined, readjusted, and, in some cases, overhauled their curriculum. If this is the case for lodging, food services, tourism, and business curricula that have been developing for decades, it should come as no surprise that developing gaming curricula poses a challenge, given that preparation of gaming professionals is relatively new. Planning and developing relevant course work, and assembling a responsive program of gaming topics, competencies, knowledge, skills, and abilities, are demanding and continuing tasks.

Gaming Course Arrangements

Depending on the number of gaming and total courses offered, gaming may be incorporated into classes in numerous ways. Main choices are to modify existing nongaming courses in order to integrate gaming-specific content, or to create separate gaming courses emphasizing content distinctive to the industry. Overall, this gaming content should better prepare students for their future gaming-relevant KSAs in order to support their long-term career success. Secondarily, the content should provide awareness of the gaming industry as a significant participant in our economic, social, and governmental milieu. As an aid to developers, examples below incorporate a variety of potential gaming and gaming-related courses in illustrating four gaming-course classifications.

Classification 1. Begin with an existing nongaming course and modify it to integrate gaming content and issues (Example: "Introduction to the Hospitality Industry."). As with all course preparation, guidance is available from numerous sources. For example, The Educational Foundation of the National Restaurant Association published survey results from 180 educator respondents, who rated 16 subject areas as "very important," "somewhat important," or "less important." For a course entitled Hospitality Industry Overview, only the following five topics received votes as "very important" from half or more respondents (at least 90 of the 180).

- Overview of segments of the industry
- Industry trends
- Guest service
- Human resources management
- Career options

Using the above as a starting point, the industry overview and trends segments could characterize the types of business and trends in gaming operations. Augmenting the *guest services* element could be a discussion or demonstration of players' clubs (a parallel to the airlines' frequent flyers clubs), emerging technology for player services, such as wireless communications, and gaming area service personnel. Challenges specific to gaming *human resources management* readily fit into a generic human resources segment (for example, the need for added employee security in cash operations, given the cash nature of many games). In turn, human resources discussions shift easily into *career opportunities*. Here, typical gaming organizational structures may include descriptions of the roles and potential educational requirements of persons holding particular titles. While the gaming subject matter integration in this example is limited, it is focused appropriately on key subject areas and services the stated gaming education objective of career support.

Classification 2. Provide a gaming course that is a parallel or offshoot of another nongaming course offered in the unit (Example: "Introduction to the Gaming Industry"). A course focused entirely on gaming may parallel an existing course, as main topics in Introduction to the Gaming Industry may resemble those in Introduction to the Hotel Industry (if offered). Expanding discussion on the subjects noted in the first classification to topics unique to gaming and the gaming industry could provide a good starting point and seed for developing an introductory gaming course.

Another consideration that may arise in this course classification is "Who gets course credit and under what circumstances?" Planners should establish explicit credit criteria; for example, "available for credit in addition to the required Hospitality Orientation course," or "not available for credit to those with more than one year of gaming industry experience."

Classification 3. Provide a gaming course that builds on a nongaming course or another prerequisite such as experience, and/or curriculum "standing" (e.g., junior level in major) (Example: "Accounting in the Gaming Industry:; Prerequisites: "Accounting I" and "Managerial Accounting"). A gaming course with prerequisites enables the instructor to build on previously gained knowledge relating to the topic. For the course "Accounting in the Gaming Industry," the designated two semesters of college accounting should provide students with an appropriate foundation in accounting standards, practices, reports, and analysis. From this point, the course can concentrate on *gaming* distinctions in accounting, its applications, and advanced concepts.

Classification 4. Develop a course dedicated to gaming subject matter that has no parallel courses, prerequisites, or restrictions on enrollment (Example: "Security and Surveillance for Gaming Operations"). An advantage of well-publicized gaming courses with no enrollment criteria is that they *can* attract student "shoppers" who are either exploring different areas or looking for an interesting elective. Their involvement can broaden exposure to, and enrollment in, a gaming curriculum. Consider the content of the example course, "Security and Surveillance for Gaming Operations" and its potential for drawing student interest with topics such as cheating techniques in casino games, prevention of crimes against games, and legal issues of surveillance and apprehension. A second advantage of offering gaming courses with no prerequisites is that, without the need to build upon other courses, the freedom exists to develop a course on separate aspects of the gaming industry.

A drawback of gaming courses with no eligibility requirements can be the necessity of beginning at a very basic level because the instructor cannot assume that students share any type or level of background in the subject. This necessity can cause a course to be objectionably slow-moving for enrollees who do possess a gaming background.

Stepping into Gaming Courses

This section suggests a systematic five-step approach to developing gaming courses. The basic steps remain similar in each of the classifications outlined in the previous section, but each step may be applied differently or to a different extent for each classification. Despite the similarity in planning and development steps, no two gaming courses on the same subject (in different programs) are likely to be, or should necessarily be, alike.

Step 1. Determine the fundamental subtopics and associated KSAs that the conventional subject has in common with the subject in a gaming setting. Subtle differences separate even traditional courses from those that include topics applicable to gaming. Further, establishing the specific subject matter comprising such a course should emphasize the integration of the hospitality and gaming venue. It then becomes important to isolate the critical elements of the customary course, or rather those that apply to all hospitality venues. The following example modifies an existing course in alcoholic beverage management or bar tending. The first step is to ascertain the relevant KSAs that overlap and extend to the educational preparation needed for any beverage supervisor, manager, and service person, regardless of setting. Examples of universal subject matter for this course include liquor liability, sanitation, product and mixology knowledge, cost and cash controls, human resources issues, customer service know-how, menus, pricing, merchandising, beverage systems, and risk and crisis management.

Step 2. Identify relevant topics that need to be added, modified, or differentiated for a gaming industry setting or orientation. Continuing with the alcoholic beverage example, the second step is to identify new subject matter applicable to the gaming environment to incorporate into the existing course. In this case, a beverage operation may be located in, nearby, or otherwise associated with a gaming operation. Keep in mind also that the reverse may occur when the gaming operation is located within the beverage operation, as when a roadside tavern houses several video poker machines and/or other games. In this case, the unique qualities include gaming-related subjects, skills, facts, regulations, orientations, practices, policies, philosophies, issues, and so forth, or modified emphases. Listed below are a few examples of the integration of gaming with an alcoholic beverage management course.

- Typical ways gaming beverage "comps" and player discounts are handled.
- Administration of transactions of cash substitutes (e.g., gaming tokens).
- Technology to document player beverage preference data for "players' club members."
- Familiarity with beverage service policies for "high-rollers" (gaming VIPs).
- Ethical issues on alcohol service to patrons/players.
- Distinctions from usual beverage server assignments—for example, that servers in casinos generally do not rotate beverage stations

Step 3. Examine the curriculum and, if possible, the course syllabi of other courses to determine what, if any, of the course content has been addressed through general or specific prerequisites. While the foundations and content students may already have encountered would be less important for a course with no prerequisites, step 3 should not be omitted completely. Curriculum planners must be attentive to fine-tuning the topic mix within and across gaming and nongaming courses. For effective and efficient gaming education, the ideal is *seamless* subject and course sequencing. *Seamless* describes the gaming program in which integrated gaming topics and, if applicable, required gaming courses blend and dovetail into one another, as well as into and from other program course work. Especially in a curriculum with multiple required or elective gaming courses, it is a serious pursuit to see that the topic treatment and topic relationships within and across courses be coordinated so that students experience a cohesive, consistent, building-blocks succession rather than inconsistencies or contradictions in the subject matter, language, or other gaps in the subject matter progression, or duplication.

Step 4. Based upon the results to this point, decide on learning objectives for students. Beginning with the expected outcomes or "what the student should know after taking the course," specific educational objectives should be written. These objectives should define clearly, in performance terms, the KSAs the students will master. When written, these objectives will use actionable learning expectations such as, *calculate, explain, decide, create, orally present an analysis of, evaluate,* and *write a report of possible future scenarios*. Examples are given in Table 12.3.

Step 5. Develop the course or course content additions to instruct and motivate students for success in the planned gaming KSAs. The fifth and final step develops the gaming content, either as an entire course or merged into an existing one. When integrated into an existing course, the

Table 12.3   Course Development Outline

Financial Accounting in the Gaming Industry	
Prerequisite:	Two years of college accounting.
Overview:	Accounting, accounting standards, systems of accounts, budgeting, reporting and report analysis, and internal control procedures applied in gaming operations.

Selected Actionable Competencies:

Upon completing this course, students should be able to . . .

Execute appropriate accounting procedures for games, e.g., table games, slots, keno, bingo, on/off track pari-mutuel wagering, and lotteries.

Describe gaming-activity reporting regulations for the IRS and this state.

Prepare a capital budget for a gaming department.

Explain and be able to carry out appropriate procedures for handling of cash, cash substitutes (tokens, chips), and noncash receipt income.

Calculate and interpret variances from planned budgets.

Develop a system of records and controls for credit extended to players.

Outline a basic handbook for primary internal control procedures.

Give an oral report on typical audit targets and procedures for a gaming department.

content may be brought in as a separate unit, interspersed as related topics arise, or incorporated as a combination of both. With most subjects, if time allows, the combination approach can permit the most thorough and realistic treatment of gaming subject matter.

The approach to developing courses suggested above should prepare educators to deal with the issues of legal oversight, certification, and professional development that will inevitably arise with the growth of gaming as an entertainment industry.

RESOURCES

Publications and Media

One of the challenges facing faculty in the development and implementation of gaming courses is locating appropriate resources. The following is a list of books, journals, and trade publications that can assist in course formation. While certainly not exhaustive, the list should provide a starting point for many content areas. It includes additional reference information to help faculty locate still other resources. *Casino Gaming: A Resource Guide* by Mirkovich and Cowgill is particularly notable. This manual lists not only books and publications, but agencies, state information hotlines, and other sources not typically found in a bibliography. Also included in the information below is the address of a specialty bookstore, The Gamblers Book Shop, that stocks a wide variety of books on gaming, and delivers worldwide.

Books—Games

BlackJack Dealer Instruction Manual, by Wanda Russell. Las Vegas, NV: Casino Executive Training Center, 1993.

Techniques of Casino Games, by Ralph Cutolo and Vic Taucer. Las Vegas, NV: Casino Creations Inc., 1993.

Craps Dealer Instruction Manual, by Wanda Russell. Las Vegas, NV: Casino Executive Training Center, 1993.

Reference Guide to Casino Gambling, by Henry Tamburin. Mobile, AL: Research Services Unlimited, 1993.

Lady Luck: The Theory of Probability, by Warren Weaver. New York: Dover Publications, 1963.

On Casino Gambling: The Complete Guide to Playing and Winning, by Darwin Ortiz. New York: Lyle Stuart, 1986.

Roulette Dealers Instructional Manual, by Wanda Russell. Las Vegas, NV: Casino Executive Training Center, 1993.

Scarne On Dice, by J. Scarne. Harrisburg, PA: Stackpole, 1962.

Scarne's Guide to Modern Poker, by J. Scarne. New York: Simon and Schuster, 1980.

Scarne's New Complete Guide to Gambling, by J. Scarne. New York: Simon and Schuster, 1974.

Slot Machines: A Pictorial History of the First 100 Years, by Marshall Fey. Reno, NV: Liberty Belle Books, 1991.

Books—Management

Casino Accounting and Financial Management, by Malcolm E. Greenlees. Reno, NV: University of Nevada Press, 1988.

Casino Supervision: A Basic Guide, by Peter G. Demos. Atlantic City, NJ: CSI Press, 1983.

Casino Management, by Bill Friedman. New York: Lyle Stuart, 1982.

Casino Customer Service: The Win Win Game, by William N. Thompson and Michelle Comeau. New York: Gaming and Wagering Business, 1992.

Casino Marketing, by John Romero. New York: Gaming and Wagering Business, 1992.

Cheating and Detection: Gambling Protection Series. (four videotapes), by Steve Forte. Las Vegas, NV: BTA Joint Ventures, 1984.

Gaming Control Law: The Nevada Model, by John Goodwin. Columbus, OH: Publishing Horizons, Inc., 1985.

Getting Started in Indian Gaming. Rapid City, SD: Sodak Gaming Supplies, 1991.

International Casino Law, by Anthony N. Cabot, William N. Thompson, and Andrew Tottenham. Reno, NV: Institute for the Study of Gambling and Commercial Gaming, University of Nevada, Reno, 1993.

The Business of Risk: Commercial Gambling in Mainstream America, by Vicki Aby, James Smith, and Eugene Christansen. Lawrence, KS: University of Kansas Press, 1985.

The Mathematics of Games and Gambling, by Edward Packel. New York: The Mathematical Association of America, 1981.

Books—Sociology/Psychology

Compulsive Gambling, (Theory, Research, Practice), by Howard Shaffer, Sharon Stein, Blase Gambino, and Thomas Cummings. Lexington, MA: Lexington Books, 1989.

Gambling and Commercial Gaming: Essays on Business, Economics, Philosophy and Science, edited by William R. Eadington and Judy A. Cornelius. Reno, NV: Institute for the Study of Gambling and Commercial Gaming, College of Business Administration, University of Nevada, Reno, 1992.

The Last Resort: Success and Failure in Campaigns for Casinos, by John Dombrink and William Thompson. Reno, NV: University of Nevada Press, 1990.

Books—Reference

"1993 Gaming Issues," *Legislative Issues Series 93-3,* by Craig Christopher: Center for State Policy Research.

A Glossary of Terms Used in the Casino Gaming Industry. Chicago, Il.: Alexander Grant and Company, 1978.

Casino Gaming: A Resource Guide, by Thomas Mirkovich and Allison Cowgill. Metuchen, NJ: Scarecrow, 1995.

Encyclopedia of Gambling, by Carl Sifakis. New York: Facts on File, 1990.

Gambling and Society: Interdisciplinary Studies on the Subject of Gambling, edited by William R. Eadington. Springfield, IL.: Thomas, 1976.

Legalized Gambling as a Strategy for Economic Development, by Robert Goodman. Northampton, MA: United States Gambling Study, 1994.

Myths and History, by Peter Arnold. Secaucus, NJ: Chartwell Books, Inc., 1977.

The Indian Gaming Regulation Act. State Legislative Reports: Vol. 17, (no. 16). National Conference of State Legislatures.

The Dictionary of Gambling and Gaming (1st ed.), by Thomas Clark. Cold Spring, NY: Lexik House, 1988.

The Gambling Papers: Proceedings of the Fifth National Conference on Gambling and Risk Taking. Reno, NV: University of Nevada, Reno, 1982.

The Gambling Studies: Proceedings of the Sixth National Conference on Gambling and Risk Taking. Reno, NV: University of Nevada, Reno, 1985.

Periodicals

Casino, Casino Magazine. Waseca, MN

Casino Journal, 3100 W. Sahara Ave., Suite 207, Las Vegas, NV 89102.

Casino Journal of New Jersey, 2524 Arctic Ave., Atlantic City, NJ 08401.

Casino Player, ACE Marketing, Atlantic City, NJ.

Casino Securities Watch, Rouge et Noir, Inc., Midlothian, VA.

Gaming Technologies, Public Gaming Research Institute, Rockville, MD.

Indian Gaming, Public Gaming Research Institute, Rockville, MD.

International Gaming and Wagering Business, Seven Penn Plaza, New York, NY 10001-3900.

Journals

Gaming Research and Review Journal, UNLV International Gaming Institute, 4505 Maryland Parkway, Las Vegas, NV 89154-6037.

Journal of Gaming Studies, Human Sciences Press, New York, NY.

The BottomLine, The Journal of the International Association of Hospitality Accountants, P.O. Box 203008, Austin, TX 78720-3008.

Retail Gaming Book and Periodical Outlet

Gamblers Book Shop, 630 S. 11th St., Las Vegas, NV 89101 (ships worldwide).

REFERENCES

1. E. Paul Durrenberger. *It's All Politics*. Urbana, IL: University of Illinois Press, 1992.
2. William R. Eadington. *Ethical and Policy Considerations in the Spread of Commercial Gambling*. Reno, NV: Institute for the Study of Gambling and Commercial Gaming, College of Business Administration, University of Nevada, Reno, 1993.
3. *Gaming Industry Update: The Next Stage: Gaming Comes to Where the People Are*. New York: Wertheim Schroder, 1994, p. 99.
4. *The Harrah Study of U.S. Casino Entertainment*. Memphis: Harrah's Casino Hotel, Gaming Division of Promus Companies, 1994, p. 4.
5. *Gaming Industry Update*; p. 11.
6. J. Popkin and K. Hetter. "America's Gaming at a Glance," *Gaming & Wagering Business*, September 15, 1993, pp. 52–62.
7. Patricia A. McQueen, "North American gaming at a glance," *Gaming & Wagering Business*, September 15, 1993, pp. 52–62.
8. *The Harrah Survey of U.S. Casino Entertainment*. Memphis: Harrah's Casino Hotel, Gaming Division of Promus Companies, 1995, p. 4.
9. *The Harrah Survey of U.S. Casino Entertainment*. Memphis: Harrah's Casino Hotel, Gaming Division of Promus Companies, 1995, p. 16.
10. *The Harrah Survey of U.S. Casino Entertainment*. Memphis: Harrah's Casino Hotel, Gaming Division of Promus Companies, 1995, p. 15.
11. *The Harrah Survey of U.S. Casino Entertainment*. Memphis: Harrah's Casino Hotel, Gaming Division of Promus Companies, 1995, p. 15.
12. *The Harrah Survey of U.S. Casino Entertainment*. Memphis: Harrah's Casino Hotel, Gaming Division of Promus Companies, 1995, p. 15.
13. *The Harrah Survey of U.S. Casino Entertainment*. Memphis: Harrah's Casino Hotel, Gaming Division of Promus Companies, 1995, p. 22.
14. *The Harrah Survey of U.S. Casino Entertainment*. Memphis: Harrah's Casino Hotel, Gaming Division of Promus Companies, 1995, p. 20.
15. *Kiplinger Washington Letter*, Vol. 71 (no. 3), New York: Kiplinger Washington Editors,
16. Personal correspondence, The UNLV International Gaming Institute, August 1994.
17. D.J. Christianson. *Gaming Education: An Analysis of Professional Preparation for the Casino Industry*, W.R. Eadington, in *Proceedings of the 5th National Conference Gambling and Risk Taking* University of Nevada, Reno: Reno, 1982.